THIS COUNTRY

— My Life in Politics and History —

CHRIS MATTHEWS

SIMON & SCHUSTER

New York London Toronto Sydney New Delhi

Simon & Schuster
1230 Avenue of the Americas
New York, NY 10020

Copyright © 2021 by Christopher J. Matthews

All rights reserved, including the right to reproduce this book or
portions thereof in any form whatsoever. For information, address
Simon & Schuster Subsidiary Rights Department,
1230 Avenue of the Americas, New York, NY 10020.

First Simon & Schuster hardcover edition June 2021

SIMON & SCHUSTER and colophon are
registered trademarks of Simon & Schuster, Inc.

For information about special discounts for bulk purchases,
please contact Simon & Schuster Special Sales at 1-866-506-1949
or business@simonandschuster.com.

The Simon & Schuster Speakers Bureau can bring authors to
your live event. For more information or to book an event,
contact the Simon & Schuster Speakers Bureau at 1-866-248-3049
or visit our website at www.simonspeakers.com.

Interior design by Kyle Kabel

Manufactured in the United States of America

1   3   5   7   9   10   8   6   4   2

Library of Congress Cataloging-in-Publication Data has been applied for.

ISBN 978-1-9821-3484-6
ISBN 978-1-9821-3486-0 (ebook)

All photos courtesy of the author unless otherwise noted.

These pages are dedicated to the faithful fans of *Hardball*.
For twenty years we shared a nightly quest for truth.
You were always great company.

CONTENTS

CONTENTS

BOOK II

BOOK III

CONTENTS

There are some things which cannot be learned quickly, and time, which is all we have, must be paid heavily for their acquiring.

—Ernest Hemingway,
Death in the Afternoon, 1932

INTRODUCTION

Almost a half century ago, I was working in a congressional race in Brooklyn. It was a case of my doing what I was afraid to do. My instinct told me that an election campaign in the old borough might be rough, scary, even life-changing.

Brooklyn electioneering back then wasn't on the level. It was not the place for the young, clean-cut candidate I was helping make his start. Only later did the campaign's hard-boiled strategist tell me he could have bought the seat for a "quarter million." It didn't shock me. A reporter for a borough weekly had previously warned me that if our candidate wanted any coverage at all, he had better pony up some ad money.

That seedy business in Brooklyn didn't kill my lifelong romance with politics. Just the opposite. As those harsh winter months of 1974 passed, I made the bold decision to make a go of it on my own. I would head home to Philadelphia and run myself.

On the face of it, the idea made no sense. I would be running against one of this country's last big-city political machines and an entrenched US congressman who was one of its top leaders.

What gave me hope was what was happening in the country. The Watergate scandal was all over the news. Wasn't this the perfect time, if there ever would be, to offer myself as an alternative to the old ways?

Who knew? Maybe the voters were in a mood to, in that time-honored phrase, throw the bums out.

What made driving across the Verrazzano-Narrows Bridge toward the New Jersey Turnpike that morning so gutsy-crazy were the hard facts. I had no money—*really* no money—and no political backing whatsoever. I hadn't even lived at home since heading up to Holy Cross College in Massachusetts at seventeen, and, outside of my family, I didn't know a single person in the city of my birth who could help me.

The strange thing is, it wasn't all that strange for me. My life at this point had already begun to etch a pattern: take a leap, live the adventure, learn what I could. Here I was making another dive into the unknown; yet another case of doing what I was afraid to do.

What I had going for me in this instance, perhaps all I had, was a message. It was the corruptive influence of money in politics. To dramatize my crusade, I would declare that I would accept no campaign contributions whatsoever. Not only did this grab the attention of the newspapers, but it also was the heartbeat of the effort—especially among our hearty brigade of young volunteers. It put wind in my sails. While I didn't come all that close to beating the incumbent, it confirmed some powerful lessons. One is to *ask*. Just as I'd started in Washington, DC, three years earlier by asking for someone to hire me, I learned that basic willingness to ask is what campaigning for office is all about.

A second lesson is to *show up*! If you want something, you have to go where it's available and grab for it. Nobody's knocking on your door to connect you to your dreams. You have to knock on theirs.

With that perilous decision to drive home and run for office in the winter of 1974 I was diving deeper into the world of politics. It's a place where, having seen both the good and the bad, I still recognized the essential promise. I knew that the whole process of going out and asking someone to vote for you is the heart of our democracy. It's how the American people choose not just their leaders but also the kind of country they want to live in.

So much of what I've written in newspaper columns and books over the years and said on *Hardball* for a generation comes directly from such personal adventures as that race for Congress. There were the years I spent in Africa, the campaigns from Utah to Brooklyn, my time serving the US Senate and later as a White House speechwriter for President Jimmy Carter.

It was that latter experience that continues to stir golden memories: of writing alone in my grand office in the Old Executive Office Building, having lunch at the roundtable in the White House Mess and hearing the scuttlebutt from other staffers, of working at the typewriter on Air Force One writing the president's remarks for the next campaign stop.

Next came my once-in-a-lifetime role as a top aide to Speaker of the House Tip O'Neill from 1981 through 1986. Following that were the exciting years of reporting on great historic moments, such as the Democratic and Republican conventions, the fall of the Berlin Wall in 1989, the first all-races election in South Africa in 1994, the Good Friday peace accord in Northern Ireland in 1998, and the funeral in Rome of Pope John Paul II in 2005.

More than anything else, of course, it's been a life spent watching the people running *this country* and those who wish they were.

I owe this life and its lessons to a half dozen leaps into the unknown. Africa leads the list.

In June 1968 I sat alone on a public park bench in Montreal a block up from Sainte-Catherine Street and decided where I was going to go in my life. My graduate school deferment had expired. Rated 1-A in the military draft, I now listed on the back of an old business card my limited options regarding a war I opposed. I could join VISTA, the domestic volunteer program; teach high school; or enlist in the army as a public information officer. That last choice, though it required a four-year hitch, would have one big advantage: it would help me really learn how to write.

My only moral claim is that I had ruled out becoming an army finance officer and similar routes. If I didn't face the fighting in Vietnam, I would not act as if I were doing my bit.

Finally, there was another option; a truly positive one. It carried the advantage of being a true adventure: the Peace Corps. The challenge was to get the right assignment. For me, that meant going to Africa and working on economic development.

All this became miraculously possible when a young recruiter showed up that summer at the University of North Carolina at Chapel Hill, where I'd been pursuing a PhD in economics. He handed me a colorful brochure about a new program in Swaziland.

That pamphlet became my plan. I would go to Africa and work at something I had been already thinking about doing once I finished my doctorate. It would be doing something good for the country and the world; a positive alternative to what had become this country's death grip on Vietnam.

So much of my life has arisen from that decision. Those two years of service as a trade development officer took me to a wider world. It allowed me to view my country at a distance. It opened me to a common humanity with people whose lives were separated from us by continent and culture. It was a spiritual experience, too, like being alone in an empty church.

Perhaps as important, it freed me. Before I joined the Peace Corps, I was trudging toward a PhD. I found myself buried in econometric models for which I had neither the gift nor the enthusiasm. My decision to head off to Africa—made the same horrid June week that Robert F. Kennedy, still hoping to be the Democratic candidate for president, was assassinated in Los Angeles—liberated me to explore my hopes for a political life.

The decision to head to Washington, DC, in the winter of 1971 was my life's second big leap. With $200 left of my Peace Corps "readjustment allowance" in my pocket, I began knocking on doors on Capitol Hill. My goal was to become a legislative assistant to a US senator. It's the role young Ted Sorensen played for newly elected Massachusetts senator John F. Kennedy in 1953.

This became my route, too. After weeks of strolling the corridors of the Senate and the House of Representatives, I managed to wrangle a job with a senator, and then, thanks to him, with another. I had begun my climb in politics. One successful leap of faith, to Africa, had led to another, to Washington. It was my Northern Irish grandmother who saw the connection. An immigrant in her youth, she knew the strength that emerges when a person is forced to adjust to a distant land. "It was Africa," she confronted me. "Wasn't it?"

That first job hunt just back from Africa would become my primer in Washington politics and how it works. Its first, durable lesson was the power of *patronage*. Every job on Capitol Hill was controlled by a senator or a member of Congress. To get the job, you needed that person's blessing. Just like my grandpop's street corner politics back in Philadelphia as a local Democratic committeeman, it was who you know.

To this I would coin a corollary: it's who you *get* to know.

My Capitol Hill job search that winter of 1971 meant going from office to office, dropping off my résumé and asking the receptionist if she'd heard of any openings. It eventually yielded unlikely pay dirt. Wayne Owens, a young chief staffer for Democratic senator Frank Moss of Utah, liked something that he saw in me. He had worked on Robert Kennedy's 1968 presidential campaign and later served for his brother Senator Edward Kennedy in his US Senate leadership position. A devout Mormon, Wayne seemed taken with my being a Catholic who had gone to college in Massachusetts and served in the Peace Corps, as well as the fact that I knew something about economics, which, he confessed, he didn't.

All that Wayne had to offer, however, was a patronage appointment to the US Capitol Police. I *took* it. Soon I was beginning my mornings in Senator Moss's office answering legislative mail from Utah, then reporting for my eight-hour shift at three in the afternoon. For those months, I faced only one real danger: my nightly walk up Pennsylvania Avenue for dinner. Back then there was a lot of street crime on Capitol Hill. Suppose

I'd been taken for an actual policeman? What if someone were pulling a holdup? Or a victim yelled to me for help?

Fortunately, before summer was over, Wayne brought me into Senator Moss's office as a full-time legislative assistant. Soon, I was drafting legislative amendments on minimum wage, government spending, and other matters. One afternoon I found myself sitting on the Senate floor amid the men I'd heard about for years. The issue was President Richard Nixon's call to freeze federal salaries. "I'm stickin' with the president," I could hear old Senator John Stennis of Mississippi muttering. Such die-hard loyalty, and the fact he was partly deaf, would explain why Nixon later selected him, and him alone, to listen to his incriminating Watergate tapes.

I soon had my eyes opened to the Democrats' own shenanigans. One favorite was a bill called the Ironclad Ceiling on Federal Spending. It was, I would discover, nothing of the kind. Thanks to a series of unnoticed amendments, it was no "ceiling" at all. Its sole purpose was to give cover to Democrats from folks back home worried about out-of-control government deficits.

When my job in Senator Moss's office ended, he urged me to "dip a little deeper into these political waters." While following that advice in 1974 didn't make me a fellow officeholder, it must have earned his respect. Senator Moss now persuaded his colleague Edmund Muskie of Maine, who had run for president two years earlier, to hire me for the new Senate Budget Committee he was chairing. That appointment put me on the road to the White House, to becoming a presidential speechwriter, and then to becoming top aide to the Speaker of the House of Representatives, the legendary Thomas P. "Tip" O'Neill Jr. My half dozen years with O'Neill would accord me in itself an on-the-job doctorate in American politics.

When the Speaker retired in 1986, I took a job as president and CEO of a big Washington consulting firm. With a staff of fifty, many of them policy experts, we serviced large corporations wanting an edge in knowing what they were talking about. Though it was a highly credible think tank, it wasn't for me. Like my time in economics grad school, it was another case of finding myself in the wrong place. That summer, fortunately, brought a better offer. *Far* better. Larry Kramer, a friend from the *Washington Post*, had been recently named executive editor of the *San Francisco Examiner*. After I'd moonlighted writing some columns for him, Larry called and asked me to become the newspaper's Washington bureau chief. Known as the "Monarch of the Dailies" since the late 1880s, it was the flagship of William Randolph Hearst's empire—the *Citizen Kane* newspaper. With my wife Kathleen's agreement, I quit the high-paying consulting job with its impressive title and took my friend's offer. Larry predicted that my column would quickly be syndicated nationally, and I'd find myself appearing on television as a political commentator.

Larry was right. It all happened quite soon. Some thought *too* soon.

For the next fifteen gutsy years, I knew the excitement of covering historic events.

Having experienced the early Cold War as a boy, hiding under my desk at St. Christopher's School, I got to cover the beginning of its end in West Berlin. As a former Peace Corps volunteer working across the border from South Africa, I got to watch the first election in which its black majority could vote. As an heir to Irish immigrants both Catholic and Protestant, I saw the end to the armed struggles—the Troubles—in Belfast.

Just as important was the feeling of having just the right position for me: newspaper columnist. It was the great New York writer Jimmy Breslin who encouraged me to go for it. He'd won fame writing about the unfamous: the working people of his city's neighborhoods. Instead of sharing the spotlight with the news-making elite, he became legendary writing about those too often overlooked.

"Be a columnist," he said, walking up Sixth Avenue from our meeting at a midtown bar. "You'll walk taller."

My next leap was to anchor a political news show. I christened it *Hardball,* after the book I'd written about real-life politics in 1988. When the program debuted, cable television wasn't the opinion showcase it would eventually become. People in Washington had gotten their political excitement Saturday nights from *The McLaughlin Group*, which I loved and eventually joined as an occasional panelist. There were other programs offering commentary like I was doing for *CBS This Morning* and then ABC-TV's *Good Morning America*, but nothing like the big prime-time shows that came later.

This book is about learning from history, from *life*, sometimes the hard way, as it takes place around you. *Hardball* spanned more than a generation. My ambition with the program was to drill down to the truth, especially in those cases where I suspected something was being withheld. It was a vital position to hold, and I refused to abdicate it by pitching softballs. I sensed there were many viewers out there with a hot question in their heads, perhaps even on the tips of their tongues. What they hate is when the person sitting in my chair won't ask it. Nothing is more maddening to know that a politician is hiding something, and the person tasked with getting it out of them doesn't even try. My job is doing what the viewer can't.

"What I like about you," people would tell me through the years, "is you don't let them get away with anything." Those occasions when I was able to deliver were points of pride.

That and my obvious candor. What you heard from me on TV is what you'd hear sitting next to me at dinner or in an airport waiting area. I called it as I saw it. There was no calculation on what would sound right, no filter. That goes beyond asking the tough, uncomfortable questions. I have this compulsion in me, evidenced through the years, to try to enliven the moment, to entertain those I'm with, to shake things up. That penchant for relentless commentary with no punches pulled has been part of my success on TV. It's also been getting me into trouble since I was supposed to be sitting quietly at my desk in St. Christopher's grade school.

As I retrace my steps in this book, I want to display the same candor. These pages are a celebration of this country and of the rich role I've enjoyed in sharing its politics and history. I got a lot of it right, but not always. I'll try to do better here in this book. Sadly, there's no Delete button for live television or for a career lived largely in public. In those cases where I wish I'd had such a button, I'll try to get it right here. That includes all the intriguing details of how everything fit together, the backstory to what you saw on television.

As you will read in these pages, there are things I've said on *Hardball* that, upon reflection, I shouldn't have. Some are simply embarrassing: such as, after hearing Barack Obama speak with patriotic fervor in 2008, I reported that I "felt a thrill up my leg." Or when I signed off at three in the morning following the 2012 presidential election results and quipped, "A good day for America. I'm so glad we had that storm last week." I was focusing on President Obama's well-celebrated handling of the cleanup following Hurricane Sandy, which had pummeled the Northeast just days before the country rewarded him with a second term. In eyeing the politics, I was ignoring its tragic effects on people's lives. Rachel Maddow—thank God!—was there to try to rescue me and return the focus sharply where it belonged. I will get to some other episodes, on and *off* the air, where I sincerely wish even now that I'd had that Delete button to hit.

One message I've managed to get across crystal clear over the decades is my passion for this country and its politics. Like Hillary Rodham Clinton, I grew up in a Republican family and carried a youthful torch for Barry Goldwater. Then it was my anti–Vietnam War hero Senator Eugene McCarthy; still later it was Barack Obama. With every twist and turn, I have reveled in the democratic contest itself. The great *Washington Post* editor Ben Bradlee best captured the personal excitement in my writing. "Matthews writes about politics with relish," he once observed, "the way sportswriters cover boxing." He *got* me. At age seventy-five, it's not a politician or a philosophy that drives me. It's my concern for our American system of self-government. That's what holds my political heart. I want this country's vigorous, back-and-forth competition of ideas and ambitions to serve a great democracy and keep us together.

I finished this book in the shadow of a president who refused for critical weeks to accept popular and Electoral College defeat. It never occurred to me that our system of self-government, ruled by elections held predictably and reliably since 1788, could be challenged by a serving chief executive. Perhaps this makes it an important time to look back on how we found ourselves here, from my earliest memories, born just after World War II, on through the Cold War, the civil rights and Vietnam War crises, as well as the high ideals of the 1960s to the spectrum of competing movements of this twenty-first century—from Trumpism to Black Lives Matter.

The narrative traces my political interest from the time I reached, as we said in Catholic school, "the age of reason." It captures all the great moments of our times as I witnessed them.

You might say writing this book is my latest leap of faith. It is my bet that you the reader will be intrigued, even inspired, by seeing this country's modern history as it charged its way through one American's life.

– BOOK I –

Think you're escaping and run into yourself. Longest way round is the shortest way home.

—James Joyce,
Ulysses, 1922

CHAPTER ONE

IRISH ENOUGH

My parents met at a dance hall in North Philadelphia just before our entrance into World War II. It was on a second floor overlooking Broad Street. Dad pointed to it one day as we drove through a run-down part of North Philly. There it was, my beginnings.

Mary Theresa Shields and Herbert Matthews were married on Saint Patrick's Day 1942. The wedding was held in the chapel at the Philadelphia Navy Yard, where Dad was serving as a first class petty officer in the intelligence outfit. The rub was that Dad was raised Episcopalian. That explains why no one was there from either family but for Mom's loyal sister Catherine.

Those trying to position me politically might find a clue in this mix of cultures: tribal row house Irish Catholic Democrats on Mom's side, and self-reliant, individualist Protestant Republicans on Dad's. In any case, the mix has made a certain sense to me.

My oldest memory is of Mom's old Hunting Park neighborhood. My older brother, Bert, and I are out on the porch, swaying on the davenport. We're watching the horse-drawn wagons come up the street, delivering milk in the morning and collecting trash later in the day. Bert pointed out how the horses pulling the milk wagons knew exactly which houses to stop at.

The smells of that old neighborhood are also memorable. There was the odor you knew crawling under the kitchen table amid the grown-ups' feet; the coal smell from down in the cellar, where Grandpop would go

13

to shovel it into the furnace; the aroma of burnt coffee from the kitchen; the strong fish scent wafted up from the Delaware River; and that of the horses that rose up from the cobblestones when it rained.

Grandmom was the lady of the house. Growing up, I would marvel at her ability at any hour of the afternoon to create a hybrid meal of lunch and supper: cold cuts, dinner roast beef, and lots of vegetables. Even after mustering together this spread, she never sat down at the table until well after the rest of us had started. Only when everyone was well into the meal would she pull up a chair to the table corner nearest the kitchen. It must have been the old Irish way.

I often think back to those old days near the busy corner of Broad Street and Hunting Park Avenue. There was the big water trough next to the subway stop and the newsstand. I can still see the horses splashing as they drank. Bert and I would sit on that porch on long afternoons, helping Grandmom make supper for Daddy at six o'clock. We would snap open the peas, shuck the corn, and cut the green beans. Everything was fresh. No cans, no frozen food. All would be prepared and boiled the Irish way 'til supper time, still hours away.

Besides family, which was a world unto itself, the main conversation at Grandmom and Grandpop Shields's was about church. Perhaps it was an upcoming novena at our cathedral-like St. Stephen's Church. I remember the morning devoted to all of us faithfully watching Dennis Cardinal Dougherty's funeral on television, when I was five. It is not surprising that two of Mom's three sisters, Aunt Eleanor and Aunt Agnes, joined the convent, becoming Sisters of St. Joseph.

Grandpop—Charles Patrick Shields—was a figure out of a Eugene O'Neill play, with special reference to *A Touch of the Poet*. I loved him and Grandmom both. He seemed always stuck a few notches below his meant-for station. His emblem of status, unlike in the O'Neill drama, wasn't a horse but the three-piece gray suit he wore Sundays after walking to St. Stephen's. One time, he arrived late for Mass. I'm sure it wasn't five minutes, but he sent us all home while he stayed for the next one.

Grandpop worked as an inspector at a fabricated-steel plant a few subway stops away. Leaving for the night shift in his cap and peacoat, clutching his lunch box, he could have been hurrying to a shop in Donegal, Ireland.

But Grandpop's pride and his claim to higher status was his role as local Democratic committeeman. On Election Day, it was his job to get out the vote on the neighboring blocks. Back in his day, that meant earning $35 in what we now call walking-around money. It was supposed to help in rousing the party faithful. He grandly put it in his pocket.

Grandpop considered it his due. He would brag to my brothers and me that he delivered "the best division in the city" for the Democrats. If it was true, it may have been helped by the division's changing demography. By the 1970s, the area around Fifteenth Street had transformed from mostly Irish American to African American. The remaining exceptions included the Shields family and the guy next door. "Nice fellow," Grandpop would say of that next-door neighbor, adding after a pause: "Polish." He didn't want us to think, even for a moment, he wasn't keeping tribal watch.

There was a legendary side to Grandpop's, and therefore the family's, politics. It was a holdover from the Great Depression. While Grandmom faithfully pinched pennies and kept food on the table through those hard years, he made the nine-mile walk back and forth to city hall, looking for a job. As kids, we never thought to ask why someone would go there to job hunt. It never occurred to anyone that it needed explaining. It was contained in a single word: patronage. Grandpop was part of the reining political machine, which would rule Philadelphia for much of a century. He figured he was owed a job.

That patronage job finally arrived decades later, after Grandpop had retired from his position at the plant. It came from his new party, the Democrats. It was a sinecure with the election commission, a no-heavy-lifting city hall slot reserved for the party faithful. I loved the fact that Grandpop, though a lifelong teetotaler, always met his turn to bring a fifth of whiskey to work—a beverage to lighten the chores of his fellow Democratic loyalists. He was a party man to the end.

Oftentimes I think back on those long evening walks when my brother Bert and I would join Grandpop, his thoughts, and his Phillies cigar. On the way home he'd stop at the corner of Broad and Hunting Park and pick up the first edition of the next day's *Philadelphia Inquirer*. Later, after turning the last page, he would look up from his chair under the mantelpiece, fix me in his gaze, and declare with total delight, "Christopher John!" It was a ritual of recognition. He was according me, a young Irish boy, a dignity often reserved for grown-ups.

We called Dad's mom "Grandmom-in-Chestnut-Hill." An immigrant in her teens from Northern Ireland, Matilda Gardner was destined to be a housemaid for one of the old-money families in Philadelphia's affluent Chestnut Hill neighborhood. Orange to the core, she was a proud member of the local Presbyterian church. She was a strong, industrious woman who never gave up her native accent.

The fact that our beloved Grandmom was not Catholic remained for Mom a snag of inconsistency in our family's faith. Having won over Dad to Catholicism not long after the wedding, she felt the need to explain to us boys why our dear Grandmom-in-Chestnut Hill wasn't in the fold.

She once told us that Grandmom went to the Presbyterian church because there wasn't a Catholic church in Chestnut Hill when she first arrived. But when Bert and I tried that out on Grandmom, she refused to play Mom's game. "I'm a Presbyterian," she declared with full authority. "I've always been a Presbyterian!"

My paternal grandfather, Robert Bruce Matthews, came from Dover, England. A chauffeur for the wealthy, he spent his life getting fired and sent packing, along with his family, usually after telling off yet another boss. This pattern tended to drive his seesawing politics. When he liked an employer, he'd adopt his aristocratic views; when not, he'd turn angrily left.

Grandmom-in-Chestnut Hill eventually had to make it on her own, which she did with impressive self-reliance. When Grandpop died in the early 1950s, she carried on, establishing her own laundry business. We'd see the butlers and other servants of the old families come to pick up their pressed shirts in those stately brown cases. It allowed her to send me a book on American history every birthday and Christmas. With the help of her reliable Frigate Book Shop, she kept my brother up with the Hardy Boys, and me with George Washington at Valley Forge.

Her world and her house, where Bert and I would spend a week each summer when Mom and Dad were on vacation, was also a lesson in history. Its walls were lined with vintage paintings and engravings from pastoral England, reminders of life's trials and poverty's curse.

Grandmom's bedroom, on the other hand, was a tribute to her new country. Three photographs looked down from the wall over her bed, those of her wartime sons: Uncle Bob, who served as a colonel in the US Army Air Forces in Australia; Uncle George, who commanded a tank in Europe, where the GIs killed countless Germans and liberated concentration camps; and Dad in his sailor's uniform. What pride she and her husband must have felt. Immigrants from the United Kingdom, they had three sons fighting alongside it. It was just as Winston Churchill had prophesized in 1940: a conflict in which "the New World, with all its power and might, steps forth to the rescue and liberation of the old."

CHAPTER TWO

GOD'S COUNTRY

Mom and Dad's decision in 1950 to leave the old street-corner world of the row houses and head for the outer territory of Philadelphia was part of a national movement. They were able to do it for the same reasons as other young families of that era. Thanks to Dad's service in the navy, the GI Bill financed his way to an engineering degree at Drexel, a house in the suburbs, and from there to the middle class.

The greater driving force in that direction was Mom's maverick spirit and ambition for better things. As a teenager, she disobeyed her mother's order not to go roller-skating, broke her arm, then spent a week suffering in secret. It took the same courage for her to marry someone from outside the church. Her daring was about to produce the first of us, Bert. I was number two. I recall Grandmom Shields scraping the wheels of a baby carriage for Jim, Mom's third. This rapid enlargement of our family may have had something to do with the decision to move to greener pastures. Mom, Dad, Bert, and I had been squeezed into a minuscule apartment around the corner from our grandparents, and we were bursting at the seams. Stuck above a grocery store, I remember rocks being thrown by the landlord's children at our glazed bathroom window. I think we'd become unwanted tenants.

It was at the dawn of a new decade that Mom and Dad took the great leap of purchasing an acre of property in Somerton, on the city's border with Bucks County, and building an eight-room Colonial. Like other postwar couples, they were breaking free of the old neighborhoods and heading out to the fresh air and open spaces. That made the young Matthews family part of history, one of the many bugle calls of the baby boom. It was five years after the end of World War II. The Yanks had come marching home, and children, lots of them, had been marching out. And thanks to President Franklin Delano Roosevelt's thoughtful commitment to raise up the men who had fought and won the war, and Mom and Dad's ambition, our family was now inhabiting what Grandpop christened "God's country." We three boys, Bert, I, and Jim, were, in his words, "the young princes." Bert was the leader; I was the challenger. He was the North in the Civil War; I was the South. He was the navy man; I was the army. Along with Jim, the youngest, we imagined a world of our own, each with his own role to play.

But it must have been a shock, especially for Mom. There were cows out back, farmhouses in five directions, and Protestants. Only a small chapel a mile away stood as an outpost of her true church. There were just twenty-five Catholic families, including us, when we arrived in Somerton, back then a distant hamlet; a rural stop on the Reading railroad line to West Trenton.

There were other things making it hard for Mom. For one thing, she didn't drive. That meant everything, not just the morning milk, but diapers, soda—even potato chips and pretzels—arrived by truck. When Mom went to the A&P grocery store, Dad had to take her. I think of her stuck up there in God's country all alone with Jim and, then, her newest, Bruce, with the rest of us at school and Dad in his new job downtown as a city hall court reporter.

For Bert and me, it was fun. Practically every day, we were in the endless field out back playing war games. In the beginning, that meant the US against the Germans in World War II. Then came the new war in Korea. This made it the US against the Commies.

Bert and I were, looking back, wildly precocious regarding world events. For that, I credit Bert, not just for the war games but also for his fascination with the navy (in which he would one day become an officer) and his lifelong love of history. Back then I was just trying to keep up.

With four young boys in the family, there was a regimen to our lives out there in the country. This was especially the case at bedtime. It was teeth brushed, prayers said, and under the covers by seven thirty, or we couldn't listen to *The Lone Ranger* on the radio. Back then, television was nowhere yet in sight, at least not in Somerton.

There was never any question that we boys would go to parochial school. That's how Mom grew up and how most Catholics in Philadelphia raised their children in those days. But it must have been quite a challenge for those nuns at the Maternity of the Blessed Virgin Mary Boys' school to handle that first-grade class of ours. There were a hundred of us—so many that they had put us in the school auditorium. Everything was done with West Point discipline. We were to line up for everything. Little colored squares pinned on each of us denoted which bus we took home at three o'clock. The drilling went on all day: "No talking!" "Hands folded!" "Single file!"

My first dispute with a Sister came early on. We were learning pronouns. Aiming her long wooden pointer my way, Sister instructed me to identify a two-letter word up there on the blackboard. Now in the spotlight, I recited what I thought was the answer: "U . . . S."

Sister corrected me, first mildly. "Yes, but what is the word?"

I repeated what I'd just said: "U . . . S."

"Us!" She finally pronounced the pronoun she was seeking.

For me and my brother Bert, the US was the American army in the war. US was on the uniforms of our soldiers. The US was our side in the great conflicts that we'd acted out in our daily war games in the backyard. That explains my persistence with Sister that day. I was speaking of a larger world; Sister was dabbling in pronouns!

I like to think that early, larger point of view of mine was the beginning of it all.

One day I walked across the small creek to our little branch of the Philadelphia Free Library. I got my first library card and took out a picture book on Alexander the Great, the young Greek leader, son of King Philip II of Macedon, who conquered the known world while still in his early twenties. Three-quarters of a century later, I still know the smell of that book. We were small, after all, but our souls were large. I was thinking of this young man who led his country to greatness.

For whatever reason, I had this early curiosity about politics. I have this clear notion of when it started. I was sitting next to Dad in a downtown movie theater. We were about to see a matinee. When the newsreel started, I saw a high-ranking military officer boarding an airplane. Something in the announcer's stentorian voice got me to ask Dad if that impressive man boarding the plane might be president. "No, but he will be!" he answered. The man in the newsreel was General Dwight D. Eisenhower, supreme commander of the recently founded North Atlantic Treaty Organization, or NATO. He was getting ready to answer the Republican Party's call to lead the country.

Politics was all around us. In March 1953 Sister solemnly declared that Josef Stalin, the Soviet dictator, had died. She then led us in prayer. I wondered what we were praying for. What was the "supplication"? Did we want the evil Communist dictator to go to hell? Was it to limit his time in purgatory? Or was Sister thinking of a simple prayer of thanksgiving that the shadow of this terrible figure had left us for good?

CHAPTER THREE

A TRIP TO WASHINGTON

In second grade, Mom and Dad took Bert, me, and Jim on a trip to Washington. Mom had an intriguing excuse to give the sisters for our absences. She said that it was because of Dad's "business." She justified that dodgy alibi to us by saying those were the only days our father could get off. Our parents' true business was teaching their children about their country.

For that, I say three cheers.

The excitement of the adventure grabbed me and still does. It was May, when Washington is at its best, sunny and starting to get warm. It was like arriving in a different climate and a separate, gleaming world. For me, it was an eye-opener to a city that would become my workplace, my discovered home, my love.

Like any tourist, I can ring off the unforgettable sights that won me over: the tour of the White House, then occupied by—just as Dad had predicted—President Dwight Eisenhower; the dozens of old-time bicycles lodged at the Smithsonian Institution; the slave quarters at George Washington's Mount Vernon estate; the Doric columns of General Robert E. Lee's mansion; the changing of the guard at the Tomb of the Unknown Soldier; the elevator ride up the Washington Monument; the Lincoln and Jefferson Memorials. I even spotted the small Liberty Bell alongside the Treasury Building, only to have Dad tell me that the real one was back home in Philadelphia.

Those days made *Washington* a dazzling word to me; a place in the sun that radiated history and honored the country's great leaders. If I hadn't been taken to Washington that spring of 1953, when I was seven, I don't think I would have followed the same road in life. Seven decades later, there remain the memories of my first visit to this city that George Washington and a French-born military engineer named Pierre L'Enfant once envisioned on horseback as they looked down from the site of the future Capitol. I cherish the photograph Dad took of Mom and us before the Lincoln Memorial, this country's great temple of hope. It says so much about our parents' love of our country. They wanted their boys to see our nation's capital and find a feeling for its history.

In that, they succeeded.

CHAPTER FOUR

WE WERE THE KIDS WHO HID UNDER OUR DESKS

During my early school years, I had a dream of leading a cavalry charge across the fields of Russia. It was an anachronism, of course. I knew full well in the age of atomic bombs that great wars were no longer won by attacks on horseback.

The reality of atomic hell was in fact a recurring lesson at the new St. Christopher's School in Somerton. A certain alarm bell would send us ducking under our little wooden desks. Once there, we were to recite what could be our final prayers. Fifteen minutes! That's how long it would take, Sister said, from first warning to when the bombs began dropping. This was only an estimate, she allowed. What we had to expect, nonetheless, was that the bombing of our new four-room school would mark the outbreak of World War III and with it the end of the world. Following that would come the General Judgment in which all of us would be standing in a long line before God and His verdict.

Those doomsday exercises were but one intimation of the Red menace. Every Sunday, we would pray at the end of Mass "for the conversion of Russia." This signified the Roman Catholic Church's recognized role as "the greatest bulwark" against Communism. Weekdays at school, we honored another anti-Communist ritual. It was called "ransoming pagan babies." A $5 donation would bring a poor Chinese baby into the Free World and out of the hands of the Communists. Anyone who brought the $5 would be celebrated throughout the day as a liberator of an unbaptized child in Red China.

Many Catholics of the early 1950s believed that the country's governing elite had "sold out" to the Communists by letting them grab control of Eastern Europe. I remember Sister speaking disparagingly one day of President Franklin Roosevelt. The very next day, she tried to soften her judgment. It seemed that an influential family in the parish had intervened. FDR had done "some good things" before World War II. She said it was later, when he was tired and sick, that he gave away Eastern Europe to the Communists.

This belief in FDR's betrayal was widespread among Catholics. I came home from St. Christopher's School one afternoon to find our new Admiral television on. The black-and-white screen showed a trial of some kind. It was the Army-McCarthy hearings pitting the Wisconsin Communist-hunting senator against the government. Mom wasn't rooting for the army. I remember Dad was more measured. A loyal but reserved Republican, he held that Joe McCarthy was right about Communist influence in the United States but had "gone too far."

One Saturday afternoon in 1955, I went with some friends from St. Christopher's to the movies. The film was *Jump into Hell*. It was about a war I hadn't heard of before: the French army's conflict with the Communist rebels in Indochina. The action centered on the battle of Dien Bien Phu, the final French defeat. The "Commies" that Bert and I had taken turns playing in our war games out back of our house had just won a big one on the other side of the world.

CHAPTER FIVE

CATHOLIC SCHOOL
BACK THEN

When Charles joined us in 1953, Mom and Dad had five sons. They raised us with many of the benefits of the comfortable middle class: private high school, private colleges, piano lessons, and eventually a summer house on the Jersey Shore. They managed to do it through a self-denying frugality and serious discipline. I doubt that Dad bought so much as a Coke on his way home from work, and I know that Mom was as deliberate as a diamond cutter with the weekly grocery shopping.

They were just as generous teaching us about their world. Many a dinner ended with our parents discussing their generation's experience. It was often defined in terms of World War II. The quality of home construction, they would say, had dropped "since the war." Mom, especially, reminded us that the treatment of Catholics was far worse "before the war." She reminisced how the job application for the big Philadelphia milk company included "religion" on its questionnaire. Writing "Roman Catholic" meant you didn't get the job.

We Catholics, even "after the war," lived in our own prescribed world. The week began, of course, at church on Sunday morning. The earlier the Mass, Dad and Mom clearly believed, the better the Catholic. Eight o'clock was for the truly devout. Those who barely made the eleven o'clock service were assumed to have been out at a nightclub the night before.

Monday night was Dad's night for the Holy Name Society, a fraternal group for men committed to not taking the name of Jesus "in vain." Tuesday night was Mom's Sodality night. Joining this spiritual organization was simply what the good women of the parish did, like obtaining the church's blessing after childbirth.

Wednesday was the odd night off. Thursday evening was reserved for the Knights of Columbus meeting, another fraternal organization where Dad made most of his friends. Friday night was K of C bowling and, after that, a poker game into the morning.

On Saturday morning, even after that long week of work, relentless evening events, and the previous night's poker, Dad went off to play golf, usually with Gene Shields, who was no relation but known widely and well as our father's best friend.

The favorite time of the week for me was Friday night. I remember waking up in the dark of night still wearing my dungarees; this meant I had fallen asleep watching television, and Dad had carried me to bed. This told me it was Friday. It meant I could look forward to two days without having to go to school. That's how much I must have hated it.

Parochial school in the 1950s was hard and tedious, with discipline encased in the aroma of disinfectant. You spent six hours a day sitting at a desk, your hands folded, not saying a word, not laughing, not showing a hint of spontaneity. If you mastered this docility, you were rewarded with As in "conduct" and "attention during class." If you were like me, you took home two Cs on your report card, both written in red.

There were also summary punishments. The ruler, especially the metal-edged type, was not just for measuring or drawing straight lines. Another punishment for misconduct was being ordered to stand in the back of the classroom with your arms outstretched while holding up a heavy stack of textbooks. You have to wonder from what gulag the sisters got hold of that sugarplum.

The default punishment remained those grades on our report cards, which had to be signed and returned the next day. Since parents in those days were at least as tough as the nuns, this meant there was no escape. You were trapped in a closed penal system. This is what electrified a command to "go stand in the corridor." That banishment to the hall could be followed by whatever punishment might come to Sister's mind. It was like being imprisoned until a set time of execution. It compounded the punishment with the dread of what we would face at home should Sister refer the matter there.

I record these memories with some reservation. The strictness of the nuns needs to be balanced against their selfless gift of education, teaching us to read and write, and cheering us through the wonderful weeks of Advent leading to the pageantry of Christmas.

That lifetime commitment to God and the children they taught was personified in our own family. Two of Mom's younger sisters were nuns. I truly loved Aunt Eleanor and Aunt Agnes. Their countless prayers, arriving in spiritual bouquets on birthdays, Christmas, and Easter, blessed my life. I could never reconcile them with some of what happened at St. Christopher's.

Part of the problem for me, I must confess, was *me*. Objectively speaking, I must have been a difficult case back then—a real troublemaker. My restless need for action or attention, whatever it was, clearly didn't thrive in the dungeon-like discipline of a Catholic classroom in the 1950s. I wasn't the sort to sit quietly in my little seat with my hands folded obediently. Even then I may have offered, free of charge, a running commentary, an up-to-the minute report of whatever came into my uncharted mind. I'd say something or laugh or otherwise break ranks and, just like that, find myself in trouble. Again.

Was there a world beyond our Catholic one in those long-ago days? Yes, we were to call those people "non-Catholics." I remember Sister instructing us on that. She said they didn't like being called "Protestants." We were to call them "non-Catholics."

There were strict rules of engagement for such interfaith dealings. It was nonengagement. Mom wouldn't let us go to the Friday-night dances at St. Andrew's-in-the-Field Church. They were "Episcopals." She was forever defending the moat that protected us from that other world. Even Dad, raised in his father's Episcopal faith, remained vigilant. "These things can get out of hand," he advised me soberly when I began seeing a nice Protestant girl in my senior year of high school.

In the summer of 1956 we were coming up our driveway in our Chevrolet, listening to the Democratic National Convention. It was the roll call on the vice presidential nomination, a battle between Tennessee senator Estes Kefauver and someone I'd never heard of named Kennedy. I rooted for Kefauver, the one I knew, and even made up a pun: "Keef-all-for Eisenhower."

When Kennedy conceded, Mom said it was the same old anti-Catholic story. It was just like 1928, when New York governor Al Smith, the Democratic candidate for president, was rejected on account of his religion.

Mom was hardly alone with those feelings that young Jack Kennedy had just been robbed of the vice presidential nomination for the exact same reason in 1956. Four years later, millions of Catholics were going to make sure he wouldn't get robbed again.

In the fall of 1956 I was pulled further into politics by what was happening in Hungary. Its people and its army, trapped behind the Iron Curtain, were rebelling. We who prayed each Sunday for the fall of Communism were now forced to watch Moscow clamp its grip on one of its captive Eastern European countries.

We Americans were frustrated by our inability to help the courageous Hungarians. How could we, if any fight with Russia could lead to a nuclear World War III? That said, what we saw happening in Hungary proved everything we'd been taught about the evil of the Communists. Even at ten years old, I could see it.

CHAPTER SIX

KENNEDY VS. NIXON

My first job in the news business was with Philadelphia's *Evening Bulletin*. I was paid one and two-thirds cents for each five-cent newspaper I delivered to people's driveways. It took a lot of bike riding: two miles to pick up the papers, two more miles up and back on the route, and then two more to get home.

One intriguing bit of economics I learned later was the three-way connection among newspapers, department stores, and politics. For whatever reason, Wednesday was the big sales day in Philadelphia stores such as Wanamaker's. That explained why the Tuesday afternoon newspapers were so heavy with full-page advertisements. Those fat *Bulletin*s were the reason I needed to double back on those days to fill my bicycle basket a second time. Those big sales explained, too, why presidential candidates always scheduled their big motorcades through downtown Philly at Wednesday lunchtime. This allowed them to grab credit for crowds that were already on the sidewalk.

I suppose everyone has a moment that wins them over to a lifelong enthusiasm. It might be a popular song heard in your teens, a local sports hero. For me, it was the 1960 battle between Vice President Richard Nixon and Senator John F. Kennedy that got me truly excited about politics. The real fight began in Wisconsin with the hot primary contest between Kennedy and Senator Hubert Humphrey from neighboring Minnesota.

It featured a contest of the glamorous, young Catholic against the old-shoe Protestant. All the magazines—*Life, Look,* the *Saturday Evening Post*—did big pictorials on the race. The article I remember most was the one in *Columbia*, the magazine of the Knights of Columbus. It reported proudly of the progress of Jack Kennedy, a brother Knight.

The nuns at our church were also excited about the prospect of a Catholic winning the presidency. Kennedy liked to joke that his way to estimate a crowd's size was to count the nuns, still distinctive back then in their traditional habits, and "multiply them by a hundred." That was not so bad a method. Not long before the November election, a sister from St. Christopher's called our house wanting to know how to get herself and others at the convent registered to vote. She had Dad mixed up with Tom Matthews, the local Democratic committeeman.

They were not the only partisans moved by religion. Several religious people knocked at our front door to warn us of the dangers of having a Catholic president. It only made Mom feistier.

Kennedy's Catholicism became an even bigger issue after he won in Wisconsin and had to compete with Humphrey again a month later, this time in heavily Protestant West Virginia. When Kennedy pulled off a win there, upsetting the odds, the nomination was his. After winning at the Los Angeles convention on the first ballot, Kennedy picked Texas senator Lyndon Johnson for his vice presidential running mate. When Johnson and his wife, Lady Bird, came out to meet the press, I sensed there was something not quite settled about it. Something sweaty.

As the country would later learn, it was for Johnson the weary end to a daylong struggle. Whereas Jack Kennedy saw the Texan as necessary for victory, his brother Bobby saw the selection as a betrayal to their liberal allies, especially those in the labor movement.

In any case, the Democrats now had their ticket for 1960, and I, at fourteen, swung hard for it. It was not just Jack Kennedy himself but also the whole "dynasty" thing. I wanted him first to serve two terms, then Lyndon Johnson, then Bobby, and, finally, the youngest brother, Teddy.

But I was still in a Republican family. Dad saw Richard Nixon as a common soul. Both were the first in their families to wear suits to work. Like Dad, Nixon had to make it himself into the middle class. When the Republicans convened in Chicago, and I began hearing "California, Here I Come," I veered back into the family's GOP ranks.

For me, it was the Cold War that decided it. Like most Americans back then, I could see our country losing ground to Russia. First came the shock of *Sputnik*, the Soviet satellite that beat us into space, in 1957. Two years earlier, having watched the US rocket expert Wernher von Braun speak with such enthusiasm about the quest on Walt Disney's TV program, I'd just assumed that we Americans would be the first to launch a satellite that could circle around Earth. But Disney and von Braun were now proven wrong.

Then came Cuba. When the bearded Fidel Castro overthrew the dictator Fulgencio Batista on January 1, 1959, after six years of revolution, we applauded. When Castro sat for media interviews with journalists such as Edward R. Murrow, then toured New York City, we clung to the hope that he was on our side. Then came the firing squads, the taking over of American businesses, and finally the realization that he was a Communist and had been all along. Suddenly we had an ally of Moscow just ninety-four miles offshore of Florida.

So when Nixon picked former Republican senator Henry Cabot Lodge Jr., our tough envoy to the United Nations, as his running mate, it won me over. By the time the Republicans left Chicago, I was with Nixon all the way. When the first great debate between Nixon and Kennedy aired in a historic national broadcast on September 26, I rooted hard for the vice president and thought he'd won. Most people didn't. It was the first time I realized that people watching broadcast debates—which clearly included me—tend to think that *their* candidate came out on top.

By the third of the four debates, Nixon had found an issue: Quemoy and Matsu, two tiny groups of rocky islands located just off the southeastern coast of mainland Communist China but belonging to our Chinese

Nationalist allies on the island of Formosa (now Taiwan). In 1958 China laid claim to Quemoy and Matsu and began bombarding its inhabitants. Although both Nixon and Kennedy were committed to defending For- mosa in the event of a Communist attack, they differed on the United States' responsibility regarding the islands. Kennedy's view was that we should come to their aid only if Chinese aggression there was part of a broader attack against Formosa, while Nixon stated we should defend them in any case; that it was a matter of Cold War principle.

That struck the country as the stronger position, and Kennedy recog- nized the fact. Conditioned by world war to view the ideological struggle in territorial terms, we saw every advance forward by the Communists as a threat to us.

These were the days when politics involved hoopla. People wore large campaign buttons and plastic boater hats bearing the name of their can- didate. There were big rallies, downtown parades, and street corner rallies.

At La Salle College High School, where Bert and I were by now enrolled, my homeroom teacher polled students on the upcoming election. It was twenty-four for Kennedy, nine for Nixon. I was surprised it was that close. Everyone around me seemed to be for our fellow Catholic. At lunchtime, I'd argue with Chris Hartman, a friend who'd grown up Republican but switched to Democrat. He was a huge fan of Franklin Roosevelt's, perhaps from public speaking classes. He was the class's ora- tor and debating star. I gave him big odds that Kennedy wouldn't win by more than two million votes.

I was doing some polling of my own. Well before Election Day, I asked Dad if he was going to vote for Kennedy. Weren't we Catholics? "I'm a Republican," he answered. Irish Catholic Mom kept her own counsel. Drying dishes alongside her at the sink after supper one night, I challenged her for being for Kennedy just because he was Catholic. That hit a nerve. With a flash of anger, Mom said that Grandmom-in-Chestnut Hill had become a US citizen after decades in this country only so she could vote for General Eisenhower, who was known to be attending Presbyterian services.

In the end, my heart was deeply for Nixon, the guy with the five o'clock shadow and the resentment. I remember him standing before a crowd in his raincoat laying out the class bitterness. "You know it's not *Jack*'s money they're going to be spending," he said. He was the underdog against the rival who had it all: Kennedy had the looks, Jacqueline, the money, and yet Nixon nearly pulled it off. Again, he reminded me of Dad, a middle-class guy trying to make it.

Election night was brutal and unforgettable. It seemed like the world had closed in on me. Kennedy won Connecticut early, then the returns from the big Democratic cities, Philadelphia and Chicago, came pouring in for him. It was the last time I cried on election night, even as Dad tried to console me. Nixon came on television late that night to say, "if the present trend continues, Mr. Kennedy, Senator Kennedy, will be the next president of the United States." In the end, although Kennedy won the Electoral College handily, 303 to 219, he only squeaked past Nixon in the popular tally by 112,827 votes, or 49.72 percent to 49.55 percent.

Such rituals of defeat are perhaps the most poignant, honest moments in politics. It's when fact crushes hope, when truth cannot lose the argument. In normal times, it's when the losing candidate learns what people truly feel about you, and it hurts far too much to hide. And that's the way it ought to be, because it's the one sure way we know it was a true electoral verdict.

The next day, I delivered the *Bulletin* with the front page declaring Kennedy the winner. In the months after Nixon's defeat, I continued my political shift to the Right, becoming a backer of Arizona's hawkish senator Barry Goldwater. In those early months of the Kennedy administration, I was fully aboard with the conservative call to arms against big government at home and stopping the Communists abroad. Dad bought me a copy of Goldwater's *The Conscience of a Conservative* at a downtown bookstore. I became a regular reader of *National Review*—even went to a speech by New Right journalist William F. Buckley Jr., sponsored by the Young Republicans. During a visit to Washington during my sophomore year of high school, my friend Tim Urbanski and I paid a special visit to Senator Goldwater's office on Capitol Hill. Though the Senate was not in session, it didn't lessen our excitement.

At fifteen, I was a true-blue, young conservative.

All this was a vital part, I suppose, of my political growing up. I was taking a strong stand against Communist aggression around the world and a strong stand for individual freedom and against big government here at home. The important thing for me was that I was now taking the philosophical part of politics seriously.

CHAPTER SEVEN

LA SALLE

Going to La Salle College High School, a private all-boys Catholic school, was a privilege. It was a great school. In my first year, the classes were held on the La Salle College campus—quite a jump from parochial school. I loved the place, its old buildings, its courtyard, the campus bookstore. Before La Salle High School moved to the suburbs in my sophomore year, it meant going to school in North Philadelphia, just a few subway stops up from Grandmom and Grandpop.

The teacher at La Salle who changed my life was Gerald Tremblay. I had him for English and remember how he told us on the first day that he had no interest in instructing us in grammar. He said if we hadn't known the basics, we wouldn't have gotten into La Salle in the first place.

What he taught was English and American literature. I will never forget him standing in the aisle during a class on Shakespeare, reading dramatically from a paperback of *Henry IV, Part 2.* There we were in the closeness of the Boar's Head Inn with jovial Jack Falstaff. The excitement of his robust recitation was that real.

Mr. Tremblay was the moderator of the school newspaper, the *Wisterian,* named for the wisteria vines that clung to the building walls of the old college campus. In the autumn of my senior year, I began working in the *Wisterian* editing room, writing articles, basically making myself at home. One day, Mr. Tremblay made a personal declaration. "If you're

going to spend all your time around here, you might as well be an editor!"
And thus it began. For much of my last year at La Salle, my name was
on the *Wisterian* masthead.

It's impossible to measure Mr. Tremblay's influence. He was the first
person I knew who drove a Volkswagen Beetle. He was the only grown-up
I knew like him. Life, as he lived and gloried in it, was about reading,
about Broadway, about culture. It was most definitely not about making
money and driving big cars. We had a record player in the *Wisterian* office
and one 45-rpm record: "Silver Dagger," sung by Joan Baez. It was 1962,
and we were being lured already by the spirit of the sixties, learning to
reject everything bourgeois.

That same senior year, I wrote to the State Department asking why we
were fighting for South Vietnam. The answer I received from the Office
of Media Services was contained in a single word: *rice*. South Vietnam
was the "Rice Bowl of Asia." Communists in China wanted South Vietnam to get its rice! It told me that our bureaucracy was under pressure to
explain a conflict to the American public that it didn't understand itself.
I had thought this war was being fought to stop the spread of global
Communism.

Mr. Tremblay, for his part, did more than instruct; he opened windows
for me. One was on New York. He took us to the Scholastic Press Association convention at Columbia University. I recall the entire weekend
from the time boarding the train at the old North Philadelphia station
through all the nights at the Hotel Taft, where each room door still had
a compartment for leaving your shoes to be shined overnight.

We saw three Broadway shows that weekend: *A Man for All Seasons, A
Thousand Clowns*, and *Stop the World—I Want to Get Off*, starring Anthony
Newley. Just as Mom and Dad introduced my brothers and me to the
nation's capital, Mr. Tremblay was introducing my fellow editors and me
to Gotham.

There was another honor I won at La Salle that I hold dear. It was
earning a spot on the school's College Bowl team moderated by Tremblay

and another English teacher. Based on the popular TV quiz show that pitted two teams of students from US colleges and universities against each other, it allowed me to show what I knew beyond the latest class assignment. For example, I was able to identify the year of the "Disputed Election" and the names of the presidential candidates involved. It was 1876, Rutherford B. Hayes versus Samuel Tilden. Spouting those answers on the spot accorded me a celebrity usually reserved for the stars of varsity basketball.

Mr. Tremblay's own politics were a matter of physics. His guiding principle was to keep the country in balance. When politics headed too far in one direction—right or left—he voted to pull it back. He had one hard-and-fast exception, however: he believed Richard Nixon was what was *wrong* with American politics.

Early in the spring of my senior year, I was accepted to the University of Notre Dame and then to Holy Cross College, where my brother Bert was attending. Mr. Tremblay, who, as a student, read every novel in the Villanova University library, argued for Holy Cross, on the grounds that the Jesuit school in Worcester, Massachusetts, was better in the liberal arts.

It's an example of how a single person's influence can shift another's life direction.

In my case, it was far from the last.

CHAPTER EIGHT

HOLY CROSS

"Wall to wall Irish." That's how Catholic tribalists bragged about the place. Founded in 1843, the College of the Holy Cross was located in central Massachusetts to protect it from the anti-Catholic mobs that had attacked their schools in Boston.

A political lesson one picked up early at Holy Cross was that inherited pain of Yankee prejudice. It was a Holy Cross alum who, in 1910, wrote the ditty: "And this is good old Boston / the home of the bean and the cod / where the Lowells talk to the Cabots / and the Cabots talk only to God." Perhaps it was that David-versus-Goliath spirit that attracted me to a small college that each fall scheduled itself against football powerhouses such as Penn State and Syracuse Universities. I joined Mom and Dad to visit Bert at Holy Cross on a parents' weekend and found something cozily inviting about the place.

I'd been a freshman only a few months when, checking my mail after lunch on Friday, November 22, 1963, a classmate confronted me with the flash news from Dallas. "I'll bet you five dollars that Kennedy has been shot!" he exclaimed. After being taken aback by the gross tastelessness of the remark, I was struck by the news itself.

I had read something of the president's planned trip to Texas. There'd been reports of the nasty treatment that Kennedy's United Nations ambassador, Adlai Stevenson, had received there earlier. "Shot." It carried a torturous ambiguity that followed me as I headed to World History. When I arrived in the classroom, James Powers, the professor, announced we could skip his lecture without getting a "cut." We were allowed just three cuts a semester. Struck by how many stayed, I headed to the basement of a sophomore dormitory that I knew had a television. I spent the rest of the afternoon watching CBS newscaster Walter Cronkite, absorbing the coverage and imagining a different world, one without President Kennedy. At noon our time, JFK was the country's elected leader. Now, in the space of an early afternoon, the man who had been the focus of all our political conversation was as gone as Abraham Lincoln.

A few days later, on the way back home to Philadelphia for Thanksgiving, I met a woman at New York's Port Authority Terminal. As we were going down the escalator together, she asked where I went to college. When I told her Holy Cross, she said, "It must be very sad up there." I believe she was expressing a special sympathy for the Irish Catholics who had lost one of their own. I wish I could thank her again. Decades later, I received similar sentiments from inside the Kennedy circle itself. New York senator Daniel Patrick Moynihan, who'd served as JFK's assistant secretary of labor, told me, "We've never gotten over it." After a solemn pause, he added, "*You*'ve never gotten over it." I felt admitted to a brotherhood.

Winters in Worcester were cold and dark, like a dank factory town in England. This was especially true in the weeks after the assassination. Perhaps it was this gloom emanating from Dallas that explains the glee that arose with the arrival to this country of the Beatles. On an unforgettable Sunday night in February 1964, they appeared on *The Ed Sullivan Show*. Our entire corridor managed to pack itself into the resident assistant's suite to watch. Anyone who says that the Beatles' arrival in this country was a historic pick-me-up from Dallas has it right. We needed a testimony to life, and the four fellows from Liverpool sang it right at us!

After a dreary first semester, I had decided to give myself a needed break. I quit the Air Force ROTC. The weekly drills and the simplistic ROTC class on civics seemed ridiculously basic, certainly to me.

"What are you going to do for your Uncle Sammy?" the ROTC commandant asked. If only to get out the door, I said I was going to join the Peace Corps. The good colonel known for having "the best boots in the air force" found those words somewhere beneath pathetic.

My ambition that spring semester was to win election for treasurer of the Student Congress, the highest collegewide office open to a freshman. It was a case of sheer ambition; an early chance to distinguish myself at something I thought I understood: politics.

My campaign tactic was basic "retail." Starting at nine o'clock each night, I would visit every corridor of every dorm, knock on every door, meet every student, and ask for his vote. Since I was a waiter in the campus dining hall, I took advantage of that, too. I had a "Matthews for Treasurer" card printed up and asked each of my fellow waiters to wear it on his uniform. I wanted everyone to see that name at every meal.

My touch-all-bases strategy worked. I won the election by almost a hundred votes over a popular rival. I did it by going door-to-door and asking people to vote for me. Life, I would learn, could be as basic as that.

There was other political news at Holy Cross that spring of 1964. President Lyndon Johnson would be speaking at the June commencement. Joseph Califano, a Holy Cross grad, was working for LBJ, who was then enjoying the national goodwill as Kennedy's loyal successor. Like the rest of the country, my sentiment about Kennedy's assassination was a huge catalyst for my own shifting political loyalties.

That summer, the Democratic National Convention came to Atlantic City, New Jersey. Working as a busboy in a restaurant near our family's summer home in nearby Ocean City, I headed there as soon as dinner was over. Up on the boardwalk, I came across a lavish fund-raiser at the Shelburne Hotel. I waited outside, watching the wealthy contributors emerge, then began asking them for their plastic admission badges. Finally, a well-dressed woman said, "Take it; I can't use it anymore."

It got me in the door. Wearing a blue blazer, I could have been just another son of a serious Democratic donor. Inside, I found myself face-to-face with the celebrities of national politics. I shook hands with Hubert Humphrey, Henry "Scoop" Jackson, Adlai Stevenson, and Eugene McCarthy, who seemed happily surprised that a young person like me even knew who he was. I, of course, was in heaven.

On the night of Johnson's nomination, I stood on the Atlantic City boardwalk looking up at the president on the balcony. That night, I drove around Atlantic City in a friend's convertible showing off the life-size "Missouri Mule" I'd picked out from the rubble on the convention floor. It was a souvenir from my first Democratic convention.

By then, politics had become my running conversation. Through my four college years, I could be found after dinner down in the snug basement coffee shop of Kimball Hall talking politics over a Coke. It was a precursor to what I would one day do professionally at that time of day. Massachusetts senator Edward Markey, who attended Boston College, once said I was getting paid all those years by MSNBC for doing what I did for free night after night in the Holy Cross cafeteria.

The distinguishing feature of our Jesuit college was the number of required courses in philosophy and theology. They dealt with elemental questions that could find their way into late-night dorm conversations. These bull sessions faced a surefire fact-check. It was entirely monetary. Nothing shut someone up more abruptly than that most primitive of challenges: "How much you want to bet?" In those many decades before Google, the bet challenge was our primitive search engine.

Holy Cross equipped you to argue your case. My favorite classes were in the history of economic thought. Discussions of Adam Smith, David Ricardo, Karl Marx, and John Stuart Mill often dealt with the conflicts between the individual and society, a topic I would never exhaust.

The Holy Cross grad who had the most influence on me was Joe McGinniss, who graduated only a couple of years ahead of me. While I was still in Worcester, McGinniss was already writing three columns a week for the *Philadelphia Inquirer*. His pieces were so provocative that local radio talk jocks could use him to light up the phone lines. It would be nine in the morning, and you'd hear one say, "So, what did you think of Joe McGinniss this morning?"

I remember the time McGinniss traveled to Vietnam to report on the war. Where others headed to the front lines, McGinniss went to report on the army unit that prepared American soldiers' bodies for shipment home. He described in deliberate detail how the US Army packed them in human-size tuna cans, designed to be stacked one on top of the other. McGinniss ended that column praising, with obvious derision, the cold, state-of-the-art efficiency of the operation. He said it enabled the army to get the bodies home in time for Christmas.

It was Joe McGinniss who made me aspire to be a ruddy Irish Catholic columnist; a guy who could walk into his favorite saloon and have the bartender yell something about what I'd written for that morning's newspaper. It didn't matter whether people liked the column or not. What mattered is that it *got* to them. McGinnis went on to write big bestsellers, especially *The Selling of the President*, which described how Richard Nixon both exploited the media and dodged its scrutiny in the 1968 campaign.

By junior year, 1965–66, I was clearly changing my views on politics. I had arrived on campus with a framed photograph of Senator Barry Goldwater in my suitcase. What had changed me? Perhaps it was my father's case against Goldwater's everyone-for-himself libertarianism, especially with regard to his opposition to Social Security. Or what I accepted as the historic necessity of the 1964 Civil Rights Act, which the Arizona senator opposed. Or it could have simply been the sudden escalation of the Vietnam War. The fact is, I was now wearing an army surplus jacket, an overt statement against it. My reading, too, was drifting leftward, from Arthur Schlesinger Jr.'s *A Thousand Days*, about the Kennedy presidency, to Harrison Salisbury's *Behind the Lines—Hanoi*.

Not all the campus was moving with me. In my interview to be a resident assistant in my senior year, I was asked what I would do if I had someone on my corridor who was getting hassled for being antiwar. I responded that I had several friends who were antiwar and didn't think it would be a problem. To the right-wing guy interviewing me, that was clearly the wrong answer. Nevertheless, I got the job and loved it.

CHAPTER NINE

CHAPEL HILL

A few days after graduating from Holy Cross, I received a late letter from the economics chair at the University of North Carolina at Chapel Hill. The offer was a full assistantship, with money to cover everything toward a PhD. I figured it had to be that 99 percent score I'd gotten on the math section of the Graduate Record Examination. I had also been accepted to the University of Minnesota. The attraction there was Walter Heller, who had been President Kennedy's top economic advisor. I decided on Chapel Hill. It was closer to Washington. Maybe I could one day land a consultancy with a federal agency or find some other way to DC.

Nineteen sixty-seven was the "Summer of Love." Scott McKenzie sang, "If you're going to San Francisco / be sure to wear some flowers in your hair." When it comes on the radio nowadays, I still stop what I'm doing and listen. It captures the lightness of that time.

I would spend that summer not in San Francisco but in Ocean City, New Jersey. The chairman of the economics department at UNC said that, despite the generous assistantship he'd awarded me, I'd be smart to make some money; I might need it that winter.

That's the "dismal science" for you.

So, I took a job at a gas station, then I got a gig as a singing waiter at Your Father's Mustache, a beer and burger restaurant with an 1890s theme, across the bridge in Somers Point. Besides serving tables, it involved clapping along with the banjo and baritone, acting jovial with the older crowd of customers, and, yes, singing along. I may not have been very good at it. "Maybe this isn't your cup of tea," the regional manager from New York suggested gently. It was like the priest who said he didn't hear me reciting my Latin as an altar boy. It was another case of me thinking I was doing okay, and the boss coming out with a different verdict. The manager's humor-deprived deputy had already told me I didn't clap correctly. How could I have been so mistaken?

Anyway, I spent that summer pumping gas, changing oil, and, on one glorious occasion, getting a guy's car started by jiggling with the carburetor.

That autumn I found an intellectual life at Chapel Hill. I devoured the *Daily Tar Heel,* the student newspaper that had been famously edited by Thomas Wolfe and years later by notables such as Charles Kuralt, later with CBS News, and Clifton Daniel, later the managing editor of the *New York Times.*

There was also, I soon learned, a northern political subculture and, with it, a strong campus political activism—something beyond what I'd known at Holy Cross. It was the first time I'd heard the word *Fascist* used to casually describe an American with establishment political leanings. It was from a guy dressed in the smartest of antiwar attire: jeans, a perfect plaid shirt, and well-polished boots. A fashion statement.

There were other signs of pretense and stylized bravado. "No pictures!" someone barked at one antiwar meeting. It was as if FBI director J. Edgar Hoover himself had deployed agents ready to jump us. What justified this theatricality, perhaps, was the reality of the draft lurking beyond the campus. Any one of us could be grabbed and sent to Vietnam. One antiwar speaker told the story of the draftee who simply sat waiting for the authorities to come and get him, then, when his time of service was over, put a sign on himself: "Take this body to where you found it." As far as it went, that was the anti–Vietnam War humor.

I remember the more serious words on a bulletin board at the campus center where I went for coffee and donuts each morning. It said that

Allard Lowenstein, a political activist and future Democratic congress-man from New York, was coming to speak that February. I didn't realize at the time that Lowenstein, who had graduated from Chapel Hill in 1949, was leading an effort to "Dump Johnson." His goal was to recruit a strong candidate to run against the president in the upcoming 1968 Democratic primaries. Given my opposition to the war, I was all for it. What had started as a mission to protect South Vietnam from going Communist had become a horrific stalemate, with the US backing one corrupt Saigon regime after another.

In October 1967 I drove up to Washington, DC, with a friend, Glenn Morris, for the March on the Pentagon. The crowd of fifty thousand anti-war protesters included Norman Mailer, who would write about that day in his book *The Armies of the Night.* He would become one of my heroes, especially after reading his first novel, *The Naked and the Dead* and, later, *An American Dream,* about a former congressman who hosted a red-hot radio program.

What I remember most from the march was the smell of trampled grass, the innocence of the crowd, the old leftists with their card tables and literature, the beautiful Washington weather, and the scary sense of mob mentality as the military police moved against the protesters with cold efficiency. The pictures that made the newspaper and weekly magazines, however, showed the young protesters offering flowers to those troops, including the young guy who put a carnation in the barrel of a soldier's M-14 rifle. Of course, Mom didn't like it a bit when I told her I'd been part of the protest. She said I'd been "down there with the Communists."

My real hope in those last months of 1967 was centered on Minnesota's Eugene McCarthy. He seemed to come out of nowhere, the one politi-cian courageous enough to take on Lyndon Johnson and the war. Just as important, he was the one grown-up who told us we weren't just trying to duck the fighting in the jungle—that we were right. What I didn't know at the time was how personal this fight with LBJ was for McCarthy: how three years earlier, Johnson had asked him to join up with him at the 1964 Democratic convention in Atlantic City, fueling speculation that the choice was down to either he or his fellow Minnesotan Hubert Humphrey to be Johnson's vice presidential candidate. McCarthy pulled himself out of contention when he learned the president had already selected Humphrey and was simply using McCarthy as a decoy duck to build suspense.

It was this cruel exploitation by Johnson, which McCarthy called "sadistic," that may well have encouraged the Minnesota senator to take on a mission that everyone else, especially Senator Robert Kennedy of New York, had rejected. For the next weeks, I went each evening to the student union to watch CBS newscasters Walter Cronkite and Eric Sevareid narrate the story of McCarthy's campaigning through the snows of New Hampshire on his road to embarrassing Johnson in the state's primary.

The campus had an edge to it in those months of late 1967 and early 1968. It was the awareness that the draft was not far away.

It drew dangerously closer in February, when General William West-moreland, following the North Vietnamese Tet offensive, requested two hundred thousand more troops for the Vietnam campaign on top of the five hundred thousand already in-country. It was now clear that the increase in numbers was not to win the war but only to sustain it. It fell to CBS's Walter Cronkite, who'd flown to Vietnam to assess the situation, to deliver the verdict on a special hourlong report on February 27, 1968: "It seems now more certain than ever that the bloody experience of Vietnam is to end in a stalemate."

So would the generational divide that was already there. Fathers like mine, loyal to the World War legacy, continued pushing sons like me to do their "duty," and sons like me felt more and more deserted.

Like most times, those months at Chapel Hill had a soundtrack. Every time I crossed Franklin Street, the main drag through Chapel Hill, I could hear a Beatles song wafting from the record shop: "I am the walrus / Goo goo g'joob."

That March brought stunning news for hope. McCarthy pulled out an electoral miracle in New Hampshire. He won 42.4 percent of the primary vote to Johnson's 49.5. Counting the write-ins for him on the Republican ballots, he lost to the president by just 230 votes. Within days, Robert Kennedy was also in the race. Two weeks later, Johnson, facing defeat to McCarthy in the Wisconsin primary, announced to a stunned America in a televised address that he would no longer seek reelection.

Then came a historic horror at home: the assassination of Dr. Martin Luther King. I got the news about the death of the country's greatest civil rights leader when I was deep in the stacks of the UNC's Wilson Library. Once again, the horror had reached me. Nor was it the end. A bitter fight continued to rage between McCarthy, Humphrey, and RFK. It went all the way to California, where tragedy would again take charge.

CHAPTER TEN

MONTREAL

By the end of my second semester at Chapel Hill, I had managed to earn a more than decent grade average, but my grad school deferment had run out. I was now facing the draft and Vietnam. That June of 1968, a friend was planning a trip to Montreal to look for a job. When he invited me to join him for the long weekend, I jumped at the opportunity to visit a foreign country on my own.

Montreal, sparkling and sunny, was politically alive with the elevation of the country's new prime minister, Pierre Elliott Trudeau. The city itself was a perfect hybrid of North American commerce and French charm.

Sitting in a public park, I charted out my life's direction on an old business card. Because of my new draft status, I-A, Available for Military Service, it demanded immediate attention. I had spent months cheering for Gene McCarthy and standing weekly vigil against the war on Franklin Street. Meanwhile, the American war in Southeast Asia continued even as increasing numbers of its citizens saw it as unwinnable.

I saw how others around me were dealing with the dire situation. One housemate became a finance officer in the army. That was okay for him; I didn't think it right for me to put on a uniform if I wasn't facing the actual fighting. It would be pretending to be part of the war effort, something I refused to do. Nor did I want to wait and risk getting drafted.

The Peace Corps and, hopefully, economic development in Africa, seemed the right course.

That Saturday night, my friend and I searched Montreal restaurants for a TV showing the long-awaited debate between Eugene McCarthy and Bobby Kennedy. The California primary was coming on Tuesday, June 4, and this was the last crucial test. Having spent months rooting for McCarthy, I now prayed for Bobby. He was the only candidate who could beat Hubert Humphrey, who was running on Johnson's Vietnam policy, and end the war.

I went to bed that Tuesday night hoping to get some sleep before the results came in. Several hours later, I awoke in the darkness and turned on the bedside radio only to hear what I thought was a tape from the station's archives. It sounded like the broadcast coverage I'd heard five years earlier during the afternoon President Kennedy had been shot and killed in Dallas.

Then the reality hit me. This wasn't a replay but another horror. Bobby had been shot, perhaps mortally.

"The giant has stubbed his toe," the taxi driver pronounced the next morning as we headed to the airport. "The giant," he repeated, warming to his imagery, "has stubbed its toe." Incredibly, he was using this first shock of news to savor his nationalist resentment.

As Wednesday evening came and went, Kennedy was still hanging on to life. It fell to Frank Mankiewicz, his press secretary, to make the final announcement in the early hours of the next morning that Robert F. Kennedy had died at the age of forty-two.

Back in Chapel Hill, I sat that gloomy Saturday watching the Robert Kennedy funeral train trudge south through New Jersey to Washington's Union Station. It was only a week since I'd been exploring Montreal hoping to catch his TV debate with Gene McCarthy. All that hopeful suspense had now vanished.

Unlike his brother's, Bobby Kennedy's funeral had none of the poet

William Butler Yeats's "terrible beauty." It struck me then as a mere sub-traction. The week before, we had a hero to lead us; now we didn't.

For whatever reason, I was still taking risks about my future. When the Peace Corps accepted me for an assignment in Venezuela, I turned it down. When a second offer came, this time to a water project in Kenya, I rejected it as well. Then, one fine day a young Peace Corps recruiter came to Chapel Hill. He had a brochure about a new program in the southern African country of Swaziland. It offered a chance to do what I'd been training to do: economic development. In this case, it was to help rural African traders become a greater force in their country's economy. I would be working with owners of small stores, teaching them book-keeping and marketing. I'd be playing a genuine, on-the-ground role in a newly independent African country. In a larger sense, I'd be engaged in the third-world struggle between "command" and free economies.

The political battle over Vietnam became a firestorm that August when the Democrats held their convention in Chicago. My housemates and I watched every minute from our apartment, rooting for the antiwar delegates, watching the police battle the protesters.

The violence on the streets soon found its way into the convention hall itself, with CBS correspondent Dan Rather getting punched in the stom-ach by a security agent. Watching live, anchor Walter Cronkite declared famously, "It looks like there are a bunch of thugs down there." It was a four-day drama of good guys—the antiwar delegates such as Connecti-cut senator Abe Ribicoff—against the forces loyal to President Johnson, against the war protesters in the streets, against the police led by Chicago's law-and-order mayor, Richard Daley. I couldn't turn my eyes from it. It was the most stunning week of television we'd seen in our lifetimes.

Even back then my long-term career eye was on broadcast news. Any number of times, walking across the UNC campus, I would look over at the studio of WUNC, the Chapel Hill TV affiliate, yearning to work there—even sweep floors, anything to get in the door.

In those last bittersweet summer days of 1968, as I was saying good-bye to friends and heading off to a distant continent, I caught something stirring in the country. It was reflected in the best new movies. *Bonnie and Clyde*, starring Warren Beatty and Faye Dunaway, had audiences cheering for the troubled bank robbers rather than the dutiful lawmen chasing them. *The Graduate*, another great film, had us admiring a troubled college graduate rebelling against the conforming world of his parents. It introduced a young Dustin Hoffman in the role of antihero, the character daring to take on the ascribed social order. Something was changing in the country I'd grown up in, something coming apart, perhaps getting angrier.

As I prepared to leave for Africa, I felt myself standing at an abyss. For the first time in memory, I had no short-term worries, no near-term decisions to make. The course was set. My next two years were to be in Africa. What lay after that was beyond reckoning.

Before leaving that November, I got to vote for president for the first time. For me, it was complicated. A Peace Corps guidebook to our group of volunteers described me as someone whose "foremost area of interest is politics." That was certainly true, but it didn't mean I'd gotten my politics figured out. I never did get back that passion for Richard Nixon I had at fourteen. His rerun in 1968 seemed to lack the underdog, gritty quality that attracted me to his race against the glamorous, well-off Jack Kennedy. There was something too staged about his campaigning now, something plastic. He was like the Count of Monte Cristo—a man who'd survived endless years in prison but had lost his soul.

That said, it wasn't an easy decision. In a ruthless sense, I thought Nixon a better bet than Hubert Humphrey to end the American war in Vietnam. What political reason did he, a Republican, have to continue Johnson's war? But I admired Humphrey's civil rights record stretching back to the 1948 Democratic convention. I also admired the senator he'd picked as his running mate. Maine senator Edmund Muskie spoke with the same understated liberalism as my hero Eugene McCarthy. I cast my first presidential vote for Hubert Humphrey.

By late November, after training on the campus of a historically black college in Baker, Louisiana, our contingent of trade development advisors was ready to depart for Africa. For me, it was a sublime time. I was about to leave everything—my parents, my brothers, my grandparents, my friends—and head off to a world far away. I remember the view of the Washington Mall from the plane as I flew home to Philadelphia. I said goodbye to my loving grandparents and wondered if I'd see them again. They were old, and I was going far away—in fact, beyond even that "Timbuktu" that Grandmom spoke of as the farthest place imaginable.

On the day I left from the Somerton train station that Dad took to work, I could see Mom crying as she disappeared behind a familiar telephone pole.

CHAPTER ELEVEN

SWAZILAND

"If you are lucky enough to have lived in Paris as a young man," Ernest Hemingway wrote, "then wherever you go for the rest of your life, it stays with you, for Paris is a moveable feast."

Hemingway was writing of the twenties in Paris. My "moveable feast" was the sixties in Africa. It was my years in remote Swaziland on a 120 Suzuki motorbike, traveling around my district teaching a group of two hundred African traders how to be better businessmen. Often on those panoramic rides through the African veld, with the escarpment high in the distance, a fantastic notion would come to me. I remember imagining that while Che Guevara had been selling revolution and Communism in South America, I was there on another continent, selling free enterprise. Even from a more humble perspective I was doing things I would never have expected. One was hitchhiking by myself up through East Africa. It would get me to the foot of Mount Kilimanjaro.

My adventures of those two years included a close encounter with a deadly black mamba—when the fast-moving snake leapt up at my car window. It meant falling in love with Indian Ocean port cities such as Lourenço Marques, Mozambique; Dar es Salaam, Tanzania; and Mombasa, Kenya.

I wasn't alone on my Peace Corps assignment. There were some interesting people with me. A law graduate from San Francisco was posted with the foreign ministry. Another, my lifelong friend Frank Orban, had the task of reconciling the laws of Swaziland, which had gained its independence from the British in September 1968, with its new Westminster-style constitution. Then there were the four of us assigned to the Ministry of Commerce, Industry and Mines as trade development advisors.

I was driven to my posting by the minister himself, Simon Nxumalo. As we arrived in Goedgegun, the capital of the Shiselweni district, he gave me a pair of instructions: develop the province economically and "Don't eat at the hotel." That first commission showed a high faith in my ability. I suspect that second command reflected a bitter memory of the too-recent colonial days. In any case, my assigned apartment mate, Cliff Sears, an architect from Chicago, arrived a few days later. He carried with him none of my Catholic school obedience training. When he declared, "We're eating at the hotel tonight," I joined him.

A few of my American companions were maddeningly good at siSwati, a language similar to Zulu. We all took our jobs seriously. This commitment to help the Swazi people made us especially unpopular across the border. The South African "apartheid" government wouldn't even let us enter its country. Soon after we arrived, a commentator on official South African radio derided us as "do-gooding intellectuals."

We had met similar mistrust by the left-wing governments of the region. On the way down to Swaziland, the plane stopped for gas in Brazzaville, capital of the former French Congo. The entire time of our layover, we were guarded by armed, hard-faced troops. That country had chosen its side in the Cold War. By the looks of things, it wasn't ours.

At Jan Smuts International Airport in Johannesburg, we were also met with a tight escort. Yet even as we were trooped off to a remote room for isolation, we saw the uniformed white schoolchildren heading past. Even at the airport, the official system of strict racial separation was on vivid display.

I have always wondered about Washington's involvement. Our suspicion was that the US government had provided the South African capital of Pretoria with the names of the Peace Corps volunteers. We heard it was the price exacted by Pretoria for it to ensure the future evacuation of a volunteer in a medical emergency. In other words, our own government was somehow in cahoots with the right-wing South African government.

It may have contributed to our sense of isolation. We had left a country where fathers fought sons over the Vietnam War. That door had been slammed behind us. Now we faced hard evidence that our government was part of the banishment. Altogether, it might explain why some of us identified with the expatriate writers of the 1920s we found ourselves reading so intently: Hemingway, F. Scott Fitzgerald, and other members of that earlier "lost generation."

I discovered there are two kinds of jobs you can get in the Peace Corps. There's the *job* type, such as teaching high school. With that kind of assignment, you know the drill. Five days a week you show up in the classroom prepared to teach. At the end of the day, you know you've done what you could. At week's end, same deal. At semester's end, you're on record as having done exactly what you were sent to Africa to do.

Then there is a second kind of posting: my kind. That's when you're given a wide-ranging assignment such as "rural development," or what I was doing. In such cases, you invent your job and keep a personal score for how well you're doing it.

There were times when I wished I'd had the first type of assignment, when I could have ended the week with a sense of achievement. But maybe the better course for me was that mix of frustration and success—of being under self-imposed stress—that truly made all the difference to me as an experience. Why? Because it's what life is like and what the *choice* of careers is like.

Like others, I did my job, traveling out there on the veld on my Suzuki, visiting traders' shops, holding weeklong business "short courses" in Goedgegun, ultimately producing a first-ever national industrial show on the national fairgrounds that was attended by King Sobhuza II himself.

I did it on my own, with each day a design of my making. It was person-on-person work, encouraging rural Swazi men to better organize their businesses, keep books of receipts and expenditures, and think about their stores as enterprises.

It taught *me* as well. One lesson was that being a rural trader in a culture such as Swaziland's is not all about what gets counted in a ledger book. It can also be about serving your neighbors and holding a position of local distinction.

"The last stop in Africa!" the British expatriates called Swaziland. The early 1970s was an interesting time for us, as Peace Corps volunteers, to overlap with the British government holdovers, in the inevitable afterglow of their empire.

What we American guests of Swaziland learned quickly was how its people were every bit as proud of their young country as we were of ours. Small in geography, the Kingdom of eSwatini, as it has been known since 2018, has held a distinctive identity since the eighteenth century. For one thing, it is a land with a common culture and language. And unlike other peoples of the region, such as the Zulus, the Swazis have kept their independence from the Republic of South Africa.

The Swazis' feelings on this matter lay close to the surface. Their patriotism was every bit as strong in their hearts and reflexes as any American's. Our group was commanded from the start not to mess with the local politics. The prime minister used a welcoming reception to make that crystal clear. *"No politics here!"* he warned us in words that made the *Times of Swaziland*'s front page. That admonition was underlined when one of our group got sent home after being reported for having talked local politics in a saloon. I felt it myself when I joked to a Swazi friend about my being in the CIA. Suddenly turning solemn, he said I must never do that again. It told me that even the notion of the United States nosing around in their affairs was no laughing matter.

But during my two-plus years in southern Africa, I learned what it's like to be an American in a time and place that bore us no grudge. Americans were strangers to Swaziland. There was no colonial experience to overcome.

From my observation, that went for Africa in a broader sense. To many living on the continent, the USA was a land of wonder. I hope to never forget the young guy I met on the island of Zanzibar on my long way home. His apartment walls were covered in rock 'n' roll posters. It was his altar of devotion to Western pop culture. Or the street kids in Cairo who asked if I knew John Wayne and cautioned me to never, ever say anything bad about heavyweight boxing champion Muhammad Ali.

I had gone off to Africa at a particular time as well as to a place: a historical meeting point between the end of the continent's colonial past and the rise of "Freedom" in Swahili. For me, it was *my* time, too. It is one thing to leave your country to get away. It is better yet to live life on the road: the youth hostels, the local cigarettes, the trading in local knowledge. It's better still to go to a country and find a home there.

This is what we did. Did it change me? Certainly it had an influence.

I remember being in a room of Swazi traders, realizing that I knew each one of them—all seventeen—personally. It struck me that this, above everything else, was the heart of the Peace Corps mission: the human connection. Time and time again, I would arrive on a hot day to a rural trading shop and be greeted by the owner with the offer of a "cold drink"—a Coke or an orange Fanta—even if he had no fridge to make it cold. Some of those guys treated me like a son, this young guy from far-off America out there all by himself. This is the treasure I took home with me from my two years in the Peace Corps, that affection.

In December 1968, the month of our arrival in Swaziland, our country launched *Apollo 8,* the first manned spacecraft to orbit the moon, and a warm-up for the culmination of the space program promoted by John F. Kennedy in 1961. When JFK took office, the US had been behind in the space race since 1957. That's when the Soviet Union launched the first satellite, *Sputnik,* followed in April 1961 by its orbiting the first man around the Earth. Kennedy's bold strategy, announced in a stirring speech later that year, was to win the space race with a feat far beyond either country's previous achievements: landing men on the moon and returning them home safely by the end of the decade—which was now just twelve months away.

The December launch of Apollo 8 caused considerable talk in Goedgegun, recently renamed Nhlangano—"the meeting place," in English—for the 1947 visit of King George VI of Great Britain to King Sobhuza II. One local woman, speaking at a new debate club, attacked the US space program as a global menace. She accused our country of planning to use space travel as an "escape route," that we Americans intended to colonize other planets in order to leave behind an overcrowded Earth.

When Apollo 11 headed to the moon's surface the following July, I was in Mbabane, the Swaziland capital. A British volunteer and I listened on his short-wave radio in that dangerous moment when astronauts Neil Armstrong and Buzz Aldrin prepared to take off from the lunar surface. I prayed that their fragile lunar vehicle, *Eagle,* would have the necessary thrust to clear the moon's surface and return to the command module orbiting above, waiting to carry them and the third astronaut, Michael Collins, home. Fortunately, it did.

My friend Steve Hank, I learned later, had spent the previous night with local villagers up on a hillside. He was pointing out the small spot of light moving across the horizon. It was a moment that combined Jack Kennedy's two great missions: Americans heading to the moon and others sent to work for people in distant lands in his Peace Corps.

Everybody in Swaziland seemed to be talking about the "achievement." In a letter to Mom and Dad, dated July 26, 1969, I told of one reaction to the moon landing that I saw as deeply insightful:

Some teacher here, a British friend of ours, said that Africa used to think that America was really not very different than other countries; it was just richer and had more of the things they had. The moon landing has shook these countries. While they could have deluded themselves that they were "developing" before, the gap now between the rich and poor countries looks quite unbridgeable.

At present growth rate, it would take Africa 350 years to get where the US is now in terms of per capita income. The real problems are going to come when these countries, independent for 20 or 30 years, can no longer make the excuse "We're only a young nation."

Our own travels outside Swaziland were limited by politics. We were surrounded, as I said, on three sides by South Africa, whose government refused to grant us visas. The other side, fortunately, was Mozambique, whose Indian Ocean capital of Lourenço Marques was only an hour hitchhike or bus ride to the east.

The Portuguese colony was then at war with African rebels who, by 1969, controlled a third of the country, mainly in the north. The only signs of the conflict in Lourenço Marques were the small groups of European soldiers in berets lounging at outdoor cafés. Since they never seemed to order a meal, I got the impression they weren't getting paid much, nor were they particularly happy to be in Africa, in any case.

My second April in Swaziland, I set off on my great adventure within an adventure. I decided to hitchhike up East Africa and go as far and wide as I could. The first leg of the trip was a hitch eastward to Lourenço Marques. That was followed by an overnight trip on the Rhodesia Railway to Bulawayo, Rhodesia (now Zimbabwe). I spent many of those hours reading a paperback copy of *Kennedy,* Theodore Sorensen's memoir of his service to JFK from his earliest Senate days through Dallas. I believe this is what led me later to the idea of becoming a legislative assistant to a United States senator. It was the position Sorensen filled for the eight years leading to Kennedy's presidency. It mainly involved writing speeches for JFK. For whatever reason, this is something I just assumed I could do. It would be my way forward.

My great trek up through East Africa now took me through Rhodesia, then Zambia, then Tanzania. The one time I got worried, I was standing on the side of the road above the Zambian capital of Lusaka. Of the few trucks that had passed, none stopped for me. Just as it was getting dark, I hit the jackpot. An older Irishman stopped his van, welcomed me aboard, then drove us for hours to a grand Tuscan-style mansion located hundreds of miles in the bush. It was the estate of the late Stewart Gore-Browne, a friend and supporter of the country's first president, Kenneth Kaunda. My Irish host and I had dinner in an elegant old library, a far outpost of England.

The next night, back on the road, I returned to its rugged reality. I spent the night at a rat-infested "hotel" just over the Tanzanian border, deciding moment-by-moment whether to keep my head in the stifling sleeping bag or risk being bitten by the rodents who were running both overhead and on the floor around me.

The days ahead were better. I caught a bus to Moshi, Tanzania, at the foot of Kilimanjaro, then another to Dar es Salaam. From there I flew back to Lusaka, then headed south to spectacular Victoria Falls. Finally, after another long hitchhike and adventure on Lake Kariba, I reached my destination. I walked in the dark across the bridge just below the falls and spent the night sleeping on the ground. I awoke the next morning and walked past packs of monkeys to see one of the seven natural wonders of the world.

Somewhere within me, at twenty-four, I'd gotten the confidence to undertake this wild journey. It never occurred to me at the time that it was anything but a grand idea.

CHAPTER TWELVE

AFRICAN MYSTERIES

The Peace Corps has three goals for its volunteers: help develop the country, represent your own country positively, and come home with knowledge of the host country.

That last mission is obviously open-ended. You never know what you'll learn working and living in a far-off place like Swaziland. Or how much, even after two years, would remain impenetrable.

Still afloat in my memory are the lessons that have served me since. One came from those business short courses I ran for the Swazi traders. It was triggered when Ethiopia's Haile Selassie turned up on a newsreel I was showing one night. At the first sight of the legendary emperor, Benjamin Gama, the local leader of the Swazi Commercial Amadoda Council, let loose with a full-throated *"Topia!"* Ethiopia!

Was Gama one of the Swazi men who had gone to North Africa and Sicily to fight for the Allies in World War II? Was he one of those Swazi soldiers for whom King George VI had come to thank King Sobhuza II after the war? Were all those army surplus coats I saw men wearing in winter actually their old military uniforms?

There was just so much I never learned about the country. It started and ended with how people actually survived. How did a rural family get by twelve months a year on that scraggly harvest of maize?

There were also the personal mysteries, such as the postcolonial sensitivities of my boss, Commerce Minister Simon Nxumalo. When I presented an oral report to him about my progress in the Shiselweni district, he seemed delighted. It listed the facts: the number of visits made to local trading shops and updates on the short courses and on our efforts to extend credit to purchase maize during the current famine. He even jotted down the numbers.

Sometime in my second year, I decided to write a more elaborate report, but he didn't like it one bit. It concerned foreign aid. In a multipage presentation, I argued that Swaziland should take a state-of-the-art approach to tapping into the various development funds available worldwide and that it use computers to do the job.

This did not go over well. The minister began our next meeting in Mbabane by announcing steamily that he had never in his career written a "minute," which was his term for a memorandum. When he had something to say, he had *said* it and not resorted to some typed-up document.

For a while, I battled in my head against Nxumalo's remarkably unhappy words, hoping desperately that he wasn't talking about my memo. Only belatedly did I accept the reality that he was indeed talking about that memo, or *minute* as he called it, I had spent weeks putting on paper. Here was a proud leader who had worked in the South African gold mines to earn his way, whose English was his second language. And here I was shoving it in his face.

It took me years of reckoning to fully understand my impropriety. Politics, I was learning in this far-off land, cuts at many levels. The grander lesson of my two years teaching business in Swaziland is that human beings are predictably *human*. Each of us has sides of pride, resentment, and ambition.

This is not to say all cultures weigh day-to-day behavior by the same scales. There was, for example, a good, hardworking guy I knew in Nhlangano who ran the little tearoom down at the marketplace. It was nothing more than a grain silo converted to a restaurant with a small counter and some seats. My housemate Cliff Sears would head there for supper once or twice a week. I'd have a plate of mealy rice and a bit of meat. The food was eight cents. The bottle of Coke was ten cents. Not bad.

The fellow who owned this place, whom I knew as "Mr. Dlamini," seemed to work all the time. He'd made enough to afford a pickup truck and was always neatly and properly dressed.

One day, however, I heard someone describe Dlamini as "lucky." What did he mean by that? That this hardworking, proper guy didn't deserve what he'd earned? It was another case of not grasping what I was experiencing firsthand. I once asked a student whether he preferred owning twenty head of cattle or nineteen head plus a local trading store. When he answered the former, I thought it reflected a distinctive African value system. He then quickly disabused me of that conclusion, saying that the reason he chose the twenty cattle was because owning a store would require that he keep selling cattle to keep it open. His reasoning was based not so much on a difference in values as in commercial expectations. He simply assumed that owning a store was a losing proposition.

It's remarkable how often I find myself even now transported back to that country so far around the planet. When it rains, I imagine riding my motorbike over the muddy roads, through the eucalyptus air of the town of Mankayane, with my long green army coat. On sunny days, I think of being out there on my Suzuki zigzagging the hills overlooking the *lowveld*, that panorama that looms eastward to the Lubombo escarpment. Or something makes me recall the government ministry office in Mbabane, where messengers delivered Manila folders tied with red laces, where you got offered a cigarette from a pack of Rothmans 30s just as a uniformed "tea boy" wheels in his wagon.

Or I think of the rigid, mustachioed Brit who ran the Gourmet Café at the end of Allister Miller Street, where the Swazi waiters wore fezes and where we went on Saturday morning for our grilled cheese sandwiches and Cokes.

Or that European oasis of a hotel in Namaacha, just into Mozambique, where I had to stay one night after having missed the nightly border closing. Or stopping in Barclays Bank in Mbabane, where I could draw my monthly pay of $72. Or all those Saturday mornings in the capital city when so many people came to town.

Or that first afternoon in Lourenço Marques on that wide boulevard lined with Cinzano umbrellas, an outpost of Europe on the Indian Ocean. Or the Portuguese bullfight, where they don't kill the bull in the ring. Or that offshore island where our Danish friend Britta Kjaer and Gary Rowse joined me for giant prawns and white wine before heading to a place north of the city to watch the crocodiles and hippos get dangerously near our little boat. Or that very southern tip of Mozambique, Ponta do Ouro.

And who was *I* back then? Fred O'Regan, a friend in Swaziland and all the years since, lifts my spirits when I hear him say I haven't changed a bit.

As 1970 came to an end, so did my two-year stay in Africa. Unlike the British expats who came hoping to hang on, we Americans always knew we'd be headed home. They organized clubs and put on Gilbert and Sullivan musicals. We waited for the movies, and for our time to leave.

On December 11, 1970, I hitchhiked one last time to Mozambique. Catching rides from one African country to another, both with names exotic and remote to American ears, had long since lost its remarkability. This trip to good old "LM" was touched with sadness for being the last. I took a final walk around the city, trying to save something of it for the long road.

The next day, I caught a flight to Johannesburg, where I'd arranged to meet up with Steve Hank. That night, he and I went to see *Woodstock*—or, rather, what was left of it after the South African censors were finished.

What stuck most powerfully that evening in Joe-berg was a sight that couldn't be hidden. It was the reality outside the movie theater. From an outdoor restaurant, I witnessed the stares of black passersby denied entrance by South African racial laws.

Nairobi, Kenya, was my last stop in Africa; a big-city experience on the way out. I had a slice of apple pie à la mode at the dazzling New Stanley Hotel, a sweet transition from Africa to the modern world. I found a copy of a current edition of *Newsweek* that contained a letter to the editor I'd submitted attacking the US government's cozy ties to South Africa.

From Nairobi, I detoured to Israel, where, for a month, I found home and comfort in the holy city of Jerusalem. From a dollar-a-night hotel above Damascus Gate, I spent my days in the Old City, eating in the Muslim Quarter, visiting the Church of the Holy Sepulchre in the Christian Quarter in the evening, then taking the long walk to see a movie in the modern Jewish area of this city.

Soon I was finally heading home to a life without a clear forecast. My assets were my youth and the vivid experience of having thrived living abroad. I had spent my early twenties breathing the free air of an open world, distant from the land of my birth and upbringing. I had known different peoples and had found ways to connect. I had tested myself in all those encounters, whether in a government office, a short-course classroom, or out in the African bush.

Something else: I had within me the experience of seeing my country as an astronaut does—whole and from a beautiful distance. Without knowing it, I had found a bridge to that world of politics I'd read about on that overnight train rambling through Rhodesia. It was a practical ability to confront the unknown.

I was pretty much alone on the night flight from London. The coach section of the giant jumbo jet was cavernous, with hardly another person in sight. On the screen was Orson Welles's *Citizen Kane,* that wild, classic tribute to newspapers and the human ego.

Looking back, I can see there was another presence on that plane. If I hadn't driven a Suzuki motorbike into all those villages in Africa as a stranger, I doubt I could have broken into politics as I did or, later, what I did as a journalist. It was my rite of passage. Nothing like war correspondent Winston Churchill fearlessly breaking out of a South African prisoner-of-war camp and evading capture during the Boer War, or Ernest Hemingway getting sprayed with shrapnel as an ambulance driver in

World War I, or Jack Kennedy saving his *PT-109* crew in the South Pacific during World War II, but it got me out of one world and into another.

Yes, Grandmom-in-Chestnut Hill, it *was* Africa. I did things over there that I'd have been scared for our children to do. They have chosen their own adventures. Whatever we do in our twenties has a lot to do with who we become and what, during those later nights in life, we get to remember, to embrace, to savor, to love.

– BOOK II –

Do not stop thinking of life as an adventure. You have no security
unless you can live bravely, excitingly, and imaginatively.

—Eleanor Roosevelt,
1961

CHAPTER THIRTEEN

CAPITOL HILL

Arriving home after the passage of years is to visit a country that only *resembles* the one you left. It looks familiar but is not the same. Time has left its mark, and the home-comer notices it more than those who remained. Pulling into the gate at New York's John F. Kennedy Airport on a near-empty jumbo jet on February 16, 1971, one change that confronted me through the window was the long hair on the young baggage handlers. *That* was new. My generation's working class had adopted the look of the antiwar protesters.

Minutes later came a strange encounter with a sight once so familiar, especially in my newspaper boy days. For the first time since December 1968, I held in my palms quarters, nickels, and dimes.

I took the train from New York home to Philadelphia. Along the way, I met a young lawyer who, upon hearing of where I'd been and what I'd been doing, offered me a ride from Thirtieth Street Station to Somerton. It was in the early hours of the morning that I knocked on the door and woke up Dad and Mom.

The world welcoming me on Southampton Road had changed. My brothers, like me, had advanced several steps in life. Bert, who now went by "Herb," was back from the navy. He'd been in the Pacific on an LSD—Landing Ship Dock—transport. His ship had been on patrol off the coast of North Vietnam. Jim was still at sea on a destroyer patrolling the Atlantic for Soviet submarines, which he told me later had been all too present. My youngest brothers were still in school, Bruce studying engineering at Drexel, and Charlie still heading off mornings to La Salle College High School. I tried reconciling them to their younger lives; to the house of brothers in which we had all played our parts.

In a few days, I headed to Chapel Hill to rejoin friends and meet with the professor I'd been assisting to tell him I wouldn't be coming back. An idea was already forming in my mind, and it didn't involve econometric models.

My next stop, the big one, was Washington, DC. I arrived in the nation's capital, if not penniless, perilously close to it. Fortunately, the city itself glistened, cold but sunny, matching the spirit of my fresh beginning. Invigorated by my foreign adventure, I was hoping to begin the career that had captured my heart. I had discovered a route. I was going to be a senator's legislative assistant, just like Ted Sorensen had been for the young Jack Kennedy. Adding to my confidence was some intelligence I'd picked up from an older Holy Cross grad: you don't need a law degree to be one.

Politically, I was walking into an America now more sharply divided than ever by the protracted war in Vietnam. On one side were the college campuses, now grown starkly militant. On the other side were those who'd stuck with President Richard Nixon, the working people, the "hard hats," who saw their patriotism being mocked by those privileged with higher educations.

I would quickly learn that Capitol Hill tended the national battle line. There were the "doves," who opposed the war. They wanted to cut off funding so that the president would have no forces or weapons for carrying on the fight. On the other side were the "hawks," who never quit Nixon on Vietnam.

It wasn't strictly partisan. For example, someone like me, back from the Peace Corps, might have been welcomed into the office of Senator Mark Hatfield, a Republican from Oregon who was leading congressional efforts to turn off the spigot of war funding; whereas I might have encountered a frosty reception from a southern Democratic hawk.

Signaling this division in political culture was hair length. Longer said *dove*, shorter meant *hawk*. You could see the distinction walking from one Capitol Hill office to another.

On March 1, at one thirty in the morning, came the explosion that fused the anger against the war with the Capitol itself. A huge blast went off inside the structure, causing massive underground damage. The building that George Washington raised up had been assaulted from within. A bomb placed in an out-of-the-way bathroom had come within a half hour of killing a Capitol policeman who had just been in the facility. Had it blown upward instead of downward, the historic dome itself might have tumbled down. A violent antiwar group, the Weather Underground, was happy to take credit.

It was in these very days of tumult that I entered Washington with bright-eyed hopes of finding a job, a career, a new life.

I rented a $35 per month room in a row house in the DC neighborhood of Glover Park. My daily routine soon took shape: each morning I'd get up, take the 33 bus through Georgetown, past the White House to Capitol Hill, and then start going door-to-door in the office buildings of the House of Representatives and the Senate.

Arriving at a congressional suite, I would introduce myself to the receptionist and ask if she would give my résumé to the administrative assistant, the top staffer. I owed this freedom to the lax security of those days. No one minded a young person, whose only credential was his overwhelming desire to belong, wandering the halls of the Capitol.

There was a purity and zeal in my quest that enforced its own discipline. I had no other ambition, no alternative vision for my life, nor a past to fall back on. I had done my time in Africa and had no interest in returning to the doctoral program in economics. All I saw was the road ahead, the one I'd chosen, to get a job with a senator or member of the House that would launch me into national politics. The certainty of my ambition gave me the willingness in that late winter of 1971 to endure rejection again and again.

I began my list of prospective bosses with members of the House Foreign Affairs Committee, believing that my service in Africa would appeal to them. I focused on the Irish American members, believing that service in President Kennedy's Peace Corps and graduation from Holy Cross would be tribal door openers.

There soon came a brief, shining moment when I thought I had struck gold. I was standing in the office reception area of New Jersey congressman Cornelius Gallagher. When he inquired what I was doing in his office, I told him I was just back from Africa in the Peace Corps and wanted a job on the House Foreign Affairs Committee. Taken with that hurried self-description, the congressman led me to a plaque on his inner-office wall. It held a photo of Lyndon Johnson signing a Peace Corps extension bill and included a pen the president had used in the ceremony. Then, with a warm flourish and only a few minutes of chatting together came the glorious offer. "You don't want to work in the Foreign Affairs Committee; you should be a legislative assistant in my office!" Blown away by the proposal, I left Gallagher's office bursting with joy.

It took a few days to get the bad news from his war-weary administrative assistant: "He said to tell you he couldn't work it out." I would learn over time the reason for the reversal. It turned out that finding a slot for me on his office staff was the least of the congressman's problems. Beneath his good looks, charm, and, I was to discover, splendid war record was a politician in deep trouble, legally and politically. The FBI had gotten Gallagher on tape placating a local mob boss who was seeking political protection from police on his gambling operations. The congressman would say that agency director J. Edgar Hoover had targeted him because of his legislative initiative to curtail the agency's surveillance techniques. In any case, I have always believed that this man who was so proud of his role in creating the Peace Corps didn't want to drag me into the darkening world in which he'd trapped himself.

Fortunately, I was by now getting a hang of how things worked on Capitol Hill. I was learning the ropes and how to climb them. The entire setup centered on the word *patronage*.

When I first heard that word spoken by a Hill staffer, it seemed exhumed from antiquity, as if summoned from the scandalous years after the Civil War. On Capitol Hill, that system remained very much alive. Every job in the Senate or House of Representative served at the pleasure of an elected official. There was no civil service. The staff in their offices, the professionals on their committees, the elevator operators, the folks in the mailroom, the police officers, the printers, the shoe shiners, the crew operating the automatic letter-writing and signature machines, owed their position to the same patronage system. Everyone making a buck earned that buck by serving at the pleasure of some politician or someone to whom he or she had handed the franchise. It was a world that struck me as oddly parochial, even petty. It encouraged loyalty, fair enough, but it also rewarded the sycophant. You got hired, retained, even promoted because of personal connections. Your prime job, never to be forgotten, was quite simply to keep the boss happy with you. That can be a prescription written in hell. It taught me that if you don't arrive on Capitol Hill with a strong moral sense, you are unlikely to find it there.

I wasn't thinking about that at the start. In those crisp winter weeks of 1971, I simply adapted quickly and desperately to the need to find a job. The basement of the Capitol became my stomping grounds. A series of narrow, underground passageways took you from the Senate to the House. It reminded me of the covered alleys of the walled Old City of Jerusalem. What remains clear in my memory is the strong aroma of the meat lockers serving the various Capitol restaurants and snack bars. Heading back and forth through that subterranean world, I spent my days rotating from one side of congress to the other, dropping off résumés. In each case, I'd ask the receptionists if they had heard of any job openings.

As my bankroll grew thinner, so did my standards. In addition to Democrats, I knocked on the doors of moderate, anti–Vietnam War

Republicans. Growing desperate, I met with a Texas Republican congressman named James Collins. I'd gotten word about an opening in his office for a legislative assistant. The encounter with the congressman himself was initiated through a cordial interview with his new administrative assistant, a recent graduate of Harvard Business School. The AA, who wasn't much older than me, could not have been more welcoming. He agreed to get me in to see his boss.

That's when the culture shock hit. As I said, the world back then was divided vividly in matters of personal appearance. The man now being introduced to me stood starkly on the other side of that divide. He was wearing a suit associated then with the Sun Belt. His shoes gleamed white. His haircut was short on the sides, the kind you get at a barber shop displaying the Stars and Stripes. As I stood there appraising him, he was doing the same to me. Eyeing my "northern" haircut and hearing my rapid speech, his verdict came quickly and decisively. It started with a brief preamble, its point being that his interests in filling the position of "legislative assistant" had nothing to do with its title.

"We don't do much legislation here," he said. He wanted to hire someone to write fiery conservative newsletters in order to keep people back in the district roused up. In other words, the congressman saw his only job was to keep his job. Then came the verdict on me. "I would say," he went on, "that people of my district—and I don't mean any offense by this—would be put off by your way of speaking." Then, turning to the young aide who'd brought me to him: "Roy, wouldn't you say that people from back home coming in this office would look at this young man and figure he brought back some idealistic notions with him from the Peace Corps?" What he was saying was now abundantly clear. The unpleasant way he said the word *idealistic* removed whatever doubt remained.

"Who do you know?" he asked, switching from one practicality to another. When I said, rather pathetically, that I knew a guy working a House elevator, he quickly got the picture of my predicament.

"You should try some of the northeastern, big-city offices," Representative Collins suggested. "I'll bet there are a good number of congressmen who would like to have someone with your background working for them."

Having given me directions back to the other side of the Vietnam divide, he relaxed and drew back on what he, Jim Collins, had learned about such situations that I now faced. "Politics is like selling insurance door-to-door, which is what I used to do before getting into this business. Some people will go for you, and some won't. You knock on a hundred doors and get nine people to invite you back for a sales pitch. Of the nine, three will buy the policy. You only have to sell three people to do all right, but you'll never find those three unless you knock on the hundred doors to start with."

I took James Collins's advice to heart, trying to always remember its simplicity and undeniable truth. Some people will like you, and some won't.

At last, with the further passage of days and unrequited door knockings, and with $80 left in my pocket, I found someone who did. One day, making my usual daily rounds of the Hill, I dropped off my résumé at the office of Senator Frank Moss of Utah. My rough theory was that a Democrat from a western state would be more likely to be a moderate. In any case, his AA agreed to meet with me.

His name was Wayne Owens, a devout Mormon who happened to be a Kennedy guy. He had been Bobby's Rocky Mountain campaign coordinator in 1968. More recently, he'd been a top staffer for Edward Kennedy, who'd succeeded Jack as a Massachusetts senator not long after his older brother ascended to the Oval Office. My entire background—the Peace Corps, Catholic college in Massachusetts—seemed to connect me to the family Wayne had served.

He offered me a tryout. My task was to draft an informed letter to the wife of the director of the Utah Symphony to answer her query: Which tax shelters were available to employees of nonprofits? Gung ho to tackle the challenge, I went to see Nancy Nelson, the administrative assistant to my hometown congressman, Joshua Eilberg. She had been very supportive when I first arrived looking for a job. Now she was equally helpful. She directed me to the Internal Revenue Service office, where they give taxpayer advice. With the information I got there, I spent the weekend drafting a letter for Senator Moss to send to that well-connected woman in Utah.

When Wayne read it, he offered me my reward. He said that while he didn't have a position on the senator's staff, he did have a *patronage* position on the Capitol Police. Spotting my downcast look, he tried to soften the blow, pointing out, "At least it will pay for the groceries." More than that, it was my *shot*.

CHAPTER FOURTEEN

US CAPITOL POLICE OFFICER

The deal Wayne Owens struck with me was not unusual in those days. In addition to their payroll for office staff, US senators controlled other jobs in the Capitol: working in the mail room, operating the elevators, carrying a badge on the police force. Most went to the sons and daughters of wealthy contributors. Few of the patronage jobs went to young, ambitious types who needed the salary and agreed to devote their free hours to working in a senator's or representative's office. My first assignment on the Capitol Police, which paid $8,000 a year, was to get a haircut. Next came a week of basic training. *Very* basic.

It is important to note that the Capitol Police a half century ago was nothing like the professional force of today. The shooting range was located deep in the basement of the Rayburn House Office Building. Toward the end of the weeklong training, we were taken there to be checked out for use of the .38 police special I was to carry eight hours a day. We were given a hundred rounds to fire at the targets. My best performance was hitting the moving, man-size silhouettes that came racing toward me. I suppose it was my instinct from childhood: in my day, you learned early to point your toy pistol at the bad guy.

Finally, we came to the last twenty rounds that would determine our qualification. After firing off ten of them, we were to write down our scores, then tape over the holes we'd left in the target. For whatever reason, probably nerves, I failed to perform the taping-over part. As a result, I was able to take double credit for the first ten rounds. Even after the screwup, however, my score still didn't reach the qualifying number.

It made no difference. In those days, fortunately long gone, patronage trumped marksmanship. Without a quiver of hesitation, I was thrown into the line of duty as a Capitol Police officer, issued a blue uniform, officer's hat, a .38 revolver, and five cartridges. The reason for that odd number of bullets is embarrassing in itself: the top officials of the Capitol Police feared that one of their rookie cops might trip on the sidewalk and discharge his weapon. They were giving us a uniform but with no confidence in the new guy wearing it.

My induction into the Capitol Police meant crossing the home-front DMZ from the long-haired anti–Vietnam War faction to that of the gendarmes, changing my appearance from dove to hawk.

Workwise, I split my day between the two. Each morning, I would find my way to Senator Moss's suite in the New Senate Office Building, located on Constitution Avenue, just northeast of the Capitol. My tasks were of the type I'd been tested on: answering complicated "legislative" letters from Utah constituents. These had been culled from the usual batch of letters addressing a single national concern such as the Vietnam War. That mail had already been pigeonholed, given a standardized response by the "robo" printing machine, and then sent to the "signature machine" for its final touch.

What ended up in my pile were the knottier letters that required some research and a human mind to answer.

That's how my mornings and early afternoons went during those early months of 1971. At three o'clock, I would change into my starched uniform shirt, trousers, and badge. Thanks to my new GI haircut, I looked every bit a police officer.

On many days, I would start my eight-hour shift in the Rotunda. It's where John Kennedy's body had lain in November 1963, and where the late-afternoon tourists now wandered amid the giant portraits of American history: the signing of the Declaration of Independence; the British surrenders at Saratoga, New York, and Yorktown, Virginia. Posted there one late night, I sat alone trying to exhume the spirit of John F. Kennedy. I could remember the power of that sight, the tragedy it spoke, even as I realized that it had been lost to the past.

My usual station, as night fell, was a guard post down in those meandering tunnels beneath the Capitol. I spent most of those evenings reading the *Congressional Record*—the official record of the proceedings and debates of the US Congress, published the morning after each session— trying to teach myself how to write a speech for delivery on the Senate floor. Occasionally, I would show my work to Wayne to see if it was approaching the grade.

My other effort at self-improvement was watching Wayne prepare for his own run for Congress in Utah. He'd begin each day writing on a yellow legal pad the names of the people he intended to call that morning: labor leaders, state political figures, national campaign consultants. I was learning a principle of politics: get in touch and stay in touch; firm up your personal relationships early. Don't just call when you want something. What I was watching was a young politician forging a campaign juggernaut.

In the spring of 1971, the conflict over the Vietnam War was turning ugly, and a massive May Day protest was about to take place right outside the Capitol Building. A sign of the coming trouble confronted me as I was patrolling the West Front of the Capitol. "Hit 'em once for me!" a nearby tourist said in dead seriousness. For all I know, he assumed I was some hate-filled cop out to bash the skulls of some antiwar longhair.

What he didn't imagine is that I identified more with the young crowd coming to protest. During what became four days of demonstrations, more than twelve thousand arrests were made in Washington, DC—including a Swaziland pal who'd come to town for the event.

The country never realized how the May Day protests could have easily turned out so much worse. The Capitol basement was packed with military teams in riot gear, helmet and shield, ready for face-to-face combat.

Even in my Capitol Police uniform, I must not have exhibited the same martial spirit. Democratic congresswoman Bella Abzug of New York, a celebrated opponent of the Vietnam War, came walking toward me, then stopped to rest. She told me how her feet were aching, then shared a larger concern. She was worried about what the police might do to "the kids" out there protesting. Fortunately, they were not unleashed.

In and out of uniform, I was, of course, still a Peace Corps guy, a recent grad student who felt the wide gap that separated me from the permanent police officers, many of them country boys, who surrounded me. One of them, Leroy Taylor, commuted several hours each day from West Virginia. An ex–military policeman who never let you forget it, he was forever talking about the "smoke" he was going to direct at some human target or another. Strangely, Leroy and I got along, enough for him to offer some personal tutoring on the subject of the country's cultural-political divide.

"Do you know why the little man loves his country?" he asked me one day. He wanted me to know the worldview of country boys like him who'd never known the privileges doled out to the *swells* of the world. Following a dramatic pause, he let the wisdom flow: "It's because it's all he's got!"

I've kept this wisdom close all the years since. It was much like the sentiment of another fellow officer, who told me he'd die to protect the Capitol, this living symbol of our democratic republic, even though he said he wouldn't lift a finger to defend "that riverboat down the street." He meant the White House. He said it with the gut patriotism of the man without wealth or status who had his flag and often the honor of having served his country in the military.

That May, I noticed an item in the *Washington Post* that told me that Richard Nixon, no matter how much battering he was getting over Vietnam, was not going to be easy to beat for reelection in 1972. Democrat Mike Mansfield, the Senate majority leader, introduced a measure halving the number of American troops stationed in Europe. Its dramatic defeat in the Senate showed me that the president still held the foreign policy high ground. As long as the Cold War endured, Republicans were going to hold the advantage against anyone who failed to hold the line.

June 1971 brought another event that united the world of the Capitol and the larger one beyond. One day I was led to a back stairs on the East Front of the Capitol and to an unmarked door. I was given a logbook to keep track of who entered. I was then told that *no one* was to get through that door. The official giving me those dual commands appeared unbothered by the Catch 22–like command he was delivering.

That odd assignment to guard that secret Capitol door would become odder still when I was told that the sensitive documents it held were the *Report of the Office of the Secretary of Defense Vietnam Task Force,* better known as the Pentagon Papers. Much of this top-secret report, commissioned in 1967 by then Secretary of Defense Robert McNamara and delivered in 1969, on how the United States became enmeshed in the Vietnam War had already been published in the *New York Times* and the *Washington Post*.

Those months serving on the Capitol Police made me familiar with the historic building itself. Later, when I held different positions up there, I liked showing guests the bullet holes in the "British stairs." They were reminders of how the redcoats shot their way up into the House chamber during the War of 1812, where they subsequently held a mock vote to burn "this den of Yankee democracy," and proceeded to do just that. I would also take friends to the deepest level of the Capitol, to the alcove originally intended for the burial of George and Martha Washington, who were now buried across the Potomac at Mount Vernon. The spot in the Capitol basement had become, instead, the resting place for the catafalque, the wooden platform on which the body of Abraham Lincoln and other historic figures have lain in state. It is now on display in the new Capitol Visitor Center.

I was able to glean contemporary Capitol history as well. One evening I was standing at the escalators that senators use to enter the Capitol.

They descend to the subways that cross under Constitution Avenue. A veteran building engineer was telling me about the snooty behavior of liberal senators who refused to even recognize the Capitol Police officers as they passed. There was an exception, a lawmaker who always took time to say hello to the men guarding them: New York's Robert F. Kennedy.

As spring turned to summer, I began to worry that I might never reach my next ambition. At each meeting with Wayne Owens, I pressed him for the job of legislative assistant to Senator Moss. One June day, he relented, informing me that I could join the senator's staff full-time beginning in September. In the meantime, I could take the summer off.

With the job in hand, I gave up my Capitol Police gun and headed west. I wanted to see not just Utah but a lot more of this country. It was another adventure, especially the long stretch of highway through the Great Plains. Then came Colorado and the Rocky Mountains. Again, I was out there alone like in East Africa, but this time with my own country all around me.

As I made the wide loop westward to California and back, I checked in with my Swaziland friends who had resumed their old lives. Gary Rowse was back at the University of Southern California Law School, Steve Hank was on his way to teaching film, and John Catanese had returned home to his old Pittsburgh neighborhood. On the way home I even managed to make the Omaha wedding of my Holy Cross friend Dick Pedersen.

I made a new acquaintance along the way. He was a hobo. At least, that's what he called himself when I was giving him a ride through the Nevada desert. He said he'd been on the road since the 1930s. As I listened to his story, he personified freedom itself—a man living life by his own code. I would remember him through the years, especially when I was feeling the strain of meeting others' approval. What his life told me then, and especially now, as I tell the story of my own life, is how that "hobo" had aged from weather and outdoor work. But what his face did not show was the wear and tear that comes from trying to contort yourself to the judgment of others.

CHAPTER FIFTEEN

SENATE LEGISLATIVE ASSISTANT

To land a job on Capitol Hill, I had to learn the power of patronage. Now that I had one, it was time to learn how to get things done. Here again, the tradecraft would be learned through trial and error. Fortunately, I assisted a kind and decent senator who appreciated my gung-ho energy and naïve confidence that politics is on the level.

Frank E. Moss was a true believer who had made his career with pluck and luck. He displayed his political ambition early. Elected class president in high school, he rose to become editor of the law review at George Washington University in DC. In another jump, he went from Salt Lake County attorney to member of the "greatest deliberative body in the world." Like others of that impressive Democratic senatorial class of 1958—Edmund Muskie of Maine, Phil Hart of Michigan, Eugene McCarthy of Minnesota—he benefited from a partisan wave. The election came amid an economic recession, which made it a terrible year for Republicans and a dandy time to be running as a Democrat.

Senator Moss also benefited from that old political rule: *the shape of the field decides the winner.* It was his good fortune to run against two well-known Republicans. One was the two-term incumbent, Senator Arthur Watkins, while the other was former governor J. Bracken Lee, whom

Watkins had beaten in the primary. Lee had challenged Watkins for his leadership in condemning the red-baiting Senator Joseph McCarthy.

Moss kept up his electoral luck. He was reelected in 1964, when the Republicans were burdened by the presidential candidacy of Senator Barry Goldwater. And he won again in 1970, a year when President Nixon went too far in trying to stir public opinion against antiwar Democrats.

Through his years in Washington, Moss became a significant force in consumer and environmental protection: in the latter case, by establishing national parks in Utah that guarded vast areas from exploitation.

My job in the senator's office began with the role I'd played while moonlighting as a Capitol cop. My desk remained the landing ground for those hard-to-answer letters. The other part of the job, the one I had pined for, was writing speeches for delivery on the Senate floor. Some were as basic as preparing an "insert" in the *Congressional Record*. That was a matter of finding an item of home-state interest in a newspaper or magazine, then drafting introductory remarks that headlined its importance. After Senator Moss had entered it in the Senate record, we'd have reprints made to send to voters.

Producing these "Record Inserts" was part of being a senator, more so for some than for others. Minnesota's Hubert Humphrey, known for his verbosity, was equally effusive in print. It was said that he didn't need a filing system. Whatever crossed his desk—or his mind—ended up in the *Congressional Record*.

Virginia Rishel had been Senator Moss's top legislative assistant since his arrival in January 1959. She was the first woman to hold this position in the US Senate. Watching her at work offered a first-rate education. To prepare a bill for Senator Moss to introduce, cosponsor, or simply support with his vote, she would draft the statement on her typewriter. That was often the first sound I heard in the morning. She would then pull out the sliding side table from her desk and, with a freshly sharpened pencil, begin editing. When satisfied, she'd head briskly and dramatically into the senator's office, sit there in front of him while he read the draft, and await his approval.

Her lunches also followed a ritual: first, the handbag up on the desk to announce she'd be leaving and not to bother her 'til she came back. That was a declaration to be taken seriously. For Virginia Rishel, noontime with an old friend was part of the day she'd been looking forward to and from which she would return clearly rejuvenated. Lunch was the social highlight of her day; she took her evenings quietly, with a good mystery to take her into the night.

Working with Virginia was to inherit from her generation's experience, especially her long-savored memory—for example, of President Franklin D. Roosevelt's incandescent charm, but also the admitted drudgery of redundant office work. "I can't believe I have to write another fish disease bill," she opined aloud one weekday morning, having handled the chore too many years before.

Soon it was my turn for a smelly task. It was Virginia who pulled me into it, with all the necessary cold-bloodedness. Senator Moss, she said, picking her words carefully, had made a commitment during the 1970 reelection that had to be met. The operators of mobile oil drilling equipment, the kind that can be driven from one well to another, had made a campaign donation. Now they wanted an exemption from the highway use tax. Someone in the office had to make the case.

I accepted the job despite catching an immediate whiff of its bad aroma. I wanted to do what politics required. I wanted to go *pro*. If good Virginia Rishel could do this work, so could I. The case I ended up making, taken directly from the lobbyist talking points, was that such equipment shouldn't be charged the same federal tax as any other big hauler for the basic reason that it was on the road only some small percentage—I think it was 5 percent—of its "working life." The paltry percentage attached to that felicitous term, "working life," masked a larger reality that I grasped on my first sight of one of these mammoth vehicles whose owners I had agreed to help protect. Picture the towering oil rigs in the 1956 epic film

Giant, starring Elizabeth Taylor, Rock Hudson, and newcomer James Dean. Think of a "gusher" rising up through that enormous frame. Now imagine one of these giant machines lying horizontally on the highway just ahead. Imagine a vehicle hogging the road so far ahead that you can't see beyond it. Now think of the weight of these Godzilla-size rigs and the tracks they could be leaving in the roadway.

The reckoning arrived when a major revenue bill appeared before the Senate. Senator Moss introduced what I dubbed the "Road Hog Bill" as an amendment. Hearing Moss's case for the measure, his fellow Utah senator, Wallace Bennett, the top Republican on the Senate Finance Committee, seemed bemused. While his facsimile of a smile said he knew the score, he moved that his colleague's amendment be accepted to the giant revenue bill "without objection."

I would learn more about my unloved Road Hog Bill as it made its way further up in the legislative process. It came in a phone call from a staffer on the then Joint Committee on Internal Revenue Taxation. This is the bipartisan panel that provides expertise on tax legislation. Speaking sotto voce as one insider to another, he wanted me to clue him in. Was my boss serious in pushing this loophole in the federal highway tax? Catching on to his incredulity, I let him know the amendment for the mobile oil drillers was not meant to be one of Senator Frank E. Moss's landmark achievements.

It was an early lesson for me on how a bill becomes a law—or doesn't. Drafting a case for a tax loophole, even getting it included in major legislation, is not the same as getting it enacted. Senator Moss had duly introduced the amendment. *Check.* The oil trade association could claim it got the measure through the Senate. *Check.* But the entire episode ended up being a masquerade. Moss's support for this special-interest bill, I have to make clear, was out of character. Early in his Senate career he had paid dearly for refusing to back Majority Leader Lyndon Johnson's push for tax breaks for Texas oilmen. Johnson had punished Moss with less-than-stellar committee assignments. This principled history of his was probably why his Utah Republican colleague had raised his eyebrows while listening to him make his unlikely case for the Road Hog amendment.

The last months of 1971 were a preview to the year Richard Nixon would seek reelection. Both political parties wanted to show they could solve the country's twin challenges: inflation and unemployment, both of which were at troubling levels. Senate Democrats took up a big job-creating public works bill. To make it a good sell in Utah, I was told to assemble a county-by-county list of all the state's public works projects—bridge, road, water, and sewer—that were ready to go. I was learning how to adapt a national topic to a matter of local urgency.

With a feeble economy jeopardizing a second term, Nixon now wielded his executive powers. Over the summer, he declared a ninety-day freeze on wages and prices in the country, and a six-month freeze on federal pay raises, to begin the following year.

When Senator Moss agreed to fight that last part, I became excited by what would be a clash with Richard Nixon himself. Utah was home to a high percentage of federal employees, many of them working for the Defense Department or managing federal lands. Why should they be singled out for a longer wage freeze than private sector workers? To advance the cause, I soon found myself working alongside top officials of the American Federation of Government Employees. They were the first labor guys I'd teamed up with professionally.

When it came time for Senator Moss to take his stand on the Senate floor opposing the federal employee pay freeze, he asked me to join him. There I was, age twenty-six and not a year back from Africa, surrounded by the US senators I had admired and followed growing up. As I sat there waiting for Senator Moss's turn to speak, I heard these familiar figures chattering among themselves like baseball players in the infield. It was as if the country's grand political stage had been replaced by a small gathering of men from the neighborhood. They sat there in that august chamber impatiently confined to their seats like the kids back at St. Christopher's. One voice rose above the others.

"I'm stickin' with the president!"

It was the Deep South growl of Mississippi segregationist John Stennis. His staunch loyalty would be warmly rewarded two years later when Nixon, embroiled in the Watergate scandal, proposed that "Judge Stennis" be the lone person to hear his secretly recorded presidential tapes and discern if they contained anything incriminating. By then, as I said, the old Dixiecrat was known to be quite deaf.

By December, Moss's position defending federal employee pay had prevailed. The Senate voted 77 to 1 to approve the full federal employee pay hike, with the Utah senator receiving much of the credit. "The man who must feel most like the Lone Ranger this morning is Sen. Frank Moss (D-Utah)," a *Washington Post* columnist wrote. "He stood firm on the pay raise while most of his colleagues switched sides in an almost comic parliamentary game of red rover."

With the arrival of 1972, my stock in Moss's office had clearly risen. Wayne Owens's replacement as administrative assistant informed me, somewhat taken aback by it himself, that Senator Moss was rewarding me with a $6,000 raise. I would now be earning twice what I was making as a Capitol Police officer.

To celebrate my new status, I bought a used Mercedes-Benz from an Egyptian official at the World Bank headquarters in DC. Thanks to the new AA, I had the use of his parking space in the underground lot next to the Old Senate Office Building. Things were going well.

Meanwhile, the political future for the man who'd hired me, Wayne, also appeared bright. With the warmer weather, Senator Moss hosted an outdoor fund-raiser for his former staffer at his Virginia house overlooking the Potomac River. I volunteered to help with the parking. It was my first encounter with the last Kennedy brother.

I had spotted Ted and his pal Senator John Tunney of California in Kennedy's convertible as we were all driving to the event across Chain Bridge. Now among the picnickers, I found myself directly in his company. In a cheering mood, Kennedy shared a scary episode from his brother's 1960 presidential campaign. It's one he would repeat in his memoir *True Compass*.

As he told it, Ted had arrived in Utah that autumn evening in 1960 already late for a speaking engagement on behalf of Jack the candidate. Upon landing in a private plane, he had just minutes to make it to the event. Unfortunately, no one was there to pick him up. Spotting a station wagon on the side of the road, and now desperate to meet his commitment, he brashly opened the door and reached into the glove compartment in search of the keys. It was then that he heard the click of a gun and saw a pistol being pointed directly at his gut by a very rough-looking local. Thankfully, real trouble was avoided when Kennedy's host for the event arrived just in time. The gun-toting car owner agreed to drive Kennedy to his meeting.

Senator Kennedy told all this without giving off a hint of embarrassment about going into a stranger's car and searching for the keys. But that wasn't what struck me. It was what this man had been through in life. Here was the youngest of four brothers, three of whom had died violently, two by bullets fired by assassins. Why was he sharing this hair-raising episode with me about a guy sticking a pistol in his gut?

Only later did I learn that the lighthearted youngest Kennedy was about to lead a behind-the-scenes probe that changed history. It was on June 17, 1972, that henchmen for Nixon's reelection effort burglarized the Democratic National Committee headquarters at the Watergate office and apartment complex. And it was Kennedy, through his Senate Judiciary subcommittee staff, who would map the entire chain of command from those burglars, to the Nixon reelection committee, to the White House. His months-long investigation would be the start-up manual for the Senate Watergate Committee chaired by his Judiciary colleague Senator Sam Ervin of North Carolina.

Heading toward the 1972 election, Watergate was overshadowed by the country's focus on the economy. To protect themselves from the perennial Republican charge of being big spenders, Democrats constructed the Ironclad Ceiling on Federal Spending. The bill ended up being a joke because it was immediately amended to exempt every category of government spending.

Switching from defense to offense, Senate Democrats pushed for raising the $1.60 minimum wage. In preparing Senator Moss for that debate, I discovered over time that Congress had tended to bump up the legal bottom wage to a total of inflation and the average increase in worker productivity. Why not make this automatic formula the law? Why not make what had been the periodic hike in the minimum wage automatic? Senator Moss liked the idea and introduced an amendment to that effect. To our surprise, it was defeated thanks to a large number of Democratic votes.

I didn't get it. Why would Democratic senators, who are proud supporters of organized labor, not want a law protecting the economic interests of the lowest paid? The answer, I rudely discovered, was the self-interest of senators, not the wage earners. The lawmakers wanted political credit every time they raised the minimum wage. If they made the raises automatic, there'd be nothing to crow about. The smart guys working for the Senate Democratic leadership explained all this to me afterward. They were generous to tell me the mistakes I was making, if not in time to avoid them.

Still hopeful, I dreamed up my biggest legislative effort for Senator Moss: a grand proposal to deal with the country's economic adjustment expected to come with the end of the Vietnam War. I went about researching all the various ways the federal government could assist in creating new opportunities for an economy no longer ginned up by war spending. When Senator Moss formally introduced the bill, I felt a real sense of accomplishment. While it never made it into law, the bill attracted an impressive posse of Senate cosponsors, including several top liberal icons. I felt I was in some small way influencing the course of legislative history. I began thinking of myself as a success—even something of a minor celebrity. At twenty-six, I had not yet discovered that to be a dangerous sentiment.

CHAPTER SIXTEEN

MIAMI

Still wanting to be a writer on my own, I faced an interesting choice in the summer of 1972. Should I write a freelance magazine article on Philadelphia's new law-and-order mayor, Frank Rizzo, or head down to the Democratic National Convention? Once again, the chance to be part of national politics held the strongest allure.

I drove down to Miami Beach with my Peace Corps friend Gary Rowse, who had been sponsored by wealthy Los Angeles liberal activist Miles Rubin to lobby for senior citizens' causes. With the US Senate out of session, I myself had volunteered to work at the convention for the DNC press operation.

The presidential nomination and the convention itself were now firmly in the hands of Senator George McGovern of South Dakota. His anti–Vietnam War politics had trumped the early favorite and more moderate candidate, Edmund Muskie of Maine, who had been the 1968 vice presidential nominee. McGovern's slates of delegates had also upended the forces of party leaders such as Chicago mayor Richard Daley and Massachusetts congressman Tip O'Neill, the latter of whom said, "We got beat by the cast of *Hair*."

The mission of the McGovern delegates was to change the Democratic Party into one of their liking. That meant ridding it of big-city bosses, political "regulars" who backed the Vietnam War, and the financial fat cats they saw holding the party in their pockets. The first sign of all this upheaval greeted Gary and me as we pulled in front of our hotel. Protestors wielding signs began yelling at us. I realized quickly it was the car. Yes, I'd bought it secondhand, and, no, it didn't have air-conditioning, but it was undeniably a Mercedes. To those protesting, I was the enemy at the gate, taken for a wealthy contributor, an object of infamy. The activists at the 1968 convention that I rooted for in grad school now found me wanting.

My convention job, at which I got quickly started, wasn't likely to upset either side of the divide. It was to produce "color" stories for use by wandering reporters. I was to chase after celebrities and grab something quotable.

I remember catching playwright Arthur Miller for his thoughts, only to watch him trip over a chair on his way through a dining area. I imagined Marilyn Monroe cringing at the sight of her former husband's awkward moment. Later, tagging alongside my hero Norman Mailer, I asked what he thought of the Democrats' penchant for demonizing Richard Nixon. The renowned author and activist cautioned against that strategy, "What happens when he saves a baby from a fire?" He may have been thinking of Nixon's historic achievement of opening relations with China earlier in the year.

As I raced around rubbernecking at celebrities and performing other chores for the DNC, I was able to get an up-close measure of the people I'd known only from the newspapers. One was Robert Strauss, the national party treasurer. I will never forget the small favor he paid me, demanding that I, a young volunteer, be let in a side door to the Miami Beach Convention Center. It opened a milelong shortcut on a sweltering South Florida day.

What I remember most from that week in Miami Beach was the giddiness of the affair. That certainly included the sight of the Massachusetts delegation Tip O'Neill had included in his crack that he'd been beaten by the scruffy cast of the sixties Broadway musical about hippies. The McGovern-backing delegation was dancing in a gleeful circle. Towering among them was John Kenneth Galbraith, the six-foot-eight Harvard economics professor. For these activists of the Left, victory was defeating and replacing the people who traditionally ran the Democratic Party. For them, the nomination was a victory in itself.

The frenzy in Miami Beach continued through the final night of the convention, when McGovern was to stand before the country and accept the nomination. It was then that the full absurdity of the occasion hit full tilt. As the clock neared and then passed midnight, McGovern had still not come to the podium. Instead of the presidential candidate standing at the national microphone, it was Senator Mike Gravel of Alaska, one of dozens of candidates being nominated to be McGovern's running mate.

"Who says a duly elected United States senator doesn't have the right to put his name into nomination for vice president?" It was at this crowning moment of lost opportunity that the spectacle of the McGovern campaign peaked. A national political convention meant to pick a president and vice president had become *Gilligan's Island*. "There are people who just shouldn't be here," I heard Senator Moss say. Because of this *theater of the absurd* at the podium, George McGovern didn't get to accept the presidential nomination 'til nearly three o'clock in the morning. This meant that even on the West Coast, few were watching. It was the South Dakota senator's one great chance to make the case for his election, and his party's own goofy antics had crushed it.

That week in Miami Beach showed me that a good part of politics is people simply out having fun. The 1972 Democratic convention was less a war council than a victory celebration. It wasn't meant to begin the campaign against Richard Nixon but to celebrate the victory over the Democratic establishment. It did that by behaving like it felt like behaving. Instead of putting on a convention aimed at winning over the American middle, it celebrated its triumph over the forces and candidates, such as Ed Muskie, who were most likely to appeal to the middle.

This is not to say the 1972 Democratic National Convention lacked for glamor. Thanks to Gary, I was let into a gathering of the old Bobby

Kennedy gang, with actress Shirley MacLaine and top political aides Pierre Salinger and Frank Mankiewicz. The person missing, now with tragic clarity, was the one who brought them all together and, had he lived, might well have held them together still. Instead, George McGovern, tragically, had inherited a vanished throne.

Even his last-minute selection of a running mate had come a cropper. Missouri senator Tom Eagleton, a dead ringer for actor Jack Lemmon, had kept a giant detail about himself from public view. Years before, to treat depression, he had submitted twice to electroshock therapy. Whispers about his past grew louder and louder until in late July, just two weeks after the convention had wrapped up, the vice presidential candidate had to admit publicly to the truth. While the McGovern camp attempted to deal with the catastrophe, I made the case to Senator Moss back in Washington for keeping Eagleton on the ticket. I'd always liked the forty-two-year-old Missourian and had even been talking to his top aide, Douglas Bennet, about going to work for the campaign.

Moss, in his usual gentle way, tried giving some tough advice. "You know what politics is, Chris? It's taking the littlest thing and making it into the biggest thing you ever saw." Having electroshock therapy for emotional depression, he assured me, wasn't the littlest thing in the world. Senator Moss, my first boss in politics, was trying to teach me how the world works. Indeed, although McGovern initially insisted that he backed his running mate "a thousand percent," Eagleton stepped down the following week. Before the convention, McGovern had originally hoped to convince Edward Kennedy to be his running mate; now he settled for a Kennedy by marriage: R. Sargent Shriver, the ambassador to France and the husband of Ted's sister Eunice Kennedy Shriver.

As much as I respected Frank Moss, I would never quite accept the lesson he imparted to me. In my mind, politics is about courage. It's Washington holding his troops together along the Delaware, Lincoln keeping the North together during the Civil War, FDR beginning his twelve-year run as president by telling the Depression-ravaged American people in the first of four inaugural addresses, "the only thing we have to fear is . . . fear itself." It's not about giving in to the mob, accepting the lowest common denominator of what's acceptable. I believed back then, and still do, that the great politicians are those who stand alone when everyone else is either buckling or ducking. A leader is not someone who puts a wet finger up so they can align themselves with the prevailing wind. It's those who John F. Kennedy memorably called "profiles in courage" who merit our respect.

CHAPTER SEVENTEEN

FIRST CAMPAIGN

In October 1972 I was sent to Utah along with another Moss staffer to work for the Democratic Party. The assignment had something to do with going over lists of registered voters. I didn't stick with the project long enough to figure it out. It was Wayne Owens's exciting campaign for Congress that grabbed hold of me. He had worked his way into the contest with his decision to walk nearly the length of Utah.

That hike through the southern, less populated part of the state was meant to impress voters in Salt Lake City, where the Second Congressional District was centered. It was to show voters in Utah's largest city that he was a young candidate ready to sweat for the job, a guy with the humility to prove himself worthy of public office. It was also calculated to improve his name recognition.

It was a masterstroke of political positioning. What on the surface appeared to be a case of *retail* politics—of getting out there and meeting the people one-on-one—was, in fact, classic electoral *wholesale*. The publicity from that long walk had put him on the map.

I could see how the young guy I'd known as a top Senate aide had grown quickly into a politician. Most of all, Wayne had the candidate's gift: the readiness to ask people to help. He was a natural recruiter, especially of young people like my new friend Tom Berggren, who had taken a year off from Harvard to assist Owens's run for the House against the

Republican incumbent. By the time I arrived out there, the campaign was in full stride. Salt Lake City TV stations were already airing debates between the candidates, and the city's two main newspapers, the *Salt Lake Tribune* and the *Deseret News*, were covering the race daily.

The big local news story, besides the campaign, was a massive oil spill near Utah's Lake Powell. To take advantage, Wayne began criticizing the federal government's response. I wrote press releases hitting Washington's haggard performance. They began getting reliable *pickup*, as it's called, in the newspapers and on the TV news. This was all happening in the last weeks of the campaign, a perfect time for a candidate to attract attention.

The experience taught me three big lessons: one, it's easier to piggyback on a story that has momentum than to start one of your own; two, it's hard to beat a hot *local* story when it comes to getting voters' attention; three, a candidate for office should talk like he's already won. When people read or heard about this young Wayne Owens pushing Washington to get off its butt, they saw the kind of active public servant they liked.

He was proving himself ready for the job by actually *doing* it.

Those were great weeks for me out in Utah. I was quickly invited to stay with some other young guys in the Owens campaign. It was like living in a frat house but with a common mission. One housemate was John Clark, a Yale-educated lawyer who also ran a polling company. The other was Peter Emerson, who popped in and out of the campaign and remains a great friend.

The thing I discovered early about Utah was the nightlife. Those Mormon-sensitive laws were not what they seemed. There were, for example, the "clubs." For a $10-a-year membership fee, you could order drinks like at any bar in Manhattan. These hangouts created a subculture in Salt Lake that was as lively as anywhere in the United States—maybe more so because they assumed the subversive quality of a speakeasy during Prohibition.

There was an upbeat spirit to the Wayne Owens campaign. Utah is beautiful in the fall. The air is clear and brisk just before the snow flies.

For me, it seemed like the right place to be, helping my friend Wayne, the person who opened the door for me, reach his dream.

I had just one lingering concern. Even in these years before the Watergate-triggered reforms, I didn't want my official role as legislative assistant to Senator Moss to cause any problems in the press for Wayne. I decided to protect all concerned by asking the senator to take me off his official payroll. What I didn't think about, but should have, was how he might take it. He had sent me out to Utah to work for the Democratic Party. Now I was telling him I was setting my own cause in his home state. When I got the senator on the phone, he took my request calmly but coldly. Why did I think he wouldn't? Here was a senator who had taken me into his office, afforded me real responsibilities, given me a significant raise, taught me a bit of what he'd learned along the way, and here I was heading off from the job he'd assigned me to work for someone else. Where were my loyalties? I suppose I answered that question with my phone call. They were elsewhere.

As the polls edged in Wayne's direction and his debate performances grew stronger, we began to imagine victory. To help close the deal, Ted Kennedy was coming to Salt Lake City. His advance man, Hank Culhane, was an education in himself. He showed us how to turn a one-day visit by the Massachusetts senator into a local sensation.

To build crowds along the highway from the airport, he got the nuns to shut down the Catholic schools. To make the big indoor rally more dramatic, he moved an entire wall of lockers to reduce the size of the hall. Kennedy himself hyped up the ballyhoo by delaying his arrival until you could feel the room so bursting with tension you thought it was going to *blow*. And it worked. When the last Kennedy brother finally entered the hall, the crowd *did* explode. With his booming baritone, he evoked Utah's legendary outlaw Butch Cassidy and "the Pangwatch Kid," a reference to his former aide's small-town roots.

At a glowing dinner that night, Wayne quoted a poem by Ernest Hemingway that seemed to capture the feeling of those months:

"Best of all he loved the fall / The leaves yellow in the cottonwoods / Leaves floating on the trout streams / And above the hills / The high blue windless sky."

The other celebrity to make a cameo campaign appearance was Robert Redford, the young star who played the Sundance Kid opposite Paul Newman's Butch Cassidy in the 1969 movie I'd seen in Mombasa, Kenya, on my way home from Swaziland. We picked up the actor one morning in Provo and headed to some big shopping malls around Salt Lake City. As we wandered among the young customers, I helped with the introductions. "Would you like to meet Robert Redford? What's your name? "Bob, I'd like you to meet . . ." Having conquered the malls, we headed to the highway alongside the University of Utah football stadium. It was the day of the big game against Arizona.

To take advantage of the pregame traffic, we had Redford stand facing the highway leading a Honk 'n' Wave. We held up signs inviting people to do just that as they spotted the famous actor waving back.

One of the campaign's last events was a parade through a Salt Lake neighborhood. I watched the incumbent Republican congressman riding in the back seat of an open VW convertible. I couldn't help but notice his wife prodding him again and again to get out of the car and shake hands with people along the roadway. I felt sympathy for these two who knew they were facing defeat and, with it, humiliation.

That halcyon autumn I was also trying to pick the winners nationwide, reveling especially in races for the US Senate. One contest that caught my interest was back East in Delaware. Over the summer, I'd joined some other people there in renting a place in Rehoboth Beach, on the Atlantic coast. One hot Friday night, I saw a giant billboard ad promoting a young, slightly balding candidate for Senate. He struck me as an ambitious newcomer but with no real chance, or what we call a sacrificial lamb. Now, however, I was getting word from John Clark, our pollster, that this Democrat named Joe Biden might be headed for an upset. It goes to show you that even in a year when the presidential race is going strongly in one direction, there will be candidates who buck the tide. Those, I've learned, are the ones to watch.

On the day of the election, Tom Berggren and I canvassed an area of reliable Democratic voters, persuading the dwindling number of malingerers to head off to the voting booths. We could feel victory coming. That evening, John, Peter, and I headed to a Japanese restaurant, where we sat on little cushions. I didn't realize we were engaging in what I would learn is an election-night ritual. Wary politicians tend to sneak away from the action in those evening hours. Why? Because it's when the bulk of votes have yet to be counted; when all you get is a trickle of returns, and the rumors run hot, unreliable, and nerve racking.

When we made it to campaign headquarters, the room was packed and frenzied. "Meal tickets!" Peter observed. It seemed that everyone within driving distance wanted to be seen sharing in Wayne's victory. That night, the Democratic candidate for president, George McGovern, lost forty-nine states, Utah among them. Richard Nixon's historic February trip to China loomed over the land, as did his subsequent visit to Moscow—the first by a US president—to hammer out with Soviet leader Leonid Brezhnev a welcome policy of détente between our two countries. McGovern, meanwhile, was seen as too far to the left, an insufficient Cold Warrior, just too radical of an alternative for a country content with what it had.

But that night in Salt Lake City, it was a remarkable political upset. Wayne had done it! A friend had gone home and emerged a winner. I had an enduring memory of electoral victory—even if my euphoria would last only through the night.

I was woken up that Wednesday by Frank Moss's administrative assistant, who instructed me to come to the senator's Salt Lake office by nine o'clock. Greeting me on my arrival, he told me he assumed I was now going to work for Wayne in his new congressional office. In any case, he said, I no longer had a role on Moss's staff. A new pharaoh had come to Egypt. His own work accomplished, he told me to go in and talk with the senator.

"Chris! I hear you're heading back to Washington!" was Frank's greeting. He struck me as upbeat; actually enthusiastic for me. Looking back over the decades, I have, on occasion, thought it was possible he had taken my request to remove me from his payroll as an outright resignation. More likely, he was merely disappointed, even a bit angry, that I had rejected his assignment for the Utah Democratic Party and preferred to work directly for Wayne. In either case, he was as warm and friendly as ever. After some small talk, he left me with some powerful career advice, the weight of which would take months, even years, to absorb: "Perhaps you should dip a little deeper into these political waters."

He was saying I had the stuff for a political career, and that I should get out there and run for office myself. I treasure his words, not least because he spoke them at a moment I think neither of us had wanted. But there I was, without a job, and, to use the senator's phrase, "heading back to Washington."

CHAPTER EIGHTEEN

FREELANCE

By the time I got back to DC, I had shaken off my personal defeat. In truth, I was optimistic. A friend of mine told me about a basement apartment to sublet near the main intersection of M Street and Wisconsin Avenue. With a Georgetown address, I felt elevated after my stumble in Utah.

One night at home, I watched George C. Scott in his Oscar-winning performance in the title role of the epic war movie *Patton*. It was the film we Peace Corps guys liked when it arrived in Swaziland, and now it was perfectly in sync with my fighter's spirit. I was young, single, and independent—and prepared to act it. The guy I was subletting from had also been through a campaign out West. He'd been AA to a three-term Republican senator from Colorado who had narrowly lost his seat. Having been on the losing end, he admitted that the Democrats had command of two big issues going for them: opposition to the Vietnam War and concern for the environment. Their only weakness, he said, was the big government deficit for which they were blamed.

I decided to raise the issue publicly. I went to work on an article about the Democrats' vulnerability as big spenders and submitted it to the *Washington Star*. "An Issue the Democrats Ignore at Their Peril" ran in that Sunday's newspaper. "Many Democrats today continue to ignore the genuine concern of many voters that massive federal deficits are the

109

chief cause of the nation's ongoing economic difficulties," I held forth. "They now dismiss any talk of 'fiscal responsibility' as nothing more than Republican obstructionism."

My article showcased the travesty of that disingenuous Ironclad Ceiling on Federal Spending bill Democrats had rallied around earlier in the year. I suggested it revealed the games the party played to avoid being held accountable. "You sound like a Republican," someone remarked after reading the piece. But it was the subterfuge I was attacking; the clever tricks of keeping power while ducking accountability.

I decided to keep at it, beginning the new year with an ironic piece for the *Philadelphia Daily News*, lampooning the way members of Congress answer their constituent mail; how they use those automatic letter-writing and signature machines to turn out prefabricated responses to earnest letters from voters back home. I tagged it: "Of course, if you find this all a little disturbing, you know what you can do about it. Write your congressman."

I was trying my hand at journalism. But even as I was showing off my new independence, I yearned to get back into politics. It was the first time since my early weeks in Washington that I was out of a job and out of the loop. I was outside looking in and didn't much like the feeling. But how was I to get back into a Capitol Hill position when I was out there publicly denouncing the way it does business? This would become a recurring quandary for me: the urge to tell the full story versus the allure of partisan combat, which inevitably involves pushing only one side.

Newly minted representative Wayne Owens tried to help out. He put me on his congressional staff for a couple of months mainly as a speechwriter. Unfortunately for me, he had already committed his top legislative assistant job to his well-deserving campaign researcher. When I asked Wayne if he had any career advice, he came back with something memorable:

"I always learned that it was associating yourself with the right people," he told me quite soberly.

That winter of 1973 I made a remarkable alliance. It was with my replacement in Moss's office, Richard Sorensen, whose celebrated father, Parry D. Sorensen, had once chaired the Journalism Department at the University of Utah. Rich was a Harvard grad, a Rhodes scholar, and now, most crucial to me, a faithful pal.

I had gotten to work that winter on something important I'd learned out in Utah. That oil spill near Lake Powell had shown me the federal government's inadequacy in the area. It took me a lot of digging just to find the US agency willing to accept jurisdiction for oil pipeline safety. The more I dug, the more I could see the big problem. Accountability kept shifting from one department to another. I finally came to the stark realization that oversight for the safety of 220,000 miles of oil pipeline lay not with a single agency but, incredibly, with a single government official! My exposé ran in the Outlook section of Sunday's *Washington Post*. It reappeared a week later in the *Philadelphia Inquirer*. My hard work as a freelancer was getting me into print.

I had another ambition back then: to learn how to deliver a speech. At La Salle College High School, I had dreaded the weekly class in public speaking. It petrified me, especially the night before, knowing my turn might come the next day. The fear continued to stalk me at Holy Cross. In my sophomore year, I switched out of a class to avoid the Jesuit professor of rhetoric who put an emphasis on having students stand up and speak.

Now, at age twenty-seven, I decided to meet the specter head-on and joined the Capitol Hill branch of Toastmasters International. Each week I assembled with other Capitol Hill staffers who encouraged one another to stand up in front of the group and say something reasonably remarkable. For me, it was the perfect way to get over the hump. As further evidence of my seriousness, I paid $1,000 for a weeklong professional course in public speaking. It was the beginning of my practice of accepting every opportunity that comes along to speak in public. I wanted to get so good at it that I didn't give it a thought. It was the same goal I had in my writing: to get past the barrier of fear.

In those early months of 1973, journalism had become a vital part of American life because of a young pair of reporters for the *Washington Post,* Bob Woodward and Carl Bernstein. Their investigation into the Watergate affair was causing a national obsession. In May the US Senate opened hearings on the scandal. They soon riveted the country even more than the Army-McCarthy hearings had a generation before. Chaired by North Carolina's Sam Ervin, a southern character right out of Allen Drury's 1959 political novel *Advise and Consent,* the sessions became appointment television. The star witness was John Dean, the White House counsel who had turned against President Nixon. The big breakthrough came in July, when Nixon aide Alexander Butterfield revealed the existence of the White House audio taping system that captured all of the president's conversations. Trying to control the historic record, Richard Nixon had inadvertently engineered his own destruction.

It is hard to convey today the extent to which Watergate dominated Washington. For some in DC, it became mesmerizing. A pal of mine, Frank Sullivan, then working at the World Bank, became as conversant with its figures as Shakespearean scholars are with those of *Hamlet.* He delighted in reciting the names of its Rosencrantz and Guildenstern characters.

My friend Sully was not alone: the whole country had heard those names so often in the dark context of Watergate that the very sounds of them evoked the escapade itself. Nor were Woodward and Bernstein the only investigators eager to unearth the misdeeds of politicians. By the seventies, Ralph Nader had become the country's premier consumer advocate, thanks to the 1965 publication of *Unsafe at Any Speed,* his exposé of uneven safety standards in the American auto industry. When General Motors was found trying to undermine his reputation, which Nader said included tapping his phone and hiring sex workers to solicit him, it only added to his prestige. He became David battling the corporate Goliath. Armed with a heroic reputation, Nader had extended his consumer advocacy to a wider range. The Clean Water Act, the Freedom of Information

Act, the Consumer Product Safety Act, all taken for granted today, were largely the result of his pioneering.

In the summer of 1973 I caught word that Nader was planning a start-up news service. Its mission would be to provide scrutiny of those members of Congress not getting covered by daily newspapers. Freed from the media spotlight, they were able to wield their official power without any true public accountability. By filling this gap, Nader hoped to shed light on a group of elected politicians working largely in the dark. Nader's new Capitol Hill News Service was to conduct the type of hard-nosed digging championed by Woodward and Bernstein for the *Washington Post*. It would ensure that members of Congress who failed to produce as legislators or who engaged in conflicts of interest would be shown for who they were.

The young editor-publisher of this new project was Peter Gruenstein, a former aide to Wisconsin congressman Les Aspin. "Most citizens get most of their news about their congressmen from their congressmen," he would tell *Time* magazine. "Let's face it, a congressman's nirvana is being able to write a press release and have it printed or broadcast without having the facts checked."

As soon as I learned about the Capitol Hill News Service, I jumped at the chance to join it. What helped me pass muster with Gruenstein was my recent freelance work for newspapers, especially the long article exposing the oil pipeline industry's perennial escape from government safety regulation. Nader himself interviewed me alone in the basement of his headquarters just off Dupont Circle. What struck me as we met was the man's unaffected charisma. He was both charming and a force of nature. He also asked a great question: How do you learn? My answer, grabbed from right out of the limited air of that basement, was that when I had a writing assignment and stayed up into the night to finish it, I got it done. I said that the memory of that early-in-the-morning accomplishment gave me confidence I could do it the next time. I've never discovered just what the great Ralph Nader made of that answer. Perhaps his habit of asking that question was another way to strengthen himself for battle. In any case, he had recruited a new Ralph Nader follower: *me.*

Selected as one of four news service reporters, I was to receive $8,000 a year with no expense account. Take a taxi to get back from Capitol Hill? It comes out of your pocket. My beat was the Pennsylvania delegation. Not for the first time, I realized how much the rest of the state differed from Philadelphia. There is something out there in the counties far from the city, quieter, less caught in the traffic. The members of Congress elected by these voters from the smaller cities and rural areas seem to represent all that. A formal request for an interview, especially from one working for Ralph Nader, can be easily ignored.

Once, I confronted John Saylor of Somerset County coming out of an elevator in the Rayburn House Office Building. Upon introducing myself and my employer, Saylor switched roles and began grilling me, demanding answers. What was I up to? What was this Nader business about, anyway? When I said we were trying to tell the real story of Congress, Saylor called me on it. He said only a member of Congress could do that.

At least that was a respectable position. I had another member of the Pennsylvania delegation inform me that his office hosted some "nice parties." He said that if I wrote good things about him, I might just get invited. Had some reporters actually gone for that pathetic line?

That October, not long after the Capitol Hill News Service got started, the country's skepticism toward politicians exploded in grand style. It began with President Nixon refusing a demand from Watergate special prosecutor Archibald Cox that he turn over more White House tapes. Instead, he offered to let Mississippi's John Stennis listen to them and then approve a summary of Nixon's conversations that had been written by the White House. I remembered the hard-of-hearing seventy-two-year-old Mississippi lawmaker mumbling, "I'm stickin' with the president!" over that federal pay freeze two years earlier.

The special prosecutor rejected the "Stennis Compromise" outright, demanding that Nixon relinquish the actual tapes. This triggered the series of firings known as the Saturday Night Massacre, on October 20. It began with Nixon ordering attorney general Elliot Richardson to fire Cox. Richardson refused and resigned. Nixon then gave the order to fire the special prosecutor to the deputy AG, who also refused and resigned or, according to Nixon, was fired. It then fell to the solicitor general, Robert Bork, now serving as acting attorney general, to obey Nixon's order, which he did. Within days of the "Massacre," the House of Representatives began the process of impeachment.

It was around this time that I discovered that a particular Pennsylvania member of Congress was paying a reporter from the local *Scranton Tribune* $5,000 a year. When I questioned him about the odd arrangement, he said the reporter was helping him write press releases and performing other publicity matters. It struck me as a glaring conflict of interest. I called up the *Tribune*'s managing editor and asked about the deal. His was the answer that truly threw me. He didn't see any conflict between a general assignment reporter working for a congressman. On the contrary, he said, he found it to be useful: whenever the congressman was about to do something, his *Tribune* guy was right on top of it.

While I didn't really like digging up dirt like this about working politicians, I enjoyed the life of a reporter, especially getting the job done. Each evening, I'd come back to the National Press Club, where we had our offices to file the day's story. There was a solid accomplishment in it. I was writing for a living.

I got to witness history right there from the House Press Gallery. Vice President Spiro Agnew had been caught taking kickbacks from contractors dating back to his time as Baltimore County executive and then as the governor of Maryland. More outrageous, he'd continued receiving the cash as veep. Facing prison time, Agnew accepted his guilt on a single count of tax evasion and resigned. Representative Gerald Ford of Michigan now became the first vice president sworn into office under the Twenty-Fifth Amendment. I was there to witness it.

With the House Judiciary Committee now considering the prospect of impeachment, I spotted a chance to experience history from the inside. I wanted to be the committee's press spokesman. This would let me write an insider's book on Nixon's downfall.

One day I went over to the office of New Jersey's Peter Rodino and asked to see his administrative assistant Francis O'Brien, whom I'd been hearing a lot about. On meeting O'Brien, it quickly became obvious that he had someone in mind for the position. He did, however, have a job in mind for me. His brother Jack was managing a new congressional campaign up in Brooklyn, and, as it happened, he was waiting out in the reception area. What I said in the ensuing few minutes must have displayed enough interest that I soon got a phone call from the candidate's shadow strategist. His name was Paul Corbin, who turned out to be the most ruthless and by far the most deceitful politician I have ever managed to come across.

Corbin began pushing me to fly to Brooklyn with him to meet the candidate, whom he kept insisting was top drawer. When I finally agreed to the trip, Corbin said to meet him at the seven o'clock New York Shuttle the next morning. Along the way, my new associate kept singing the praises of his candidate as if he were gangster Meyer Wolfsheim talking up Jay Gatsby.

Up in Brooklyn, Corbin switched to making promises. He clearly wanted me signed on to the campaign, and he wanted it done now. Out came his ace in the hole: he said if his guy won the race, I would be named AA. I cut him short: "If he wins," I said, "he will pick the person he wants." That seemed to impress Corbin—or at least he wanted me to think it did. He said I'd just given him more evidence that I had the savvy to sell his new guy to the New York media.

After only three months at the Capitol Hill News Service, I said yes. Was it a desire to get back in the political action? Yes. Is it that I discovered liking politicians was more to my taste than investigating them? Yes. Was it because Jack O'Brien, the titular campaign manager, struck me as being honest and possessing a good, wry sense of humor? Yes.

But I suppose what really pulled me to that Brooklyn campaign was fear. It just struck me as something I needed to do. With its ethnic factions and political clubhouses, the old borough simply scared me. Like writing and public speaking, it was daring me to meet the challenge.

CHAPTER NINETEEN

BROOKLYN

Brooklyn soon became for me an academy of politics, as well as a prelude to the gutsiest move of my life.

I found an apartment in Brooklyn Heights, a block above Montague Street. Each morning, I would trudge through the winter slush, with a black coffee and donut in hand, to the campaign's storefront headquarters. My initial quest was to promote the candidate to the borough's array of free weekly newspapers. A lesson learned quickly is how these "shoppers" made it financially: totally on advertising. That went for political candidates as well as local businesses. Free publicity, in other words, wasn't free. If my candidate wanted even a photo from one of his events in print, he had to fork over the money. Buy some ads, and you get some coverage in the news space. Otherwise, forget about it.

For Paul Corbin, who tried buying me into the campaign with his promise of the candidate's top staff job, such dealings were a matter of basic tradecraft. He told me once that the candidate "could have bought" the seat in Congress we were seeking for a quarter million dollars. Given the nature of Brooklyn politics back then, it seemed entirely possible. But our candidate wouldn't have gotten within a ten-foot pole of such a deal. Once an aide to Senator Robert Kennedy, he was as clean as they come—a born reformer. Corbin, on the other hand, seemed entirely comfortable with an outright purchase of a seat in the US Congress. He took pride in the backroom arts. One night, in a second-floor Chinese restaurant on Court Street, he shared some of his favorite escapades with me.

As I would learn later, the Canadian-born tactician started out in politics in Wisconsin. One of his early triumph's was convincing a fabulously wealthy Republican to make a big gift to Corbin's Democratic candidate for governor. He did it by convincing the rich donor that if his candidate lost the primary, the state's Democratic Party would be taken over by the "Communists." It worked.

Then, with his candidate now the party nominee, he went back to the same donor and warned him that if the Democrats lost in November, the Reds would grab control on the grounds that the moderates had blown it. He scored again: another big contribution went in the campaign's treasury. I later learned a great irony about these shenanigans. It's that Corbin had himself been a committed Communist with a long FBI file on his early activities.

The fact is, there was more than trickery in Paul Corbin's heart. He also had a gift for knowing human nature, plus a knack for exploiting it. It showed in how he treated that Republican contributor he brought over to his side in the Wisconsin governor's race. When Corbin took him into the governor's mansion to meet the successful candidate, this wealthy man became emotional. He said it showed a level of respect the Republicans had never given him, a treat he'd never been allowed.

Corbin said he worried what his benefactor would now seek in return. With the new governor standing there, he asked if there was anything they could do for him. At first, the wealthy contributor was hesitant. Finally, he said he did have one request in mind. Could he have one of those low-numbered state license plates? The point of the story: what many people want out of politics is simple human *recognition*.

It was in Wisconsin that Corbin discovered his political hero: Bobby Kennedy. He became involved with the family during the 1960 presidential primary battle between John F. Kennedy, the Catholic, and Senator Hubert Humphrey, the Protestant. This is where Corbin displayed his brand as a master political trickster, passing out anti-Catholic literature in the Catholic neighborhoods—where it would drive wavering voters to vote for their fellow communicant. That included Republicans, who, under the state's open primary law, were able to cross over and vote in the Democratic contest.

I knew the impact of such door-to-door anti-Catholicism. It's the way Mom responded when some people knocked on our door pedaling the similar warnings about having a president loyal to the pope.

That night in the Chinese restaurant, dinner long finished, the mastermind behind the Wisconsin dirty tricks spoke in his gravel-driveway voice about the manager of that 1960 presidential campaign: the man he called Bob.

Corbin was at Robert Kennedy's side when, following his brother's death in Dallas, he ran for the US Senate in New York. Hearing his friend speaking about the 1964 Civil Rights Act, Corbin became convinced that the younger Kennedy was being too legalistic. He told his candidate to think about being in an African American's situation. "Imagine driving through the South, and your wife had to go to the bathroom," he recalled telling Kennedy, "and you can't find a place that will let her use one. How would that make you feel?"

He told me of how he pushed Kennedy to get past his brother's assassination. Campaigning with him through New York State, he realized Bob was taking the same route his brother Jack had taken four years earlier. He told Kennedy to stop being his brother's ghost and be himself. Only Corbin could get away with that kind of brutally frank talk.

Years later, I would learn more about Corbin's reputation as RFK's hatchet man. Although hated by some, his hijinks made him beloved by Robert and Ethel Kennedy. Born Jewish, Corbin became so devoted to the Kennedy family that he converted to Roman Catholicism in order to have the two Kennedys as his godparents.

Conventional wisdom has it that Paul Corbin pulled his last hurrah in the dirty tricks department in 1980. Embittered by Senator Ted Kennedy's defeat in the 1980 Democratic primaries to President Jimmy

Carter, Corbin reportedly vowed revenge. In advance of Carter's make-or-break October debate with Ronald Reagan, he got hold of the president's briefing book and purportedly delivered it to Reagan's campaign manager William Casey. It allowed Reagan to anticipate Carter's strategy and be prepared with a strong rebuttal.

It had all the aspects of a classic Corbin operation. One, he got away with it. Two, most insiders, the people he wanted to impress, are convinced he did it. Three, Reagan won the debate. Four, his pal Casey became CIA chief under Reagan. Five, the perpetrator himself got his revenge.

Corbin died in 1990. It was Bobby Kennedy's widow, Ethel, who held the memorial service for him at Hickory Hill, the family home in Virginia. As an invited guest, I remember it as a grand gathering of the Kennedy political clan, many speaking with undisguised delight about the Corbin shenanigans.

As both a journalist and a lover of political combat, I was lucky to come across this creature of the partisan underworld. Political life is packed with shared exploits and those who recount them. For whatever reason, Paul Corbin, master of the political dark arts, decided in that old Chinese restaurant in Brooklyn to open his Santa Claus sack to me.

Not everything Corbin taught was corrupt. He also had vintage lessons to teach. His rule for press relations, for example, was to establish a personal relationship with the reporter covering you. If nothing else, it allows you to plea for mercy on those occasions when you're desperate to keep something you said out of the newspaper. I would know those times all too well. Another Corbin rule was the need to maintain a strict one-to-one connection between staffer and job. Anything to do with press was the sole, exclusive job, duty, and responsibility of the campaign press secretary. No one else talks to the media. The same goes for field organization and all the rest. One job: one person to do it—one—and when necessary, one person to blame.

I owe something more to Paul Corbin from those months in Brooklyn. A lifetime benefit of that short campaign was meeting Robert Schiffer, whom Corbin had recruited out of the University of Tennessee. Schiffer and I became lifelong friends.

The campaign's big event that winter was a fund-raiser at Brooklyn's old-money Montauk Club. I arranged for a contributor to make his donation in the form of a $5,000 bid on a portion of an unpublished Ernest Hemingway manuscript donated by the author's widow, Mary. It won the campaign a treasured mention in *Newsweek*'s Periscope column.

When I showed Paul Corbin the speech I'd drafted for the candidate that night, particularly the tribute to Robert Kennedy, I saw the emotion he still carried toward his fallen hero. I referred in the speech to Gordon Strachan, the young Nixon aide at the fringes of the Watergate scandal who, when asked what advice he would give a young person interested in getting into politics, said, "Stay away."

Our candidate represented the opposite. An idealist in his early thirties, he was determined to carry on the Robert Kennedy spirit. He had worked with RFK in the economic redevelopment of the poorer segments of Brooklyn and wanted to carry on his work in the borough. Unfortunately, the campaign wasn't working. Corbin would pop in now and then to enforce a nasty discipline that offered no real direction. There seemed no route for our candidate among the rivalries of the political machine of county boss Meade Esposito, the borough's web of reform clubs, or in the alternative Liberal Party.

Worse yet, I discovered one evening that the real decisions of the campaign were being made by a "kitchen cabinet" of the candidate's old friends. Nothing wrong with that in itself, but it marginalized those of us on the campaign paid staff. It was nothing like the Wayne Owens campaign, where the workers were first and foremost the candidate's personal friends. I began looking for a way out.

At this same time, I came upon Hugh Sidey's column in *Time* magazine about Robin West, a guy my age, who was taking on the Republican political machine in Delaware County, just outside Philadelphia. If this young fellow from an old-money background could do it, why couldn't

I? I called up my brother Jim and asked him to meet me at our parents' house.

What struck me when I got there was how comfortable it was to be home and, surprisingly, how open Dad was to my running. "Maybe the people are ready for something new," he said, "that they've had it with the old city politics." He understood exactly what I was thinking. He had the local perspective that I saw nationally: that Watergate had shaken things up, and that, in a time like this, anything could happen at the polls. I just couldn't bring myself to make the leap that night. After that good talk with Dad and Jim, I got in the car and headed back to Brooklyn.

A week later, Bob Schiffer and I went to the movies in Manhattan. The feature was *Walking Tall,* the partly biographical tale of Buford Pusser, an imposing small-time professional wrestler in Chicago who returns to his Tennessee hometown to find it corrupted and overrun by organized crime. He becomes the town sheriff and singlehandedly goes to war with the bad guys. Pusser survives multiple attempts on his life, but in one ambush, bullets intended for him kill his wife.

After the movie, at a bar in Greenwich Village, I became convinced I needed to break out. I remember there was some wild graffiti on the door leading down to the restrooms. "Watergate is India," it said. *Brilliant,* I thought. The scandal was as massive and unfathomable as it was endlessly entangled. But I knew that the problem lay deeper than Watergate. It was the system that locked some people into power and kept others forever locked out. It made me angry not only for the country but also for me personally. I wondered if this might be a time when all the rules would be broken; that people really would break loose from the old dark politics that had been the seedbed of this historic corruption. So, wasn't this a time to give them an alternative? To give them *me?*

The only way to test the proposition was to actually run for Congress; to put myself in the arena and, on an outside chance, win. Could this be the year that the voters actually did "throw the bums out"? Now, sitting in that saloon in the Village, I became determined. I had to do it. The next morning, I got up, looked directly into my decision, and acted.

I will never forget driving across the Verrazzano-Narrows Bridge to Staten Island on my journey home. I didn't know anyone in Philadelphia outside of my family. I was not even registered to vote there. I had nothing, really, in the form of political assets—certainly not a connection with an actual politician. Driving home that morning was the scariest thing I'd ever done.

CHAPTER TWENTY

RUNNING ANYWAY

I had seen how political campaigns begin with nothing but a candidate and the goal of election. The trappings might include a beat-up storefront with a dirty rug, a folding chair, and a phone sitting on the floor. Nearby there might be a cardboard carton holding some paper coffee cups. Except for those tangibles, the rest of the campaign starts with sheer ambition.

All I had heading over the Verrazzano Bridge that morning was the last part. My first step was to take the local commuter train downtown to city hall, where I registered to vote in Pennsylvania and collected the necessary filing papers for seeking elective office. I was about to raise myself from citizen to that lofty position known as "candidate for Congress."

My next task was to scrounge through a pile of old street lists, which recorded the names, addresses, and party affiliations of registered voters on every city block. These lists were the essential tools for collecting the necessary two hundred valid signatures needed to get on the ballot.

By moving forward, I was making a statement: that I was out to challenge the political order. The hostility now voiced itself. Standing at that desk in city hall, I was approached by an old-timer exuding the whiff of a "drone." That's what the reform-minded Democrats called the paid city hall hangers-on during the last years Republicans held power.

"Are you a lawyer?" the do-nothing demanded. "No," I answered, as if being interrogated. "I'm a journalist."

"He says he's a journalist," came his snide verdict, aimed vaguely at the power structure he confidently felt stood behind him. Was he trying to use his *attitude* to intimidate me, as if the sheer force of his questioning would send me fleeing? How dare I *think* of challenging an entrenched official in a primary! He carried the authority of a nobody defending the somebodies. It was precisely what I thought I'd be up against as I'd contemplated my decision while driving home from Brooklyn.

I was about to take on the Philadelphia Democratic political machine, each one of the last in the country. Composed of sixty-seven ward leaders each and their many dozens of local committeemen, the machine held enormous power in the city. It decided who got what jobs. It was the entrenched door-to-door network that had run Philadelphia since the early 1950s. This is what I was taking on during those winter and spring months in the contest for who should represent a large swath of Philadelphia in the US Congress.

Now, in my hand lay the road map to the individual voters. The district began in my childhood neighborhood of Somerton, the hamlet bunched up against Bucks County. Farther south, however, were the crowded, more urban row houses that stretched north from downtown. Many of the residents were Jewish. Roosevelt Boulevard was the great multilane highway running up through the district, and the east side was home to most of the city's police and firefighters. What the people of the district had in common was their moderate incomes.

The incumbent I was challenging, Congressman Joshua Eilberg, had worked his way through ward politics. A lawyer, he'd risen not only to ward leader but also to vice chair of the Philadelphia Democratic City Committee. His power lay as much in the state capital of Harrisburg, where he held the reins of Philly's legislators, as in Washington. His use of it for personal gain would eventually be his undoing.

I'd achieved my first goal. With street lists in hand, I headed to Somerton and hit the pavement, seeking signatures from voters along my old newspaper route. Maybe they'd remember me. Meanwhile, my parents were determined to do what they could to help. Dad took petition forms to the Knights of Columbus hall. When he returned, I could see that a number of his fellow Knights had filled in not just their own signatures but also the names of their family members. Right there was a problem: no way could I submit a sworn petition containing signatures that weren't actually *signatures*. So, the next morning, I was back on the trail again, this time to another part of my old *Evening Bulletin* route.

Most people didn't remember me. It had been fifteen years since I delivered them their afternoon newspaper. A few did make the connection, though one was clearly not impressed. "So what?" he answered when I reminded him of our previous acquaintance. To him, I was just another politician asking to be trusted. I attributed his reaction to the ongoing Watergate investigation, which was coming ever closer to implicating the president of the United States himself.

The most memorable encounter was the woman living a few blocks from our house who refused to endorse anyone who failed to present what she saw as the title deeds to a legitimate candidacy.

"I won't sign a petition for someone who doesn't have literature," she declared, anchoring herself to that word *literature* as if a glossy brochure lent official status to my quest. Until I could produce something printed, she wanted no part of me.

I pushed on.

By the time I took the train northwest to Harrisburg to submit my petitions, I'd reached a certain plateau. At the outset, Dad put the odds of my winning at 100 to 1. Now he reduced them to 10 to 1. What mattered is that he never once said I was wasting my time.

The fact is, I was all alone out there. It was just me and precious little money. I had my family and a car, but no staff, no literature. Then, slowly, it all began to happen. Al Bergin, an enthusiastic friend of my brother Jim, volunteered to be my press secretary. Then a married couple, John and Marilyn Funk, came aboard. They had been accepted to the Peace Corps and were waiting to go overseas. Marilyn agreed to help me in what I determined was my first and only route to mounting a significant campaign: recruiting young volunteers. She began calling up Catholic and public high schools to ask if I, a candidate for Congress, could address the students during a class period. Based on the enthusiastic response, I don't think I could have found a more compelling advocate. Thanks to Marilyn, I found myself standing in front of high school classes, one after the other, preaching the evils of money in American politics.

My pitch, more common today, was that politicians' reliance on campaign contributions puts them in hock to special interests. To that, I offered a solution. I said if young people like them would volunteer for the campaign I was assembling, then they, not the fat cats, would be the people who mattered.

What I was doing, of course, was attacking the same conflicts of interest that we reporters at the Capitol Hill News Service had been probing. The difference was that I was doing it as a candidate against one of those very congressmen. I was crusading against big money in politics, promising a way around it.

My message soon grabbed attention. On March 17—Saint Patrick's Day!—the *Philadelphia Inquirer* ran the following headline: "4th District Candidate Refuses All Money Gifts."

The Watergate scandal has filtered all the way down to Philadelphia's 4th Congressional District, with one candidate declaring that he will refuse to accept any financial contributions at all. Chris Matthews, a 28-year-old former aide to consumer advocate Ralph Nader, said Friday that he would run a "money-free" campaign for the seat held by Rep. Joshua Eilberg, a Democrat. Matthews, who filed last week for the May Democratic primary, said he would "neither solicit or accept" financial contributions to his campaign. Instead of television advertising, direct mailings, and other traditional campaign tactics, Matthews said he would rely entirely on volunteers to reach voters in the 4th District. Matthews, who was formerly employed as an investigative reporter for

Nader's Capitol Hill News Service, blamed the "whole system of private campaign contributions" for political scandals.

"If we have learned anything from these disclosures," he said, "it is that the small group of private interests that contribute the bulk of political campaign finances expect something in return."

That was me nearly a half century ago, talking about dirty money in politics. I was campaigning against not only the fresh crimes of Watergate but also the big-city corruption of entrenched power, the dark cigar smell of city hall itself, the indoor world Grandpop knew all too well, the world Dad said people were ready to dump. The first sign of deliverance came when many of the high school students I'd addressed decided to walk to the back of the classroom and pick up three-by-five-inch index cards to sign up for the campaign.

I now introduced a campaign technique I'd learned in Utah. Within days, we were out on Roosevelt Boulevard with Honk 'n' Wave signs. The weather was a godsend, and so was the long line of young high school kids waving with joyful enthusiasm to the commuters on the main route coming home from downtown. In the midst of the young sign wavers were the excited faces of Mom, Aunt Catherine, and our cousins Cathy, Teresa, and Ann Marie. We were, just by this single cost-free act of outdoor campaigning, bringing recognition to the campaign night after night. Not only that: the young volunteers loved it! They were shining attention on a new, clean way to run our American democracy. I'd taken Honk 'n' Wave from Utah to Philly.

It's hard to write now how good it all felt, how perfect. I was using whatever means I could to build a campaign for public office. A beneficiary of what I'd witnessed in Utah, I knew that the key was getting out with the people, to let them see me up close. During mornings and early afternoons, I did a lot of campaigning on my own, primarily in supermarkets. Making the rounds was a lot like traveling on my motorbike to the shops of my clients in Swaziland. One thing I learned was that people start their grocery shopping on the produce side, then work their way up and down the aisles to the other side of the store. My method was to follow a reverse course. This way I could meet the potential voters face-to-face and, just as important, not approach the same person twice. It's not good politics to fail to recognize someone you'd just met! My new arsenal of literature consisted of the impressive reprints from the *Philadelphia Inquirer* article about my not taking money. It explained the nature of my campaign in objective terms: I was a twenty-eight-year-old taking on the system.

On weekends, a crew of volunteers joined me as we hit the big shopping malls, handing out reprints of that *Inquirer* article. We even had a high school combo band playing for us, so idealistic that its members refused my offer to buy them pizza. They seemed disappointed that I'd even offered. They were that pure. How could you not love them and what they were doing?

What recharged me in those spring weeks was the faithful arrival of my pals. Bob Schiffer, now working for Congressman Hugh Carey's run for New York governor, never missed a weekend. Rich Sorensen commuted up from his job with Senator Moss.

Another DC friend, Paul Meagher, had begun digging into my rival's campaign finance records. Exhuming Eilberg's list of contributors, he spotted a number of companies. Since corporations are banned from making such donations, this looked like pay dirt. Armed with the names and contributions, I called the top investigative reporter for the *Inquirer*. He said if I wanted the newspaper to cover the story, I had to take my complaint to the US Attorney's Office for the Eastern District of Pennsylvania.

It was another case of "So, *this* is how it works!"

In pursuit of justice, I went downtown to the government office building and came across the brother of a La Salle classmate. I made the complaint. The *Inquirer* reporter put it in the newspaper.

I was raising the heat. The incumbent was soon on television saying that I was "living in the house of my father," who he said was a registered Republican and cannot even vote for his own son.

I always took this as a shot across the bow. Dad worked for the court system. The congressman was suggesting not so subtly that my father might pay the price of my campaign with his job. My rival was not just a US congressman but something more powerful in the city. As vice chairman of the Philadelphia Democratic Committee, Eilberg was the number two leader of the political machine that controlled city hall and its patronage. Dad would have none of it. He wrote a letter to the *Inquirer* stating that he was, in fact, a registered Democrat and was going to vote for me. My Republican father had, without telling me, switched parties.

Now the cavalry arrived. Tim St. Clair, then a young staffer for Congressman Owens, had decided to use their DC office printer to produce my long-sought literature. Moonlighting past midnight, after he'd run off Wayne's daily requirements, he returned to work meeting mine, which Rich delivered to Philadelphia by train. Tim sent along a personal note I've never forgotten: "Matthews, you've got steel balls."

My new literature declared:

"Chris Matthews: Democrat for US Congress.

"When Matthews worked as an investigator for Ralph Nader in Washington, he saw the high price of political corruption. It is the price you pay every time you reach for your wallet."

Inside were images of me meeting voters in supermarkets, deploring the connection between political deals and consumer prices.

"For decades, Congress—through special tax breaks—has encouraged US petroleum companies to drill for Arab rather than American oil."

The brochure then criticized the incumbent congressman for taking contributions from "insurance companies, construction firms, and other corporate sources." It hit Eilberg for continuing to represent corporate clients in his downtown law office while at the same time drawing a congressional salary.

My past association with Ralph Nader, as brief as it was, gave me a sparkling credential in the time of Watergate. A friendly ward leader yelled from his car that the Nader connection itself was worth 10 percent of the vote. It was a necessary weapon against an entrenched incumbent, a kingpin of the old political machine.

As a declaration of war, however, it was hardly necessary. The empire was already striking back. It came in a visit from the Fairmount Park Police, who patrolled the boulevard, ordering us to quit our Honk 'n' Wave events because we were causing a safety problem. Surrounded by a retinue of officers, the top official said something about the high school girls being so distracting to drivers that it might cause an accident. Openly embarrassed by his mission, he confessed to me that politics was involved. Someone big had called to complain about my campaign tactic—someone with enough clout to tell the police department what its job was in this matter. It was clear to me that his shutdown of Honk 'n' Wave had less to do with the line of duty than with the political pecking order.

I decided to go on the offensive. I had a bank of volunteers call every Democratic official in the Fourth Congressional District and invite them to a Sunday reception at my parents' house. To dress up the affair, we offered a screening of the documentary film on Robert F. Kennedy that had been shown at the 1968 Democratic convention just months after he was killed. This brought another intervention from the party machine. Many of the committee people told the volunteer callers that they would love to come; in fact, they seemed thrilled to be invited to such an occasion. But only one Democratic committeeman showed up. Word had gotten around that this was not an "official" party event, and they were not to attend. The lone arrival was the local ward leader himself, Mike Stack Jr., who I assumed was there to take names. That said, once the primary was over, Mike and I became good friends.

Days before the May primary, the *Inquirer* ran an article describing me as "an energetic young economist . . . running on a 'shoestring' campaign in which he has refused to accept any campaign contributions.

"Matthews, a fast-talking young bachelor from the Somerton section,

claims that campaign contributions make a candidate dependent on special interest. He has been relying on volunteer workers, most of them
high school students, to push his candidacy. He has been spending all
his time campaigning in supermarkets and on street corners, telling the
consumers that the high prices eroding their incomes are a direct result of
'deals' between their representatives in Washington and big business." The
reporter had clearly read my literature.

Young Andrea Mitchell, who'd graduated from the University of Pennsylvania, now reported on the campaign for KYW, which had long been
the local NBC AM radio station. Her manner of coverage was classic
Philly, a city of distinct neighborhoods: "In northeast Philadelphia, where
there are large numbers of Jewish voters and large numbers of Catholic
voters, Eilberg is Jewish and Matthews is Catholic." So much for the
melting pot!

My strategy was simple: I wanted to win. Instead of spending the last
weeks going door-to-door in the Catholic areas, I went to Eilberg's own
ward, leafleting every house. If I was to be victorious, there was no way
to do it without penetrating my opponent's base.

And so the day of the primary arrived on May 21, 1974. Under Marilyn
Funk's direction, our gung-ho volunteers were sent to as many voting
divisions as we could cover, which was a lot. Who knew if we might pull
off a miracle? I had a hunch going into the race that in this spring of
Watergate, with Richard Nixon clinging precariously to office, we might
just see the voters in full revolt. Could it really happen?

But we were up against one of the country's last old-time political
machines, where every voter is handed an "Official Democratic Ballot"
telling him or her which candidates to vote for. On the flip side, to make
voting easier, are the endorsed candidates' ballot positions. The time had
arrived for the machine to prove its resilience to our maverick campaign.

A few days before voting, a couple of party henchmen jumped out of
their car and wrestled a pile of my prized new literature from the hands of
my brother Jim. Bob Schiffer, working Eilberg's home division, watched

aghast as the incumbent US congressman began assaulting him with questions—"Who are you working for?"—and attacking me for "living with his father and mother." He then walked down the line of Democratic voters, ripping my literature out of their hands. Bob was stunned at what he was watching. "I can't believe you're a member of the impeachment committee!" he blurted. As nightfall approached, I worried that I had built up the hopes of all my young volunteers. Did they know what we were up against?

How wrong I was! On the night of the primary, we had a great party at the house on Southampton Road. Everyone seemed to be having the time of their lives. When the TV news declared that I had won roughly a quarter of the votes, it didn't cause a ripple. My worries about the high school volunteers had been in vain. Those young idealists knew exactly what we were up against. It was simply too much fun to be valued investors in an actual political campaign. They were the campaign's big shots, and they knew it.

Besides this, the volunteers could say they had rung an early bell against campaign corruption. We were battling the influence of big corporations in our political system and the effect it had on the average voter. They were getting themselves into what we, in the sixties, called participatory democracy. Mom also delivered, working our local voting station the entire day, personally steering her neighbors toward her son's ballot position. The big producer on election night, however, was my brother Jim. He had taken a bunch of friends and worked one ward extremely hard. It turned out to be our best.

The next day, Rich, Bob, and I, along with my brother Bruce, who'd been emotionally protective of my chances, all headed to New Hope in Bucks County. We just had to get away. Out there along the Delaware River, in that wonderfully artsy town, we had a big lunch during which I told my brother my theory of the campaign. It's a line from an old Walt Disney: "It's what you do with what you got that counts."

What I never got clear about the race was my reaction. Was I disappointed? Not really. I knew it was a long shot. Besides, I had gotten quite a few votes, more than some congressional primary candidates get when they win. I felt only the emptiness that came from giving my all and now having it behind me. I never once thought I shouldn't have done it. I think everyone would benefit from putting his or her heart into at least one political campaign. But, still the question: Did I like being the center of attention? Did I enjoy or feel even all right in this role of hero-champion? Did I feel morally worthy of it all? Or did I prefer the role of reporting on such people, chronicling politics, putting it together for history?

My mother, Mary Theresa Shields, daughter of Charles Shields, proud Democratic committeeman, had her own view of the 1974 primary campaign I'd come home to run. Later, Rich Sorensen told me that she'd shared this view with him, if not with me. "Do you think he's just a dreamer like my father?"

That spring, during the campaign, Mom's mom died. I remember the last time I'd seen my Grandmom Shields. I was leaving the old row house on Fifteenth Street in the Philadelphia neighborhood of Nicetown. As I was closing the front door, she softly called to me from the cot in the dining room, "Goodbye, Chris." She knew that heaven was close. I should have known it would be her last loving words to me, the grandson who loved her dearly. Grandpop, lost, soon followed her.

CHAPTER TWENTY-ONE

BACK TO WASHINGTON

For several high-spirited, driving months, I had launched myself into public view. I was a boy flying a kite with my face on it. With the primary election decided, I had to pull myself back to earth.

For a couple of weeks, I made myself at home at my parents' house. I began looking for a job: some way to make a living and stay alive politically. But absent the excitement of the campaign, life began to lose traction. I had made a leap, fallen short, and was in retreat, at home marking time.

Dad suggested I consider heading back to Washington, where he believed I belonged. He also reminded me, gently, that I had some bills to pay for that "shoestring campaign" of mine—mainly the printing costs for those 150,000 brochures. I decided to take the hint.

Back in DC, lightning struck almost immediately. Visiting Rich Sorensen in Senator Frank Moss's office, I reunited with Mary Jane Due, the Moss staffer who was now his administrative assistant. A few days later, she called to say she had a job for me. The senator had two big speeches coming up. Would I write them? I jumped at the chance.

Here was another lesson in politics. Some people see you as an ally, others as a threat. Wayne Owens had hired me and encouraged me, while his replacement didn't see me fitting into his plans. Now Mary Jane Due had the power, and with it a desire to bring me back on board. So many dynamics in life hinge on this interplay of human sentiment or chemistry. Some people like you and see a future in the relationship; some don't.

Senator Moss now presented himself as one of the former. When I encountered him in the office, he seemed entirely aware that I was working on his speeches. His allowing me back onto the team, if only temporarily, was a recognition that I had honored his call to "dip a little deeper into these political waters." Perhaps it had raised his estimation of me.

In any case, one of my joys was learning of the senator's hidden role in my campaign.

It turned out that my opponent, Joshua Eilberg, had strode into Senator Moss's office one day to register his complaint that Rich Sorensen, one of his legislative assistants, was working on my behalf. Moss told the complaining pol from Philadelphia that Rich had every right to help out his friend on his own time.

Hearing that story told me a couple of things: one, that Moss was ready to stand up for me; two, I was truly back to Washington, this land of separate vassal states, where each Capitol Hill constituency is guarded jealously by individual US senators and representatives.

Fortunately, by the very act of prosecuting that race in Philadelphia, it seemed I had earned the status of having been a *candidate*. I had entered the political arena, accepting its risks. It put me a notch above where I'd stood when I left Senator Moss's staff two years before. I had earned a knighthood, albeit a minor one.

The situation of the country had also advanced by the summer of 1974. Like the title character in Shakespeare's *Richard III*, the Richard in the White House had grown desperate. With the House Judiciary Committee opening hearings on impeachment, Nixon rode Air Force One to Egypt and then to Moscow in a vain attempt to win back a measure of presidential prestige. The chief executive was also playing for time, yielding more and more power to the Congress. In July he signed the Congressional Budget and Impoundment Control Act. Like the War Powers Resolution, passed over his veto the previous autumn, it shifted power back to the Congress. With that new power came a serious duty for Congress to keep the government's fiscal house in order.

The senator chosen to chair the new Senate Budget Committee was Edmund Muskie of Maine. Joining him on the panel would be his friend and staunch 1972 supporter Senator Moss. Soon I got word that Senator Moss had called up Muskie and pressed him to hire me for the committee's staff. Merry Halamandaris, who worked in Moss's office, overheard her boss's hardball pitch: "You want a good man? *He*'s a good man!" Overnight, I was not just back in the Washington loop but also connected to a key decision maker.

What remains remarkable in my life is Senator Moss's dramatic behavior in all this. It was obvious now that our renewed relationship had grown warm and would endure for the rest of his life. "You want a good man? He's a good man." You can't get better than that. It was with that same note of confidence that he had advised me to "dip a little deeper in these political waters."

It was another life lesson in how events follow one another. If I had not decided to stick my neck out and run for office, none of this would have happened. By the sheer act of crossing the Verrazzano-Narrows Bridge out of Brooklyn, I had advanced to a higher league.

Had the decision to return to safer harbors in Washington ended my quest for elected office? My Peace Corps friend Fred O'Regan gave me a tough time about this. When I said I simply didn't have a job back in Philadelphia, he saw it as a cop-out.

"You could load trucks!"

Yes, Fred, I could have. But now I had a bigger job in Washington and, with it, another learning experience. My elevation to the Senate Committee on the Budget resulted from a timely conversation between its chairman and a Democratic member. Had that phone call not been made, I would not have gotten the job. It was as basic as that. In any case, it landed me on the Senate's hot new committee. With it came a mandate to do what I'd argued Democrats should do: play it straight on matters of dollars and cents. Wasn't that what I'd written in the *Washington Star* in late 1972?

All this was transpiring as the country was galvanized by the spectacle at 1600 Pennsylvania Avenue. For weeks, cars had been driving past the White House blowing their horns for Richard Nixon to resign. By late July, the House Judiciary Committee had approved articles of impeachment. With transcripts of his own White House recordings exposing the "smoking gun" of his central role in the Watergate cover-up, Nixon called it quits. In a dramatic nighttime address to the country on August 8, he became the first president in history to resign. Taking the reins of office the next afternoon, the thirty-eighth president of the United States, Gerald Ford, declared: "My fellow Americans, our long national nightmare is over."

With the Democratic Party in firm control of Congress, my appointment by Muskie to the Senate Budget Committee was moving me into the political big leagues. For the first time in my career, I found myself working with top-rate staffers. The most impressive was Douglas Bennet. In his midtwenties, he had begun his professional career working in India for Ambassador Chester Bowles. After gaining his PhD in Russian history at Harvard, he'd already been administrative assistant to two senators, Tom Eagleton and Abraham Ribicoff. It was during his time with Eagleton that I'd spoken with Doug about going to work in what turned out to be the Missourian's short-lived vice presidential campaign. Earlier in 1974, Doug had shown electoral ambitions of his own. He'd sought a congressional nomination in his native Connecticut but lost at the local Democratic convention to Christopher Dodd, son of the state's former senator Thomas J. Dodd.

It was from Doug that I discovered what top-level Senate staff work was all about. With spiffy authority, he outlined how I would be selling the committee's mission to editorial writers, columnists, and other opinion leaders.

Muskie himself gave me an education. By this point, he was a major national figure. As a legislator, Muskie had played a significant role in winning passage of the Civil Rights Act of 1964. He had also been the chief senator behind the Clean Water Act and the Clean Air Act, two major environmental initiatives. Thanks to him, travesties like the 1969 Cuyahoga River fire in Cleveland, when a spark from a train ignited an oil slick, no longer blackened the sky, and smog-ridden cities such as Los Angeles could again see the stars at night. He'd been Hubert Humphrey's running mate in 1968, losing that close election to Richard Nixon and Spiro Agnew. In 1970 Muskie advanced his stature even higher with a stunning rebuke to Nixon on national television.

"There has been name calling and deception of almost unprecedented volume," he told the country. "Honorable men have been slandered. Faithful servants of the country have had their motives questioned and their patriotism doubted.

". . . It has been led, inspired, and guided from the highest offices in the land."

High toned and historical, his words had the character of nonpartisanship, but they carried the punch of being deadly partisan, causing President Nixon to fall well short of his electoral ambitions that year: the Democrats not only held on to their Senate majority but also added twelve seats to their lead in the House.

I would now get to see the seasoned insider at work. Muskie was, to begin with, physically intimidating. His six-foot-four height and craggy features were an early-warning system that he was no one to be troubled with. A workhorse, he was called "Iron Pants" by his staff for his ability to take his seat at the beginning of a legislative mark-up session, where bills are actually written, and never leave it. His strengths were patience and persistence. Other senators jumped from one committee to another, racing to catch the TV cameras that departed usually after senators and witnesses had made opening statements. Again, Muskie let his colleagues have all the time they wanted to speak in such circumstances. All he wanted was the power to shape legislation when they were done talking and had left the room.

His other attribute was his Vesuvian temper, which he saw as a tool of tradecraft; few senators were up to contending with it. Those top staffers who witnessed a Muskie outburst at close range would describe it in predictable phases: first, an explosion, then another, and finally something heading skyward in decibels and primordial human rage.

Such a temperament can be a problem when exposed to the general public. Muskie killed his presidential chances when he dissolved in angry emotion during the 1972 New Hampshire primary after a newspaper criticized his wife. But as a legislator, a reputation for having a bad temper can give a senator an edge. Few enjoyed the prospect of having to lock horns with the senator from Maine.

But the Budget Committee staff, including me, was proud of working for Senator Ed Muskie, a legislator with the political stamina to do the hard work and ask for more.

"There's not enough pressure here," I heard him say of the US Senate. He was the son of a Polish immigrant who made a life as a tailor for his family in his new country. Muskie believed in hard work and felt fortunate to have important and interesting work to do.

In November 1976, a few nights after winning his fourth term in the Senate, Muskie spoke to us staffers at a reception upstairs at the Monocle Restaurant on Capitol Hill. He'd had a few drinks and become philosophical. He had just been through a hard-fought campaign in which he didn't take any chances, nor could he afford to. In the same election, Maine had gone for President Ford over Democratic challenger Jimmy Carter. Several of Muskie's Democratic colleagues, including Frank Moss, had gone down in defeat. He left us that night with two bits of advice.

One was classic Muskie. It was about charting our careers: "Just remember, wherever you go, that's where you're going to be." In other words, before jumping to a new job, try to imagine what it would be like actually doing it day after day.

His second maxim struck me as grander but also closer to his own experience: "The only reason to be in politics is to be out there all alone and then be proven right." How could you not like a politician who so openly admired courage, so candidly admitted vanity?

On my last day with the senator in 1977, heading for a job at the White House, I had rehearsed something to impress him.

"I think that if we had a parliamentary system," I said with some pomposity, "you'd be prime minister." The idea was that he had that kind of respect from his Senate peers. I should have known better.

"But we don't—do we?" Muskie replied.

While never having given the country a president (or a prime minister), the state of Maine is so proud of Edmund Muskie that it named a permanent state holiday after him.

The author at eight.

Me in the middle of my brothers Bert and Jim. We're outside a motel Dad found somewhere between Washington, DC, and Baltimore. We stayed there during our unforgettable visit to the nation's capital, a trip I never quite got over.

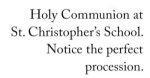

Holy Communion at St. Christopher's School. Notice the perfect procession.

Grandmom and Grandpop.
I still feel the love.

Grandmom-in-Chestnut Hill
immigrated from Northern
Ireland. When World War II
came she had three sons in
uniform fighting for her new
country. She loyally bought me
books on American history.

My Holy Cross
yearbook picture.

I love this picture. It captures my connection with the Swazi traders I'd come to teach.
Many treated me like a son.

Freshman Democratic Senators Edmund Muskie of Maine (*in the left foreground*), Eugene McCarthy of Minnesota, Philip Hart of Michigan, Frank E. Moss of Utah, and Gale McGee of Wyoming (*in left background*). Senator Moss made me his legislative assistant; his friend Ed Muskie brought me to the brand-new Senate Budget Committee. (*Credit: Library of Congress*)

Chris Matthews
Democrat for U.S. Congress

When Matthews worked as an investigator for Ralph Nader in Washington, he saw the *high price* of political corruption

It is the price *you* pay every time you reach for your wallet . . .

My race for Congress had a clear message: if you want the bigshots out of politics, put yourself in it. Volunteer to help.

On Air Force One with President Jimmy Carter and chief speechwriter Hendrik Hertzberg. That's White House press secretary Jody Powell on the right.

At the phone for Speaker Thomas P. "Tip" O'Neill Jr. Those half dozen years were the toughest, biggest job of my life.

Kathleen and I emerging together under blue skies from Trinity College Chapel in Washington. You can see me hugging God's greatest gift beyond life itself.

Speaker O'Neill's eightieth birthday!

Bob Schiffer and I worked together on a 1974 congressional campaign. That was in Brooklyn. Our next joint effort was in Philadelphia, when I was the candidate.

The *New Yorker*'s Hendrik Hertzberg made me a presidential speechwriter. Later he made me a journalist.

President George H. W. Bush gave my Dad and Mom the greatest night of their lives, dinner and a movie at the White House.

Kathleen and I in Paris for the G-7 meeting. The year was 1989, when the map of Europe lost both the Berlin Wall and the Iron Curtain.

The Queen.

Just days after accepting the 1992 presidential nomination, Governor Bill Clinton was in a bus touring Texas. He was worried that the Republicans had something ready to drop on him. It didn't stop him from waging a great campaign.

With Archbishop Desmond Tutu on a tour of voting sites the day of South Africa's first all-races election. In the background you can see the length of the lines, from one horizon to the other. This was Nelson Mandela's gift to his country, a peaceful transition to democratic rule.

Jay Leno had me on the *Tonight Show* a remarkable twenty-nine times. He was always just as welcoming, friendly, and curious in the green room as he was on camera. What a good guy! (*Credit: Paul Drinkwater/NBCU Photo Bank/NBCUniversal via Getty Images*)

Sharing thoughts with presidential candidate Barack Obama. This was our *Hardball* College Tour at West Chester State University in 2008. It was a great moment in the history of our show. (*Credit: Charles Ommanney/Contact Press Images*)

Here I am with Donald Trump in Green Bay on the eve of the 2020 Wisconsin Republican primary. I don't believe the man ever expected to be president. He certainly did not spend his life preparing himself for it.

In my quarter century anchoring *Hardball* nothing made me happier than having a viewer say, "You don't let them get away with anything." That's because I ask the question the viewer wants asked. If you don't push for the truth, the whole truth, and nothing but, you don't deserve one of these jobs. (*Credit: Ali Goldstein/NBCU Photo Bank/NBCU Universal via Getty Image*)

The Matthews family in support of Kathleen for the US Congress. Back to front, left to right: Thomas, Caroline, Sarah, and Michael (*holding Brendan*); Chris, Kathleen, and Julia.

CHAPTER TWENTY-TWO

JIMMY CARTER

A little-known governor of Georgia first crossed my radar in 1974, after I lost the primary for Congress and received an encouraging letter from him urging me to "stay actively involved in Democratic politics." Going further, it requested my help:

"I would appreciate any information or advice you might have that would help our efforts in Pennsylvania or other states. Please feel free to contact me personally or Hamilton Jordan." It was signed by Jimmy Carter, who would announce his presidential candidacy that December.

This shows the savvy that took a one-term Deep South governor all the way to the White House. Rather than throwing kisses to recent victors, he was putting out lifeboats to the shipwrecked.

Jerry Rafshoon, my close friend who was with Carter from the beginning, recalled later how that strategy took shape. Out campaigning with Carter one day, Jerry spotted a promising local candidate and said so. Carter had a totally different calculation. "It's a Republican district," he pointed out. "He's not going to win. He'd be better for us if he loses. He'll work for me. He'll bring his organization with him." An outsider himself, Carter decided his allies were among those who'd been shut out politically. He would be their door back in.

None of this came through to me at the time. At first sight, Jimmy Carter struck me as simply a regional politician with a pitchman's smile

147

who didn't want his career to end at the state level. It took me a while to develop a finer, sharper picture of the candidate from Georgia. I found it in print rather than on television. In lengthy interviews, Carter revealed what was—for me, certainly—a strong selling point. Instead of expanding the size of government, he spoke of fixing what existed. He was especially critical of regulations that simply drove up business costs and extended red tape. He used the example of a Washington regulation that freight trucks must ride empty on their return routes.

Although much of Carter's pitch was anecdotal, I found him a happy discovery. Here was a candidate who wasn't out there making one promise after another to build a bureaucracy bigger and bigger. His philosophy of government mirrored my own.

To the political establishment's surprise, in the 1976 Democratic primaries, Carter won early and hung on. He let rivals Mo Udall, Birch Bayh, and Henry "Scoop" Jackson carve up the liberal vote. As the lone moderate-to-conservative in the race, he stood out as the alternative. The peanut farmer from Plains proved an old rule of politics: the shape of the race defines the victor.

When the 1976 Democratic convention opened in New York City that summer, I joined a self-selected posse of Muskie staffers at the old Gotham Hotel (now the Peninsula) at Fifth Avenue and Fifty-Fifth Street. Beyond the media spotlight, we were running an eleventh-hour push to get the Maine senator named as Carter's running mate. Looking back, it's highly likely that he'd already chosen Senator Walter Mondale of Minnesota instead.

Carter's momentum carried him through to November, but barely. President Gerald Ford carried the enormous burden of Watergate. On succeeding Richard Nixon, he had promised the country to end the scandal's "nightmare." Then, by pardoning Nixon four weeks later, he had kept him from trial. In so doing, he had denied the American people the full truth behind the crimes of Watergate. For that, he would pay electorally. This country had been following a mystery story page by page only to have the book slammed shut just short of the last chapter. In the end, the results on election night were anticlimactic. While Carter won the close race, Ford, by coming on strong in the final weeks, received credit for his near upset.

The Democratic victor now faced an intraparty conundrum. To beat Ford, Carter was forced to win over the combined votes of all those Democrats who'd backed the more liberal candidates he'd bested in the primaries. To do this, Carter had to sound more like them. In doing so, he lost authenticity. In the primaries, he looked and sounded like a small-town farmer from Georgia, one skeptical of big-government rhetoric, because that's who he was. But campaigning in the fall, he had to talk like the big-government liberals he'd defeated in the spring.

Even though I was working for Muskie, I spent much of that autumn of 1976 out in Utah trying to help Senator Frank Moss win what threatened to be a tough reelection effort. It was to be a different campaign than Wayne Owens's victory in 1972. Four years earlier, I had shared in the quiet, calm thrill of a winning campaign. This time I arrived out West to a campaign in trouble. Seeking a fourth term in a conservative state, Moss was facing a serious challenge to his political survival. Newcomer Orrin Hatch, a hard-line supporter of former California governor Ronald Reagan, who'd challenged the incumbent Ford for the top of the GOP ticket, was running the smartest campaign ever waged against Moss. Rather than attack him personally, which hadn't worked with voters, he told audiences how he liked Moss. He said he was a "sincere" public official, a "sincere liberal."

Something else was happening out there in 1976. People in the Mountain West, certainly the business interests, had grown in their resentment against the federal government. They especially didn't like large parcels of land being designated national parks. They wanted that land for "development." That was a word they liked. *Environment* was the one they didn't like.

This rightward political wave, dubbed the Sagebrush Rebellion, would cost Democratic senators their seats in Utah, Wyoming, and New Mexico. On election night, a misty-eyed Senator Moss showed his character and true generosity. His concession speech showed more concern for those of us who'd worked for him than with his losing his own career. What a fine man.

Postelection, I was heading east toward an uncertain future. In 1972 I had lost a job with Senator Moss. Now I worried that Moss's loss might possibly jeopardize my position with Muskie. I had lost the patron who'd pushed for my hiring. But this time I was also facing the upside of a Democratic administration. Jimmy Carter's victory that November, narrow as it was, opened the door to the White House for Democrats for the first time since 1968. This included a new generation of political professionals, myself included, anxious for our shot.

I learned from Patricia Gwaltney, a policy specialist on the Budget Committee staff, that she'd just been recruited to work on Carter's pet project to reorganize and reform the federal government. She'd heard of a job she thought was perfect for me. Richard Pettigrew, the top White House advisor on the reorganization project, was looking for a deputy to help sell Carter's big effort to the media and the public.

Pettigrew had, like other Carter allies, lost a primary in 1974, in his quest for the US Senate in Florida. After a friendly interview, he decided to take me with him to the White House. Like Wayne Owens and Frank Moss, Dick Pettigrew was a clean and honest public servant who made me the beneficiary of his goodwill. Thanks to him, I was about to get an insider's look at the Carter presidency.

It's said that a soldier sees only the small part of the war he is fighting. Still, I had a pretty good vantage point. Jimmy Carter had run on a promise to make government more efficient and less aggravating. Better yet, he said he would make the government "as good as the American people."

Even in the first months, I spotted obstacles to our ambition to streamline the federal government. One was the nature of the presidency itself. The country's top leader is expected to deal, most of all, with its most urgent problems. Carter's first priority upon arrival was to get the economy, still recovering from a recession, out of a ditch. If he couldn't accomplish that, nothing else would matter. Reducing the number of chairs in the White House Cabinet Room wasn't going to dazzle the country when there weren't enough jobs. The fact is, we increased them by two, creating new departments for Energy and Education.

A lot of it was politics. Predictably, liberal groups wanted a push for more, not less, government. The teachers' unions wanted a Department of Education, and Carter needed to show his gratitude for their backing in the election. Those concerned with the energy crisis demanded a new agency in its name. Jimmy Carter, who'd run to shrink the bureaucracy, was now growing it. Most crucially, there was the party itself to deal with. Carter may have outcampaigned the liberal establishment in spring '76, but he had not defeated it. Liberal factions were not going to be denied top positions in his government. Nor was their blood to be stirred by greater government efficiency. Cutting back on regulations and reforming the civil service all became solid Carter achievements. But they never thrilled the liberal soul.

Tinkering with government was certainly not a strategy to engage the interest of Senator Edward Kennedy of Massachusetts. He did not help topple Nixon in 1974 so that he could sign up for this humble government agenda a few years later. The schism between the two men, as real as one can get in politics, would one day divide the Democratic Party.

Meanwhile, the country was heading toward a reckoning rooted in the early Cold War policy that had guided both political parties. As is so often the case, it was about oil.

In 1953 the CIA had engineered a coup in Iran, toppling an elected government and putting Shah Mohammad Reza Pahlavi in power. Now, a quarter century later, the people of the oil-rich Middle Eastern nation had suffered enough from this corrupt imposed dictator. Mobs were demanding the shah's overthrow and an end to the influence of the country that had installed him.

In the fall of 1978, the first signs of trouble regarding Iran were the flyers posted around Georgetown attacking the shah and promoting a protest against his coming visit. It seemed to me yet another foreign group in our nation's capital pushing a cause that didn't concern us. This all changed when the shah arrived. I could smell the tear gas around the White House, as the DC police tried to quell the anti-shah demonstrators. By bringing their protest here, young Iranians were also spouting their contempt for the United States.

Facing the prospect of gasoline shortages, Carter decided, however, to double down on America's bet on the shah. At a lavish New Year's Eve dinner in Tehran, he toasted Iran as "an island of stability in one of the more troubled areas of the world." He credited the shah personally for this allegedly tranquil state of affairs. "This is a great tribute to you, Your Majesty, and to your leadership and to the respect and the admiration and love which your people give to you." As I would learn many times in politics, words spoken in a room, aimed at the people in that room, can echo farther—most inevitably to those ears by which they are least well received.

That toast stamped the Jimmy Carter seal on almost twenty-five years of the United States' usurping the Iranian people's right to democratic rule. He did it with the same goal as his predecessors: to keep Iran from the Soviets and to keep its oil for us. We would soon pay dearly for the transaction.

The year 1978 would also produce President Carter's greatest triumph: the Israeli-Egyptian peace accord. Through thirteen days of talks at Camp David, the rural presidential retreat in Maryland, Carter was able to bring together Israeli prime minister Menachem Begin, a militant in his country's initial fight for independence, and Egyptian president Anwar Sadat to a historic accord between two countries that had been at war since Israel's founding in 1948 and hostile to each other ever since. Israel's greatest strategic rival hereby agreed to its sovereignty.

Carter relied on his most outstanding traits—diligence, patience, religious faith, and political cunning—to bring together the two longtime foes. He demonstrated the courage of a leader willing to take a risk. From my perspective, the successful negotiations showed me something about the president's abilities as well as his limitations. While he never could bend official Washington or the Democratic Party to his will, he proved himself a force of nature when he tackled a task he could achieve largely on his own. Coaxing these two Mideast leaders into the same space and keeping them there 'til they made peace was a stunning accomplishment.

Unfortunately, the glow of Camp David did not survive the horrors that came in 1979. In January, the mass protests in Iran forced the shah to flee the country. The turbulence in its wake drove up world oil prices and, in the United States, led to long lines at the gas pumps not seen since the Arab oil embargo of 1973–74.

By July, President Carter was back at Camp David trying to make peace between himself and the American people. It was the energy crisis and more. He couldn't seem to move the country. After days of meetings with a wide array of invited advisors, Carter delivered a prime-time address that was quickly christened "the malaise speech." He said the danger facing the country was "much deeper—deeper than gasoline lines or energy shortages, deeper even than inflation and recession." He spoke of a "crisis of the American spirit," the belief that "the next five years will be worse than the past five years." What was needed, he said, was a "restoration of American values."

The overnight reaction was positive but short lived. What killed the positive buzz was Carter's stunning follow-up: he fired a big chunk of his Cabinet.

What the public saw as an explosion, however, I had seen as the end of a long fuse. There were people who accepted jobs in the Carter administration, including those at the highest levels, who would have just as easily, or more so, gone to work for *any* Democrat elected to the White House in 1976. Their résumés simply matched the job positions. Finally, in the summer of 1979 Carter was separating the wheat from the chaff. But it was too late. It made him look angry and weak at the same time.

It was in the aftermath of all this that I reached my dream of becoming a presidential speechwriter. Again, it was a personal connection, a friend, who made it happen. Bob Schiffer, whom I'd met in the Brooklyn campaign and who came down to Philadelphia all those weekends to work hard for mine, was now working in a top budget post for New York governor Hugh Carey. Upon my arrival at the White House, Bob had gotten me in touch with Hendrik Hertzberg, a former *New Yorker* magazine reporter who had written campaign speeches for Carey in Albany and was now doing the same for Jimmy Carter.

By the turbulent summer of 1979, Rick had risen to top presidential speechwriter. He now made the case to the White House chief of staff for me to join him on the presidential team. "He's no Ted Sorensen," he wrote in his memo to the White House chief of staff. Having set the literary bar appropriately high, he said I wrote fast and knew my politics. I still needed to prove myself.

Fortunately, the annual convention of the National Conference of Catholic Charities was on Carter's upcoming schedule. I wrote the speech, Carter gave it. I had the job. I was a speechwriter to the president—the position I'd dreamed of while riding the Rhodesian Railway through the night.

CHAPTER TWENTY-THREE

KATHLEEN

In March 1978 I attended the Radio and Television Correspondents' Association Dinner. This is the black-tie Washington gala that figured in the 1987 comedy-drama *Broadcast News*. The real business of this annual event came in the hours afterward, when each of the three broadcast networks at the time—ABC, CBS, and NBC—hosted their rival receptions. Their purpose, made clear in the conversations, was to show their dominance, and for the guests to get their next job.

It was on such a night, at this affair, that real change came to my life. It's when I first stood in the presence of Kathleen Cunningham.

A Stanford University grad, Kathleen had come east from her home in the San Francisco Bay Area, lured by the excitement of political Washington. She was working as a producer for WJLA-TV, the ABC Washington affiliate. The two of us were introduced by Anne Edwards, a mutual friend who worked in the White House. From that first encounter, I was determined to ask Kathy out, a mission that took me three weeks to accomplish.

When I arrived to pick her up on the arranged night, it was for something of an audition. Before coming down from her bedroom, she deployed her roommates to greet me and, as it turned out, to *vet* me.

Since the Correspondents' Dinner had been black tie, she had no way of pegging me socially. For all she knew, I might have shown up in a leisure suit or leather jacket and engineer boots. Fortunately, I came in a blue blazer, button-down shirt, and khakis—what I had been wearing since high school. In any case, it passed muster for a first date from the woman whom I would one day lovingly call "the Queen."

We went to dinner in Chinatown and then to Matt Kane's Bit O'Ireland, an Irish hangout where we discovered a Cunningham coat of arms hanging proudly above the bar. Besides the Irish ancestry, we shared a love of politics and the experience of being one of five kids in boisterous Catholic families. Kathy and I established an early bond when she invited me to visit her parents, who were living in Europe. We began our trip in Geneva, Switzerland, where her father was working for an American corporation. From there we split off to the south of France, where Kathy shared her favorite places from a sophomore year spent studying in the country: Saint-Paul de Vence, Saint-Tropez, Haute-de-Cagnes. We stayed at a seaside apartment in Port Grimaud, near Saint-Tropez, owned by the parents of her former boyfriend.

Let me just say that the continental surroundings of that unforgettable summer of 1978 did not in the end outdo Kathleen Cunningham. Once I knew she existed, I knew I could never live without her.

CHAPTER TWENTY-FOUR

PRESIDENTIAL SPEECHWRITER

When people ask me to name my favorite job, what comes to mind is my time as a presidential speechwriter. I visualize the White House Mess, sitting at the roundtable with other presidential aides and trading the scuttlebutt of the day amid the fresh scent of the salad bar. I think of my office, that giant cube of a room in the Old Executive Office Building and the vintage table I used as a desk. I think of the fresh paint smell of the West Wing and the rhododendrons as you walk through the open colonnade and into the White House itself.

What first struck me about the West Wing was how compact it is. The Cabinet Room and the Oval Office are just around the corner from the Press Briefing Room we see on television. The Roosevelt Room, where the staff held its meetings, was right across the hall from the Oval.

Then there's the quiet of the place. It's not at all like the *West Wing* of television glory. Never once did I confront traffic, or the walk-and-talks that the show's creator and writer, Aaron Sorkin, liked to script. The hallways and stairs are empty, filled with that respectful silence that makes a statement of its own. At the heart of the White House, amid its historic trappings, was the work—in my case, writing speeches for the president of the United States.

I especially loved those rides on Air Force One. It was still the old plane: the Boeing 707 Jack Kennedy used. We would type out remarks, sometimes for the next stop, on an IBM Selectric as the air force pilot took off at what always seemed like a 45-degree angle. The best part was working under Rick Hertzberg. Call it chemistry. Carter's chief speechwriter was also my editor and my enduring friend.

Our job was to prepare the president for all his speaking occasions. They ranged from talking points for an East Room reception to major addresses. Our task was to grasp the circumstances of the event, understand the audience, and research the message. We'd get input from Cabinet members and top presidential staff. But the job of figuring out the right theme often fell to the speechwriter.

Keeping up with the assignments took a bit of organizing. It was like getting ready for college exams. You couldn't do it first things first; you had to plot your work schedule so that every speech received the right amount of time. Think triage.

It was Rick, in fact, who taught me about separating a writing project into a set of limited tasks. Rather than face a huge, formidable assignment, it allows you to face any project by attacking it one task at a time. This was the big secret about doing the job. The president of the United States is not going to sit down and tell you what he wants to say. That's not how it works. As speechwriter, that's *your* job. You write the jokes—or get them from a helpful professional. You discern the key points, refer to the relevant policies, make the historic references. You dig out what the commander in chief will most likely want to say on that day to that group to achieve a hoped-for headline.

From there, you run your draft past the top presidential staffers, including the national security adviser, Zbigniew Brzezinski; the head of domestic policy, Stuart Eizenstat; the relevant Cabinet members; Press Secretary Jody Powell; and communications director Jerry Rafshoon. You take all their notes and prepare the final version for the president.

The ideal scenario was to get the final draft to the president well before he had to deliver it. Some nights Rick and I would go to dinner with our girlfriends, often at the Old Ebbitt Grill on Fifteenth Street, across from the Treasury Building, then head back to the Old Executive Office Building and work well into the morning.

Rick, as I said, was my editor, which was not an easy task. He joked about reaching the end of my speech draft only to discover endless lines of detritus; that wild array of fragments, phrases, and false starts I'd pushed down and left behind through hours of rewriting. Fortunately, Rick found this pile of refuse a comic relief to a hard night's work.

Some mornings we didn't get done until dawn. We'd walk over to the West Wing and find our way along the basement floor to the darkened room where we left the speech in the correct pile for the president. From there, a US Marine would deliver it to the chief executive's hideaway next to the Oval Office.

One time we smelled the coffee wafting through the West Wing. Jimmy Carter, still keeping a farmer's work hours, was already at his desk. I always wondered how my jokes sounded to him as he read them in that little hideaway before dawn.

In October 1979, a year before he would face reelection, President Carter was invited to speak at the dedication of the John F. Kennedy Library. Making the event awkward was the knowledge that Senator Edward Kennedy, the honored president's youngest brother, was within weeks of challenging Carter for the nomination. The president himself had been stirring the pot. Not wishing to look worried, he'd told an audience of congressmen in June that if Kennedy took him on, he'd "whip his ass."

Now, on the eve of the library dedication, Rick came by my small town house on Capitol Hill with what he'd spent all night writing. I thought what he wrote was perfect; a light confection of history and wit. It could have been Jack Kennedy himself.

The draft opened with Carter citing the late president answering a reporter's question on whether he "would recommend this job to others?" Kennedy's answer, with Carter quoting him directly, was that he wouldn't recommend Teddy make a run for the job "at least for a while." It was a teasing, wistful appeal to JFK's younger brother to rein in his ambition.

The entire speech was as fine a tribute as could be imagined for the occasion, but especially for a president about to face the full fury of the storied Kennedy political prowess. President Carter, who tended to chop up speech drafts, using them as his own talking points, gave this one just as it was written. My hunch is he wanted the Kennedy people to be impressed that he could match the Kennedy oratory when and if he wanted to.

That November, the smoldering crisis in Iran exploded. Opposition to the shah had made his position untenable. Meanwhile, support for the Ayatollah Khomeini, an exiled religious leader, had grown enormously thanks to his recorded messages sent from outside Paris. On January 16, 1979, the shah left Iran for good. Two weeks later, Khomeini arrived in triumph to lead the Iranian Revolution.

Suffering from cancer, the shah found brief exile in Egypt, Morocco, the Bahamas, and Mexico. He now asked to come to the United States for medical treatment. Soon after President Carter agreed to the request, thousands of protesting students stormed the US Embassy in Tehran. Sixty-six diplomats and military personnel were soon their captives. The hatred I had smelled through the tear gas the previous fall was now seething.

In December came another strike at our country's global prestige. The Soviet Union sent upward of thirty thousand troops racing into Afghanistan, overthrowing the left-wing government, executing its leader, and replacing him with one of Moscow's choosing. The Russian bear was again on the loose.

Carter's response was measured. He slapped an embargo on US grain shipments to the Soviets. Then, prodded by a column by the *Washington Post*'s Robert Kaiser, he called in March 1980 for a boycott of that summer's Olympics in Moscow. The twin year-end events, especially the shocking sight of blindfolded Americans being led about by their Iranian captors while American flags were burnt and trampled, rallied the country around the president.

"Americans have been united in recent weeks, perhaps as never before in recent history," Carter told a crowd in the White House East Room that January. "We faced a common threat, and we faced it as one people."

With the first contest of the nomination fight, the 1980 Iowa caucuses, just days away, Carter was also trying to balance concern for the hostages with his domestic agenda. In that same speech, he introduced major legislation to help train and employ minority youth. "They are at a point where they can either take off and find meaningful jobs and have a productive life . . . or they can drop out into a lifetime of hopelessness and alienation." It was the president working off my speech draft. He finished with my quote from the acclaimed African American writer Langston Hughes: "Hold fast to dreams, for if dreams die, life is a broken-winged bird that cannot fly."

On January 21 Carter and Kennedy went head-to-head in Iowa. To undermine the challenger's chances, Carter spokesman Ed Jesser, who'd worked with me on the president's reorganization project, had put out word that Kennedy had the best operation "on the ground" in caucus history. That phrase, "on the ground," became the bugle call for what was now expected to be a big Kennedy win. For the Carter people, it was a classic use of political lowballing. Jesser had slashed expectations for Carter and raised expectations that Kennedy had to score a big win.

It worked. When Carter nearly doubled Kennedy's vote in the Iowa caucuses, Jesser's strategy landed with double the impact. The president, who was supposed to be trounced in his first encounter with Kennedy, had, as he had promised, whipped his rival's behind. I think it was the grain embargo against Russia that made the difference. The farmers of Iowa were willing to sacrifice on behalf of their country. Again, call me an idealist, but I think that's what did it.

The Republicans also witnessed a big upset in Iowa, with George H. W. Bush defeating Ronald Reagan. This caused real nervousness in the West Wing. Some thought that Bush, who'd been a Texas congressman, US ambassador to the United Nations, CIA director, and chair of the Republican National Committee, would be a stronger opponent.

Around this time, I checked in with National Security Adviser Zbigniew Brzezinski to get his approval for some tough presidential language attacking the Soviet invaders. I found him outfitted in black tie heading to the same Washington media dinner for which I was also in a tux. Brzezinski said he had a serious problem with the word *barbarous* in describing the Soviet actions in Afghanistan. He said he wasn't going to be rushed into okaying such a provocative word on his way out the door. He told me to come back the next morning.

Here is what made it into the president's speech that day:

Some have said—many have said—that we should not allow *politics* to interfere with Olympic competition. I agree completely. . . .

It is not *politics* when one nation sends a hundred thousand of its heavily armed troops across a border and subjugates its peace-loving, deeply religious neighbor. . . . It's aggression pure and simple.

Not every event went so well. For Saint Patrick's Day, the plan was to honor House Speaker Thomas P. "Tip" O'Neill Jr. Here again, sensitive politics were involved. O'Neill had kept himself neutral in the Carter-Kennedy fight, citing his duty to chair the Democratic convention.

In writing the speech, I decided to try to elevate the annual celebration. I wrote tributes to Eugene O'Neill; F. Scott Fitzgerald; *The Last Hurrah* author Edwin O'Connor; Daniel Decatur Emmett, who wrote the song "Dixie"; and Broadway legend George M. Cohan, famous for composing "Yankee Doodle Dandy."

That evening in the East Room, President Carter made all the points I'd drafted, but not before making an unforgettable slur about the event's honoree. I'd learned that the sons of the O'Neill clan in ancient days had been the kings of Ulster, and my remarks for the president saluted that history and the Speaker himself as a "common man" but "an uncommon leader." Then, in the presence of actress Faye Dunaway and other Irish American notables, Carter turned everyone's attention to the guest of honor's wife.

"I understand this is the first time in the forty years that Millie has ever seen Tip sober on Saint Patrick's Day.

"As a matter of fact"—he dug deeper—"this is the first time in forty years that Tip O'Neill and Millie have ever been *together* on Saint Patrick's Day evening. Right, Tip? Millie? At least before the wee hours of the morning?"

Standing in the back of the room, enjoying our first Saint Patrick's Day in the White House, Kathleen and I cringed. In fairness, Carter was under horrific pressure at the time. By March, with the Americans still held hostage in Tehran, the country's unity was giving way to anger, and it was showing up at the ballot box. I was with pollster Patrick Caddell when he had to tell Carter that he was going to lose the New York primary. Kennedy's win there and on the same day in Connecticut were his first outside of Massachusetts and signaled trouble ahead.

The time had come, I decided, to get out there on the front lines. The Pennsylvania primary was coming up on April 22, and my home state seemed the right place to go to work. Other White House staffers were being dragooned into the campaign. I figured if I went into the field now, I would be off the hook for field duty once the fight with Reagan heated up.

I volunteered to take a leave from the White House to be the Pennsylvania spokesman for the Carter-Mondale reelection campaign. Our vulnerability there was palpable. Carter was holding to his Rose Garden strategy, refusing to hit the campaign trail as long as the hostages were being held.

Kennedy, meanwhile, had the support of Philadelphia mayor Bill Green. Twenty years earlier, it was Green's late father, a powerful Pennsylvania congressman, who'd led the Democrats in giving John F. Kennedy a 330,000 plurality in the city.

The younger Kennedy brother showed himself at home in Philadelphia in a way Jimmy Carter never could. Ted made courtesy calls to John Cardinal Krol, the city's archbishop. He was seen ritually chomping on Philly soft pretzels on Broad Street and did all the popular call-in shows more than once. As the primary date arrived, it was as if Ted Kennedy had become a Philly resident. I got so frustrated by the attention lavished on him in the *Inquirer* that I called its editorial page editor, Ed Guthman, to complain. After listening calmly, Ed said he understood how I felt, adding that he'd once been "in the same position" himself. He was referring to his years as Bobby Kennedy's press secretary.

Unfortunately for the president, the battle in the spring months of 1980 was not so much between Carter and Kennedy as between the United States and those student protesters in Iran. As long as Americans were being held against their will overseas, the president of the country was not going to look strong to American voters. The only things going for Carter were Jerry Rafshoon's TV ads. His man-in-the-street interviews about Ted Kennedy painfully exposed the challenger's personal problems, especially the 1969 car accident on Chappaquiddick Island that cost a young woman, Mary Jo Kopechne, her life. Those Carter TV ads helped keep the final Pennsylvania numbers close enough that Kennedy failed to get the next morning's headlines. "Squeaker" is how the *Philadelphia Daily News* bannered it.

In any case, Pennsylvania marked the end of the Rose Garden strategy. Two days later, a secret US airborne mission to free the hostages, code-named Operation Eagle Claw, ended in catastrophe, leaving eight US servicemen dead and the fifty-three Americans still in captivity. The decision to launch the rescue mission led to the resignation of Carter's leading diplomat, Secretary of State Cyrus Vance. He had given notice beforehand, believing the mission was too complicated to succeed.

I immediately wrote a note to Hamilton Jordan urging the president to offer the post to Senator Edmund Muskie. Whether my memo ever got to Hamilton, my hunch about Muskie's patriotic sense of duty turned out to be right on the mark. When offered the job of secretary of state, Muskie took it.

As I wrapped up the campaign in Pennsylvania, Kathleen and I were getting ready for our wedding. It was held in June in the chapel of Washington's Trinity College. Our priest was the communications director for the archdiocese, Father Maurice Fox, whom Kathleen had worked with during Pope John Paul II's recent visit to Washington, DC. Her grandfather obtained us a blessing from the pope. Rick Hertzberg, who was in Venice with Carter for the G7 meeting, relayed the president's good wishes. After the reception at the F Street Club, we squeezed in a two-week honeymoon on Nantucket.

In July Kathleen covered the Republican convention in Detroit for WJLA. The Carter speechwriters watched it from Rick's office. We thought one of Reagan's riffs hit especially hard:

"Can anyone look at the record of this administration and say, 'Well done'?

"Can anyone compare the state of our economy when the Carter administration took office with where we are today and say, 'Keep up the good work'?

"Can anyone look at our reduced standing in the world today and say, 'Let's have four more years of *this*'?"

When the Democrats met for their convention at New York's Madison Square Garden, Carter's political weakness was starkly apparent. The party liberals, still clutching at hope for Ted Kennedy, had not come over to the president's camp. It was no longer the argument over policy; now it was about the fight itself. Carter's people wanted a smooth convention. Kennedy diehards wanted the opposite. If that hurt the Democratic nominee's chances in the fall, their attitude was "so be it."

No Democrat of the era will ever forget what occurred the Tuesday night of the 1980 Democratic convention. It was yet another case when the person giving the best speech at one of its conventions wasn't the party nominee for president.

"No performing elephant could turn a handspring," Ted Kennedy intoned, "without falling flat on its back." I loved the picture drawn by those words. It reminded me of what Richard Nixon once said in tribute to Jack Kennedy's speechwriters: that they gave their man great "word pictures." It was a memorable way to make fun of the GOP's effort to remake itself for the election. But it was Kennedy's poignant swan song to his defeated presidential campaign that left its historic mark.

"For me, a few hours ago, this campaign came to an end. For all those whose cares have been our concern, the work goes on, the cause endures, the hope still lives, and the dream shall never die."

I could see the tears flowing from the eyes nearby. It was Ted Kennedy—his family, his very being—who held the Democratic heart.

On Thursday night, the convention's last, things got worse for the nominee. When it came time for Kennedy to raise hands with Carter as a sign of party unity, he chose to play a game of cat and mouse on the convention stage. While finally taking his hand, he'd wanted to humiliate the nominee and did so with cruel artistry.

In August it fell to me to write President Carter's speech to kick off the fall campaign against Ronald Reagan at a huge Labor Day picnic in Alabama.

My inspiration was to tell the story of his historic meeting at Camp David with Prime Minister Menachem Begin and Egyptian president Anwar Sadat. I had Carter describe how he took the two leaders to the battlefield at Gettysburg to display our own country's bloody history. Carter liked my draft and delivered it with feeling.

That evening, Kathleen and I were walking through Georgetown and decided to duck into a bar to see how Carter's speech went over on the TV news. What we saw was Ronald Reagan standing with New York Harbor and the Statue of Liberty behind him. That picture conveyed more than the storied thousand words about patriotism and love of country. Our adversary had grabbed the flag. He was running as the American candidate for president.

For Carter, the fall campaign only got worse. For weeks, Reagan had refused to debate him one-on-one, insisting on a three-way debate that would include former Republican congressman John Anderson, who was running as an independent. By late October, the Reagan team relented.

166

With a Gallup poll of voters now showing Carter edging into the lead, Reagan agreed to a two-man debate in Cleveland on Tuesday, October 28. The tight polls and the excitement of the election coming in just a week created a prime-time audience of 80.6 million people.

Early in the debate, President Carter tried to put the spotlight on the need "to control nuclear weapons." He called it "the most important single issue" of the campaign. But the debate moderators had other issues on their agenda. After the bulk of the debate had been spent on the economy and domestic issues favorable to Reagan, Carter tried to bring it back to his preferred topic in a way the media characterized as desperate.

"I had a discussion with my daughter, Amy, the other day, before I came here, to ask her what the most important issue was. She said she thought nuclear weaponry and the control of nuclear arms."

What was remembered most from the evening, however, was Reagan's razor-like retort to Carter's charge that he'd been an early opponent of Medicare. Putting on an exasperated look, then shaking his head in disdain, Reagan said, "There you go again."

Reagan's debonair performance made it seem that Carter was being unfair in his charge. He wasn't. Reagan's frontline opposition to Medicare in the early 1960s remains to this day a matter of public record.

But how do we explain Reagan's spot-on reply to Carter's attack? Had he known it was coming? Had the challenger been helped by the debate briefing book that Paul Corbin was believed by many Carter insiders to have nabbed from the White House? In any case, with that withering dismissal, he had drawn blood. It painted the incumbent as a pathetic figure clinging to office.

Others thought Reagan had struck a deeper wound. Dad thought the killer line was contained in the riff of questions that Reagan deployed in his closing: "Are you better off than you were four years ago? Is it easier for you to go and buy things in the stores than it was four years ago?

"Is there more or less unemployment in the country than there was four years ago?

"Is America respected throughout the world as it was?

"Do you feel that our country is as safe; that we're as strong as we were four years ago?"

When I challenged Dad, saying that I'd heard Reagan deliver that same line before, he wasn't impressed. "I hadn't," he said. That taught me something truly important about politics. When you hear a candidate say something, don't assume that everyone else has heard it already. It's why they make a discipline of repeating themselves. I remember reading how Jack Kennedy would cite Coca-Cola in this regard. Everybody knows about it, knows what it tastes like. So why, Kennedy asked, did its manufacturer keep advertising it over and over and over again? It's because not everyone is paying attention. It's because people have other things on their minds besides Coca-Cola.

The same, he said, goes for politics.

CHAPTER TWENTY-FIVE

SCRAMBLE

History offers two types of American election years. One is when the country likes what it has. The other is when it's ready to place its bet elsewhere. Nineteen eighty stands high in the latter category. Any competent Republican could have given President Carter a race. All that Ronald Reagan needed to do in their single debate was pass the competence test.

When it was over, Carter knew that Reagan had met that threshold. Alone with his diary that night, the president ridiculed his rival's "Aw, shucks" performance but saw that it had succeeded. "He apparently made a better impression on the TV audience than I did."

This left only one hope for Carter. He needed to change the topic. He needed to shift the country's focus from a desire to replace him, Jimmy Carter, to a fear of putting Ronald Reagan in his place.

The next morning, Carter set out to do what he'd failed to do the night before: nail his rival as someone not to be trusted with nuclear weapons. In Pittsburgh's Trinity Episcopal Cathedral, he produced the evidence. It was a *New York Times* article from February that quoted Reagan as saying that a foreign country's decision to develop nuclear weapons wasn't "any of our business." But it was too late. The verdict on the debate was already a fait accompli. *Reagan had won.*

The spirit on Air Force One in the final week of the campaign had a way, however, of denying the outside world. Walking aboard, I would hear

Phil Wise, a Georgian good ol' boy, singing the current Willie Nelson favorite "On the Road Again." On takeoff, Phil had another ritual: he would crouch on a serving tray and surf down the aisle as the air force pilot took the aircraft steeply into the sky.

Sitting in the staff section with Rick, I was struck by the contrast between the harsh politics outside and the remarkable comforts within. The staff tables always had our name card, a restock of M&M's, and, of course, our packs of cigarettes.

President Carter, holed up in his forward compartment, meanwhile, endured the turbulence from the postdebate outlook from his pollster Pat Caddell. The poll numbers "don't look good for us" he wrote in his diary. "Reagan apparently improved more than I did." But then, hopefully: "Nobody knows."

I'd been taken with the loneliness of Carter's journey. At every stop, he had to meet with local politicians he may have met only once or twice before. To prepare himself for the critical encounters, he now worked his way through the photos of the local personages that would be awaiting him in the next receiving line. Is this what it takes to lead the United States?

The crushing blow awaited us at a campaign stop in Chicago. It began with a rush of optimism. At four in the morning on Sunday, November 2, the White House received what looked like good news from Tehran. The Iranian parliament had met and agreed on terms that teased hope for the hostages' release.

The sound of people hurrying up and down the hotel hallway woke me up. Through the door, I could make out the clipped, military inflection of the Secret Service. Someone said "Deacon," the president's code name. I called the White House Situation Room on my white "signal" phone and was connected to the National Security Council staff. What I learned was that the hostages in Tehran might somehow be released. The latest conditions from the Iranian government were no tougher than those we'd already said we could meet.

At first, the staff was euphoric. Bumped to the backup plane, Rick, White House aide Tim Smith, and I talked exuberantly about what we could accomplish in a second term.

By the time we returned to the White House, however, our hopes had turned to dust. Chances of an immediate hostage release had hit a snag. The agreement with the Ayatollah Khomeini still involved issues that could not be settled by Election Day. With nightfall, an atmosphere of doom descended. "I wish I could predict when the hostages will return," the president told a dejected and angry country. "I cannot." It was the clincher. He was admitting he was powerless.

The next day, we headed for a last-ditch race across the country to campaign in as many time zones and hit as many media markets as possible. Leaving by Marine One, I watched the White House shrink below us. Once aboard Air Force One, we faced a moment of desperation: Rick realized that the three-by-five-inch index cards with Carter's talking points had failed to reach Jody Powell, forcing Rick to type new ones from the backup copies. The snafu, but also the quick recovery, seemed a perfect metaphor for this last Monday of political combat.

First came Akron, Ohio. With Senator John Glenn, the heroic astronaut, at his side, Carter raised what he called "the overriding issue" of the election: "the issue of peace and the control of nuclear weapons and preventing the spread of nuclear weapons to terrorist countries." He quoted the words of Robert Kennedy on the last day of his fated 1968 campaign, which was also the last one of his life. "I ask you to vote for yourselves." That final RFK appeal would be Carter's refrain through every airport stop heading westward.

When we reached Detroit later in the day, Air Force One was connected to local television. Rick took notes from the *CBS Evening News*. It wasn't good. The lead story was the one-year anniversary of the Iranian hostage taking, which would be the next day. Election Day. When Carter returned to the plane, Rick had the unhappy task of telling him that the next day's presidential election had been replaced as the number one news item by yet another reminder of the country's humiliation. We reached our last stop, Seattle, late in the day, and Carter gave his most rousing performance of the campaign. Caught up in the loud reaction, he became unusually poetic. He told the crowd how he'd asked his press secretary, Jody Powell, where they were going to spend the night. "There's no *tonight* tonight!" Powell had answered. There would not be the usual overnight stop at a hotel. We were flying cross-country to Plains, Georgia, for the president to vote at dawn. This was to be Jimmy Carter's last campaign speech.

Back aboard Air Force One, Rick cheered Carter with a joke about his performance, cracking, "You finally got the stump speech down, Mr. President!" For the first time, Carter joined us in the staff section. He then asked to have the press corps come forward for drinks. Whatever result was coming from the country, he seemed serene.

We did not yet know the damning verdict from the voters. The one cause for nervousness was Pat Caddell's incessant phone calls. They were for Jody Powell, who had the seat next to me but had not been there to take the call.

With the campaigning behind us, Jody now headed to the front of the plane to take the call from Caddell, who was gathered at the White House with Hamilton Jordan and Jerry Rafshoon. They had seen Pat's final poll numbers, which showed President Carter losing in a landslide.

When Carter got on the phone, he was still basking in the rousing cheers from Seattle. His pollster had to cut him short. It was over, Pat told him. The country had turned to Reagan resoundingly. Taking the news, President Carter had one request. He said that no one should tell his wife, Rosalynn. It was important that he deliver the painful news himself.

When Rick and Jody returned to the staff section, they had fresh marching orders. Carter needed words to calm the country and lessen the partisan fury. It was the only way to curb a national mood that threatened to take not just the presidency but also the Senate. We spent the remaining hours in the air crafting words that softened the edges of the national discontent.

The scene on Marine One that dawn remains strong in my mind. Stuart Eizenstat and his deputy David Rubenstein sat across from the president, who looked frozen in his seat. As we were about to land, Jerry Parr, the president's chief Secret Service agent, was on his walkie-talkie. "Dancer's on the ground," I heard someone say. Rosalynn Carter was waiting for her husband.

When the motorcade arrived in Plains, I found myself walking past the town's train depot, and when I looked up, I saw the president and his wife through the window. Instinctively, I averted my eyes. This was a time they deserved to have to themselves.

Back in Washington that day, I witnessed what was to remain for me an enduring portrait of the 1980 presidential election. It was the sight of a man racing into the polling station, his face set in an expression of hard determination. I have always interpreted that to be the mien of the country that day—an explosive cocktail of anger, frustration, fear, and hatred, all contained in one word: *hostages*. For a year, Americans had watched our compatriots being marched blindfolded, our flag burnt and stomped on, for the whole world to see. Now they had a chance to communicate through the ballot box how they felt about it and the president who'd let this happen to their beloved country.

Taking our diplomats into captivity certainly qualified as an act of war. The president could have responded with an ultimatum that they be released. But he would have had to back up his words with action. Jimmy Carter was not willing to take the country to war, with all the lives it would have cost, in order to win reelection. That was his moral strength—and his electoral weakness.

As predicted, Reagan indeed won in a rout: 50.7 percent to 41 percent in the popular vote, and a one-sided 489 to 49 in the Electoral College. The next morning, Kathy and I drove to Pennsylvania just to get out of

Washington. Eventually we stopped at a motel, had dinner, spent the night, and then headed back home in the morning to DC.

For the last two months of the year, I did my job. Before the balloting, President Carter had committed himself to delivering a good number of postelection speeches. For me, it was a good way to keep busy and distracted, not having any idea where I was headed next. Rick Hertzberg drafted Carter's farewell address, which the president delivered the first week of 1981. It showcased his three great causes: the danger of terrorists getting their hands on nuclear weapons, the energy challenge, and human rights.

"America did not invent human rights," he said. "In a very real sense, it's the other way around. Human rights invented America."

His farewell was classic Carter. He was sticking to principle, while also sticking it to his critics. His trio of causes touched dangerously on the reasons he had lost. He had been ridiculed for referring in the debate to thirteen-year-old Amy Carter's concern over nuclear weapons. There had been the "malaise speech" driven by the gasoline shortages. Finally, there was his decision to allow the shah admission to the United States for medical treatment, a dictator no one would ever call a defender of human rights.

The preamble of Carter's speech was also classic Rick, a fine and fitting self-description for the president from Plains who'd chosen to walk part of his inaugural route to the White House. "In a few days, I will lay down my official responsibilities in this office, to take up once more the only title in our democracy superior to that of president: the title of citizen."

That humility connected Jimmy Carter with those who had worked for him. Whatever could be said against his term in office, he could never be branded as elitist. We were as honored for having been in his service as he had been in the country's. Both personally and professionally, he remained unmarred by scandal. And when it came time for him to go, he left office with his head high, his conscience clear. He'd done his best, honoring the call of the prophet Micah: "To act justly, to love mercy, and to walk humbly with your God."

On the day of Ronald Reagan's inauguration, I left the Old Executive Office Building and strolled up Seventeenth Street. Then I joined the other White House staff at Andrews Air Force Base to see the president we'd come together to serve take off for Plains. After a desultory lunch in a nearby Maryland restaurant, we all went our separate ways into that familiar emptiness that follows every great endeavor.

CHAPTER TWENTY-SIX

TIP O'NEILL

In 1980 the American voters elected both a Republican president and a Republican Senate, leaving only the House of Representatives in the hands of the Democrats. Even there, the GOP assault had left its mark. The campaign featured a nastily effective attack ad showing an overweight, white-haired politician stranded in a limousine that had run out of gas. The guy represented everything wrong with Washington: entitled, arrogant, clueless.

When the dust cleared from the campaign, the Democrats assessed the damage. The popular rejection had been thunderous. The only top Democrat left standing was the one the Republicans had targeted in their TV campaign.

In the estimation of political Washington, the caricature in that GOP TV ad was not the Speaker Thomas P. "Tip" O'Neill Jr. they knew. As a young politician, he became the first Democrat elected Speaker of the Massachusetts Legislature. In 1953 he'd taken John F. Kennedy's seat in the House of Representatives. Through his long career rise to the US Speakership, O'Neill would hold elective office continually since 1936.

While popular among his colleagues on both sides of the partisan aisle, O'Neill was not a man to cross. Richard Nixon called him "the most ruthless and most partisan speaker we have had in my lifetime. He plays hardball. He doesn't know what a softball is." When Nixon saw that

O'Neill was the Democrat leading the charge against him on Watergate, he knew his presidency was in peril.

In 1981 one partisan who saw a strong new role for the veteran O'Neill was a young congressman from California, Tony Coelho, who'd just been chosen to lead the Democrats' comeback in the next election. It was Coelho, backed by O'Neill's chief counsel, Kirk O'Donnell, who wanted the Democratic Speaker to go on the offensive. The key to that strategy, as I would learn later, was to bring *me* aboard.

As in every doorway in my life, someone had to be there to open the door from the other side. In this case, it was Marty Franks, who, as a hardworking Democratic National Committee staffer in 1980, had done great research for the Carter speechwriters during the fight with Reagan. Coelho had just signed Marty as executive director of the '82 campaign effort on behalf of House Democrats.

Marty and Tony, in a series of meetings, laid out the plan and my role in it. I would help O'Neill elevate his daily morning press briefings into a Democratic counterpunch to what Theodore Roosevelt called the president's "bully pulpit." My job was to make the Republicans' favorite target into their worst enemy.

My first meeting with the Speaker, then sixty-eight, was alone with him in his backroom office at the Capitol. I immediately felt his sheer *presence*. I suspected he knew it and how to use it to his purposes. Jacket off, shirtsleeves showing his butcher-like arms, O'Neill was comfortable in his advantage. His lone signal of vulnerability came in his words. "Tell me what I'm doing wrong and what I'm doing right," he said. "An old dog can learn new tricks."

And he did, not right away, but soon *and* when it counted. And so my life as Tip O'Neill's guy began, the education by fire that would break me or make me.

One of my first enterprises in 1981 was the Congressional News Service. I modeled it after the Ralph Nader operation but with a partisan mission. Our first news story, for example, covered Republican members of Congress attending that spring's Paris Air Show. I headlined it with a question, "Paris, Anyone?," and went on to say: "Taxpayers back home . . . might ask how a junket to Paris squares with budget cutting and federal belt tightening." It proceeded to list the Republicans who'd been lucky—or in this case, unlucky—to be aboard a government jet for that excursion to Paris. For honesty's sake, we always included a credit line, "Paid for by the Democratic Congressional Campaign Committee." It was, I admit, in smaller type. I should also confess that the Congressional News Service's edition on the Paris Air Show caused trouble. A few of the congressmen who'd flown on that US Air Force plane to the City of Lights were not, as our news service reported, joined by their wives. This left open the question of who, if anyone, accompanied those particular members of Congress—a question that caused the Republicans, who had been extremely aggressive up until now, to sue for peace. Not long after its creation, they convinced the Democrats that, at least in the case of covering junkets, the Congressional News Service should be *un*created.

The spring of 1981 was marked by much more serious news. Following a speech at the Washington Hilton, Ronald Reagan, just two months into his presidency, was the victim of an attempted assassination. The bullet wound he suffered was far more life threatening than first reported. Reagan lost a huge amount of blood through internal bleeding, and the bullet had lodged frighteningly close to his heart.

To help calm the country, First Lady Nancy Reagan and Chief of Staff James Baker arranged for the Speaker to be the first authorized public visitor to the president. Max Friedersdorf, Reagan's special assistant for legislative affairs, described to me the moments he witnessed at George Washington University Hospital: how the Speaker knelt next to Reagan's bed; how the two men recited the Twenty-Third Psalm together; and how, before leaving, O'Neill kissed him and encouraged the president to get some rest.

By June, however, the Democratic Speaker and the Republican president had gotten past what had been an extraordinary honeymoon. O'Neill criticized Reagan's proposed tax cuts as "geared for the wealthy America." The new president, he said, had "no regard, no care for the little man of America." Not liking what he heard, Reagan accused his rival of engaging in "sheer demagoguery."

The Speaker took the Reagan retort as an escalation and an attack on his constitutional role. Sitting in a small room of the Capitol, I watched him listen to the arguments pro and con on whether he should respond to the president's counterattack. For me, this was the moment of truth, the reckoning, and the reason he'd brought me aboard. Looking back, I believe he'd realized already that he had to fight or have Reagan roll over him.

With the decision to fight, O'Neill appointed me administrative assistant to the Speaker, a position he told me with some formality was "statutory"—meaning that it was created by an act of Congress. "We'll have a good time," he assured me after I'd quickly accepted.

It was a career honor, of course. I had begun in Washington as a member of the Capitol Police; a decade later, I was AA to the Speaker of the House. For a half dozen years, my days would begin with a ritual. I would awaken each morning and read the newspapers, knowing that well before noon Kirk O'Donnell, O'Neill's legislative expert Ari Weiss, and later Jack Lew, and I would be held to account.

"Waddaya hear out there? Anything I should know? Anything special? Where are we at?" The Speaker was like a vacuum cleaner pulling in the latest information.

This vetting was especially vital on Mondays. On weekends the Speaker liked to retreat to family, pals, poker, gin rummy, and golf. I consider that ability to dump the worries and leave town a key to his political longevity. It was our job to deliver nuggets at that all-important Monday-morning inquiry. Tip intended it to cover the waterfront: what someone said on *Meet the Press*, what was buried in a newspaper he hadn't gotten to, what a congressman had whispered in the cloakroom, what rumor rung true. We were there to look out for danger from any direction. A guy who'd won fifty electoral contests, been elected the youngest Speaker of the House in Massachusetts in his thirties, and then transitioned from the street corner to back room was now adjusting to the media age.

My main job those half dozen years was coming up with ammo to use in O'Neill's daily back-and-forth with Reagan. They included branding the president's fiscal policy the "Beverly Hills Budget" and accusing the chief executive of being "Herbert Hoover with a smile"—Hoover, of course, having been the president who served during the Great Depression.

I carried on the war with Reagan on other fronts. When his forces organized a Capitol rally for a constitutional amendment requiring a balanced budget, I organized a counterrally on the other side of the building that had people holding a giant banner declaring the balanced-budget push a "Sneak Attack on Social Security." On that night's news programs, the rallies received roughly equal coverage.

The hijinks continued. One time I got word that the Reagan people planned to show up on the Washington Mall with a giant apple pie stretching seventeen feet in diameter. They were going to slice it up to illustrate the benefits of the big Reagan tax cut.

I called up Mitch Snyder, the city's top activist for the homeless, and told him what was up. We had gotten to know each other when the Speaker's office encouraged President Reagan to rename a new submarine the USS *City of Corpus Christi* in lieu of just the USS *Corpus Christi*. Snyder had been on a life-threatening hunger strike over the issue.

Later that day, while watching the news, I saw a half dozen protesters with pillows stuffed in their coats to mimic fat bellies and cigars in their mouths. They were loudly declaring themselves by name as members of Reagan's millionaire kitchen cabinet. The TV news showed them crawling through that giant apple pie. Reporters trying to cover the event had a difficult time describing what exactly they were watching. It was as if the protesters and the Reagan enthusiasts were all part of the same partisan spectacle.

With the country's jobless rate on the rise, I now conjured up a plan for a middle-of-the-night rally outside the White House. I arranged for a large band of autoworkers and steelworkers from Pennsylvania and Maryland to rally outside the White House at 4 a.m. with signs demanding "Wake up, Mr. President."

To guard against any shots at the Democrats, I encouraged some members of Congress to serve coffee and donuts to the steelworkers. I didn't want any loose talk about "both parties" being to blame for unemployment. The Speaker's buddy from Pennsylvania, Democratic representative Jack Murtha, rated that event a "ten strike." It ran on the news all day long.

It was at such moments that Tip O'Neill would look at me and ask, "Is this one of yours?"

Our greatest coup was helping push Social Security to the top of voter concerns in the 1982 midterm elections. I had gotten a tip from *Washington Post* reporter Spencer Rich that the Republicans had sent out a fund-raising letter offering the option of making Social Security "voluntary." He wanted my assistance in obtaining a copy. With the help of a former colleague from the Democratic Congressional Campaign Committee, Eric Berkman, we got hold of one. On the Thursday before the election, we blasted out the news of what the Republicans were planning. To drive it home, Kirk and I put out a statement from the Speaker demanding that Reagan "repudiate" the GOP proposal. It was all over the news the entire weekend, and on Tuesday the Democrats picked up twenty-six House seats—almost the same number they had lost in 1980.

Politics is not, of course, only about winning elections. But before reaching a deal with the opposing party, you need a position of strength to deal from. It's called leverage. To get a "yes," you need the power to say "no." Because of the pressure put on by the Democrats and the resultant pickup of House seats in the '82 election, Reagan and O'Neill were able to get to the negotiating table and save the Social Security system. That wasn't the whole of it. On other key matters affecting America—a fairer tax system, bringing the dangerous Cold War to an end—Ronald Reagan and Tip O'Neill managed, together, to get the job done for the country.

In April 1985, months before Reagan's historic meeting with the new leader of the Soviet Union, Mikhail Gorbachev, O'Neill led a bipartisan delegation to Moscow. He told Gorbachev that he shouldn't try to divide us by political party; that Reagan was speaking for the whole country. Not only that: he told Gorbachev, at the president's personal request, that he believed Reagan, despite his strong condemnation of the Soviet Union as an "Evil Empire," was serious about wanting to reduce the number of nuclear weapons held by both sides. Just as another Democrat, Harry Truman, had been the first president to fight the Cold War, Tip O'Neill was determined to help bring it to an end and for equally patriotic reasons.

When Tip announced he'd be retiring in December 1985, the Speaker gave me a gavel that said "Thank you for building my image." Better yet, he signed a picture of us at a morning press conference: "The best in the business."

My real contribution was to encourage him, when others didn't, to get out there and face Reagan the Great Communicator in battle. That meant going on television, a step that made him a figure of lore for millions of Americans. His last Harris poll at retirement had O'Neill with a 67 percent job approval.

Those six years taught me lifelong lessons about character. One is the value of daily courage. Tip O'Neill showed his by getting up each morning and doing battle even on those inauspicious days, months, and years when he knew his old-style liberalism was taking a pummeling. He never quit.

The second thing he taught me was commitment. In O'Neill's case, it came from his life experience. Ever since his election to the Massachusetts legislature at age twenty-four in 1936, he was in daily contact with regular people and their problems: the sick husband who could no longer provide; the mother of the child who needed specialized health care; the out-of-work person who needed pressure applied to the guy doing the hiring. Tip O'Neill's liberalism wasn't top-down; it was bottom-up. It was less an ideology than the learned recognition of other people's problems.

I watched up close as he dutifully read the letters that came to him, the messages of people who needed help.

O'Neill had resentments, as anyone does, especially about those born with too many breaks. He would never forget being the *townie* from North Cambridge, nicknamed "Old Dublin," who had to kneel cutting the grass on Harvard Yard as the *swells* in boater hats sipped champagne during Prohibition. My years working for the Speaker were, for this reason, a challenge. It's a tricky business being in charge of another person's public image. But I had this instinctive belief that if I could get him to go out there and state his positions—even if he took some punches in the process—people would like what they saw. They'd see a big fellow from the working-class neighborhood of North Cambridge out there fighting for the little guy.

The political lesson from my years with Tip O'Neill was how two politicians, holding opposite philosophies, could sit down together and do the people's business. Part of his and President Reagan's success was their insistence on keeping open communication. For Kirk O'Donnell, my daily partner all those years, that was a rule for success: "Always be able to talk."

Reagan and O'Neill personified that ability. It was the president himself who explained their rule of engagement. It was just prior to his 1982 State of the Union address. He was using the Speaker's office as his waiting room prior to addressing the nation. As Reagan walked in, I greeted him rather abruptly: "Welcome to the room where we plot against you."

"Oh no, not after six," the president retorted. "The Speaker says that here in Washington we're all friends after six."

At Tip's big farewell event on Saint Patrick's Day in 1986, a dinner to raise money for his beloved Boston College, Reagan led the tributes.

"I'm grateful you have permitted me in the past, and I hope in the future, that singular honor: the honor of calling you my friend. I think the fact of our friendship is testimony to the political system that we're part of and the country which permits two not-so-shy and not-so-retiring

Irishmen to have it out on the issues rather than on each other or their countrymen."

I am very proud of those years and all that they taught me about how, when we choose the right people, we can carry forward our democratic business in this country. Ronald Reagan and Tip O'Neill shared something deeply personal in this regard. It was their age. Born in the early twentieth century, they had witnessed its tragedies but also its triumphs. Both didn't want to waste their time of leadership over petty partisanship. They were getting near the end of their public service and wanted it to be useful. At this point in their lives, there was an urgency to getting important things accomplished. They knew life was precious; so was their chance to get things done for the United States.

Tip O'Neill's last night in the Capitol as Speaker had the quality of the spiritual. It began with the kind of ritual that is hard to imagine in today's partisan tumult. Assembled in the seventy-four-year-old Speaker's back office that evening were the leaders of both parties from the House and Senate. No one was in a rush to go anywhere. Republican senate majority leader Bob Dole of Kansas, spotting me, asked if I could help him with the coffee urn. It took two hands to work the spigot and hold the cup. Dole had lost strength in one arm from a World War II wound. He had been shot in the mountains of Italy as he carried a wounded soldier from the line of German machine-gun fire.

That last hour with those leaders in that familiar room was warm, sentimental, and genuinely patriotic. They were honoring a man who'd served his country as Speaker of the House for ten years, the longest continuous period in history. They were doing it not as political allies and adversaries but as compatriots.

Since having moved to Washington when I was twenty-five, I'd lived and breathed politics. My world had been the Senate, the White House, the Speaker's rooms. With some interruption, I had been on the inside looking out. My life working amid the cigar smoke of the partisan back room had now run its course with Tip O'Neill's retirement. It was not an experience I was ready or willing to leave entirely behind. I kept my respect, even awe, for those with the courage to stand for election. Nor could I forget what I'd learned from watching them hold tight to the position and power that their elections had won them. Their wisdom of the game, shown to me in so many facets, was now my traveling treasure chest. It would come in handy where I was headed.

I was about to make a transition into that other imagined career, the one that had attracted me since my days editing the *Wisterian* at La Salle College High School. I was about to become a full-time journalist, in a town where a few top broadcast reporters, print reporters, and columnists ruled the political arena. They decided who was "being mentioned" for the coming presidential nominations, they declared the "front-runners" and spotted the "comers" to watch in the stretch. With newspaper readers following the horse race, hoping to get an early pick on the winner, they were the track touts over in the paddock. They were the ones in the know who told you where to place your bets. More important, they were the cognoscenti the candidates needed to impress. At the time, the stars were the *Washington Post*'s David Broder and the *New York Times*'s R. W. "Johnny" Apple. Having survived the loss of the Senate legislative job, defeat in my race for Congress, Jimmy Carter's defeat for reelection, I was about to make another career leap, this time from the high dive.

– BOOK III –

You have to tell the whole truth, the good and the bad, maybe some things that are uncomfortable for some people.

—US Congressman John Lewis, 2015

CHAPTER TWENTY-SEVEN

WRITER

Even while I did battle by day for Tip and the Democrats, I moonlighted at night penning articles in my own name. Early in 1983 a short article of mine ran in the *New Republic*. Entitled "Citizen Reagan," it chronicled my day-to-day job as Speaker O'Neill's wartime lieutenant. "I don't know how you spent 1982," it began, "but I spent it Reagan watching."

The magazine article went on to describe what had been my combative days dealing with a president who portrayed himself as an armchair critic of government even as he held its highest post. It was the Teflon shield that allowed him to lead rallies against government deficits at the foot of Capitol Hill even when he'd been the chief executive presenting those budget deficits to Congress.

The *TNR* article brought a remarkable bonus. Within days, I was looking at a callback slip from James Silberman, editor of Summit Books at Simon & Schuster. When we got on the phone, Jim came promptly to the point. He asked if I was interested in writing a book about day-to-day Washington politics. He had a particular model in mind. He wanted a how-it-works portrait of the political world to match a best seller he'd edited in 1968, *The Money Game*, which exposed the inner world of Wall Street. I was excited by the idea of writing a book about the rules politicians play by; those backroom maxims I'd picked up over the years that separate winners from losers. Kirk O'Donnell was a huge believer in

189

these rules. Tip O'Neill himself was known for arguing that "All politics is local," saluting the key motive for how he and other politicians made their decisions: how it will affect the people back home.

The person who got me truly started on the project was the most celebrated journalist of our time: Bob Woodward. Hearing me talk about the book project at a Saturday-night party, Bob told me to come by his house on Monday after work. When I arrived, he was all business. He had a tape recorder placed on the coffee table in front of me. "Tell me all about your book," he said.

For the next forty-five minutes, I ran through my ideas of a chapter-by-chapter manual of how politicians guide themselves in battle. I'd write about how they preserve alliances ("Dance with the One That Brung You"), contend with adversaries ("Keep Your Friends Close, Your Enemies Closer"), make deals, and build reputations.

That Thursday, Bob surprised me again. A big envelope arrived containing a verbatim transcript of my run-through with Woodward three days earlier. His cover note read: "Here's your first draft. Now go ahead and write the *book*!"

With no more excuses, and not wanting to let Bob down, I went on to populate the book with the stories of people and politics I'd picked up during the past decade. I infused my firsthand knowledge with that of the masters such as Lyndon Johnson. One source was Republican tactician Lee Atwater, who could be quite ruthless in political contests. He suggested I study *The Prince*, a sort of playbook for heads of state on how to establish power, maintain it—or seize it, if necessary—written by the wily Niccolò Machiavelli in 1513. (Atwater recommended relying on the CliffsNotes version, which he said was better organized and more straightforward than the master's text.)

It was from Machiavelli that I gained the golden wisdom that people are as loyal to those *they* help as they are to those who help *them*. "For it is the nature of men to be bound by the benefits they confer as much as those they receive," he declared. From this comes the governing rule:

ask someone for help, and it yields a bonus. On top of the help itself, you win the future goodwill of the person who helped you. People may forget that someone did them a favor; they rarely forget having done one for somebody. This explains the value of political contributors lists. Once someone has given money to a Democratic or Republican candidate, that person is a good prospect for future contributions or to back another candidate from that party.

The critical help I got from Bob Woodward confirmed another lesson in power. In all my years in politics and journalism, it has been my experience that the people to count on for help are those most confident in their own capabilities. Such people are not haunted by fear of the next rival. It's those worried about holding their place that you have to watch out for.

I called the book *Hardball*. The title traces back to the character Mr. Dooley in a series of nineteenth-century columns by Chicago-born journalist and humorist Finley Peter Dunne. His Dooley, a bartender, would spout street corner political wisdom in his Windy City establishment. One of his maxims was "Politics ain't beanbag." No, it's hardball! It *hurts* when you get hit with one of those hide-covered balls.

While writing *Hardball*, I continued to turn out articles for the *New Republic* and other periodicals. It was clear that after years of writing for others, I was eager to write for myself. I also yearned to *talk* for myself. All those years since walking past the WUNC-TV studio at UNC Chapel Hill, I clearly had my eyes on a role in television.

My first reconnaissance in this direction began in the weeks before the 1984 Democratic Convention. To prepare for Speaker O'Neill's coverage in San Francisco, I went up to New York to speak to NBC news anchors Tom Brokaw and John Chancellor. I wanted not only to case out the convention coverage but also to meet these iconic figures. Tom's welcome could not have been warmer. A guy who loves covering politics seemed happy to host someone working for the legendary Tip O'Neill.

In 1986, with Tip about to retire, I made a return trip to New York, this time adding CBS to my stop. I suggested to Howard Stringer, soon to become the network's news president, that he give me the backroom role Tim Russert had secured for the president of NBC News, Larry Grossman, after serving as the top aide to both Senator Daniel Patrick Moynihan and New York governor Mario Cuomo. Stringer said he didn't think CBS would be willing to spend the money for such a position, but then said something I was not likely to forget. He suggested I consider going on-air, becoming a network correspondent.

I had another encouraging meeting on that trip. I had asked Jimmy Breslin, the great New York columnist, if we could get together to discuss careers in journalism. He named a Midtown Manhattan bar and told me to meet him there.

When we settled into a booth, Jimmy found just barely enough light to pour through the articles I'd brought along. Then, suddenly on a mission, he escorted me uptown to the city room of *New York Newsday* to meet its executive editor, Don Forst.

Walking up Sixth Avenue, Breslin kept making the case. "Be a columnist," he said, "You'll walk taller."

Breslin was talking about his craft and how he went about it. He urged me to find the angle that reporters and other columnists tend to overlook. This is what Jimmy was known for. It was the way he'd covered the funeral of President Kennedy. While others wrote about the ceremony, he'd gone out to Arlington National Cemetery and interviewed the guy who was digging the lost president's grave. The legendary columnist was telling me to do the same. I should get away from the pack and go for the little, personal story that everyone else ignores.

When we walked into Forst's office, Jimmy told him to give me a column, just like that. Though Forst didn't fork it over, Breslin made quite a case for me. I have always wondered about that day. Here was the best in the business telling his big-city editor that I should be a columnist. Was he doing it for the hero of his book *How the Good Guys Finally Won: Notes from an Impeachment Summer*, which celebrated Tip O'Neill's role in Richard Nixon's downfall? Had my longtime boss said something to him about my writing? Or was Breslin doing all this out of simple, human generosity?

The closing days of 1986, with Tip O'Neill leaving the stage, were another one of those times in life when I needed some direction, just like that day when I sat on a park bench up in Montreal to ponder joining the Peace Corps. In January 1987 I would no longer be the administrative assistant to the Speaker. That big desk of mine in the Capitol was going to be someone else's.

With no door to journalism swinging open, I decided to accept a very attractive offer to run a Washington, DC, consulting company. I became president and CEO of the Government Research Corporation, a for-profit think tank. The job came with attractive perks: a huge salary, an expense account, an impressive office overlooking Connecticut Avenue, and a team of fifty people, many of them experts in their areas of national policy. Since GRC was owned by a large Toronto-based public affairs firm, I would travel to Canada's provincial capitals—Regina, Edmonton, Victoria—to meet with the premiers who were our clients.

But, much like that singing, hand-clapping waiter's job in Somers Point, New Jersey, being head of GRC did not turn out to be my "cup of tea." Having lunch with prospective clients, acting chiefly as a "rain-maker," was no way to quicken my heart. Hearing me complain one day on the phone that I didn't have much to do, my old boss Tip O'Neill told me to keep it to myself. I suppose it's in the unwritten code of former members of Congress who go to work "downtown." You must never admit that, with all the money and trappings, you'd much rather be back in the action, back in the politics of this country, the mission that brought you to Washington in the first place.

But that was precisely my feeling in those months of 1987. I was nursing this sense of lost destiny when I planned a June trip to San Francisco for Kathleen's sister's wedding. To get some work done for GRC, I decided to add on stops in the Bay Area to meet business prospects at the Clorox Company in Oakland and Apple in Silicon Valley. To add some sizzle to the loop, I decided to have lunch with my *Washington Post* pal Larry Kramer, now executive editor of the *San Francisco Examiner*.

It turned out to be a helluva lunch. After we'd shared a carafe or so of white wine, Larry popped the question. Was I interested in writing a column? We ended the historic lunch with Larry telling me to send him some columns and we'd meet again in a couple of weeks when he was back in Washington.

When I showed up for our meeting in DC, I brought along a column he liked. I'd entitled it "That Doleful Wit." It profiled Kansas senator Bob Dole's penchant for the one-liner, a reflexive habit that won hoots from the audience but was far less successful in advancing his ambitions. It was an impulse for the unfiltered comment I could relate to.

Larry offered me a deal. He would pay me $200 for each weekly column. I could keep my big-paying position at the Government Research Service. That's how it went until later in the summer. It was then that Larry sent me a letter for the ages. He said his Washington bureau chief was heading to the *New York Times*. He wanted me to take his place. He said the timing was perfect. By signing on to the *Examiner* now, I could grab an early start covering the 1988 presidential election.

Here was the offer: write two columns a week plus longer articles on the big political story of the week for the Sunday edition. Larry assured me that this was just the beginning: that my column would be syndicated in no time and that I'd soon be on television commenting on the national political scene. All I had to do was give up that lucrative consulting job and become a full-time journalist. What Larry didn't have to say was that I'd be working for the real-life flagship of the Hearst empire. He did tell me that William Randolph Hearst III, the press baron's grandson and now the publisher, was eager to have me come aboard.

When I asked Kathleen about giving up the big job with GRC, taking a wallop of a salary cut, and joining the *San Francisco Examiner*, she said to follow my heart.

I also reached out to George F. Will, a top columnist with the *Washington Post* who was syndicated across the country. When I asked whether I should take the offer, he answered with a question of his own. "How much do you like to read?" It echoed the counsel of the late Harry Golden, who published a newspaper called the *Carolina Israelite*. Asked one time how to become a writer, his advice was simple: *read*! My brief conversation with Will left the matter in the air. A few minutes later, he surprised me with a second call. Pushing me to make the leap, he gave me some advice: don't miss this chance to be in the fight.

Larry Kramer's offer was, once again, a case of meeting or knowing someone who could make all the difference. Just as I had made my start on Capitol Hill thanks to Wayne Owens, now it was Kramer and that lunch in San Francisco. He was offering me my chance. He assured me that it would all come quickly together for me.

And it did, though some thought *too* quickly.

CHAPTER TWENTY-EIGHT

SAN FRANCISCO

To welcome me to the *San Francisco Examiner*, publisher Will Hearst hosted a luncheon out there at the Washington Square Bar & Grill, known locally as the Wash Bag. Included around the table that early afternoon were former mayor George Christopher and other figures I'd read about over the years. The guest who left the strongest impression was the one who'd called earlier to say she might not be able to make it due to a noon event in Chinatown but would try. About forty minutes into lunch, I spotted her heading our way across the square. Newly elected congresswoman Nancy Pelosi had made it after all. With her arrival came a new rule: never accept an invitation unless you're sure to make it. It's far better to admit a prior conflict. That way when you do manage to show up, everyone is happy.

Even as I began my new role as a journalist, I was still sharpening my knowledge of the world I'd left behind. Unlike those who spent their careers reporting on politicians, I kept looking at life through their eyes. For better or worse, it was the old case of "what you do with what you *got*." What I had that most journalists didn't was a memory of the politician's life. I knew what it was like behind those closed doors; knew the life's hopes and daily fears. Yes, I would be judging them as a columnist and reporter, but I also maintained a heart for them. I knew the guts it took to choose such a life. I had felt it myself those months in Philadelphia walking through supermarkets and standing on the boulevard asking people to vote for me.

The Hearst bureau was at 1701 Pennsylvania Avenue, diagonally across the street from the Old Executive Office Building and the White House. I found myself driving into the same parking lot that I had used when working for President Carter.

Soon I was pursuing precisely the career Larry Kramer had foreseen. My columns were being syndicated in dozens of newspapers, and I was being invited on Larry King's late-night radio show on the Mutual Broadcasting System. Back then, Larry hosted the broadcast from his studio in Crystal City, Virginia, across the Potomac River. Listening to him on my cross-country drives to Utah, I had always considered Larry the best in late-night radio. What I discovered doing his show was Larry's amazing ability to sleep during the commercials. I don't know how he did it!

Listening to me in those days, you heard the voice of a political insider; someone who spoke the language of politics and loved the contest. The great Benjamin Bradlee of the *Washington Post* said that I wrote about politics with the same "relish" sportswriters do about boxing. I think I talked like that, too, especially in the middle of the night with Larry King.

The '88 presidential campaign was well under way. By the end of September 1987, Delaware senator Joe Biden was found to have plagiarized large portions of a campaign speech delivered before by British Labour Party leader Neil Kinnock. It got him scratched from the race.

With Christmas coming, I wrote a holiday cover for the *New Republic* called "Carnival of the Candidates." Working with our close friend Margaret Carlson, the magazine's managing editor, and cartoonist Vint Lawrence, we depicted Jesse Jackson as "the Savior," Michael Dukakis as "the Management Consultant," Vice President George H. W. Bush as "the Loyalist," and so on. The article took me to a career milestone, my first TV interview, on *Good Morning America*. Again, it was a friend who made it happen: the show's producer, Rickie Gaffney, had worked with

Kathleen at Washington's ABC affiliate. She booked me to talk about my *TNR* article on the '88 presidential candidates with host Charlie Gibson.

With the wind at my back, I went up to New York for another meeting with CBS News president Howard Stringer. Taking advantage of his earlier suggestion that I go on-air, I asked him to hire me as a political commentator. He introduced me to David Corvo, executive producer of the network's morning news program. David put me on *CBS Morning News*, kept putting me on, and soon gave me a remarkable contract for once-a-week appearances at CBS News headquarters in New York.

Besides the weekly trip to New York, what I liked most about the CBS gig was the political freedom. Unlike my later appearances on *The McLaughlin Group* or on cable, I wasn't asked to argue with someone. Nor was there the expectation that I take one political side of a debate. I was simply there to help viewers get their heads around a story and do my best to bring a news item alive.

By the time of the 1988 New Hampshire primary, the Republican battle to succeed Ronald Reagan had grown heated. Bob Dole started the season winning the Iowa caucuses. He then took a beating from Vice President George Bush in New Hampshire, one he seemed to know would knock him out of the race. When NBC's Tom Brokaw asked Bob Dole if he had anything to say to Bush, his answer was typically bare-knuckle: "Tell him to stop lying about my record."

That line made the Kansas senator the bad guy, which he wasn't, though it certainly captured his resentment. Just as Dole had declared in a 1976 vice presidential debate with Walter Mondale that World Wars I and II were "Democrat wars," it didn't help him with voters. It was "That Doleful Wit" I had described in my first *Examiner* column.

My book *Hardball* came out that spring. Working at night and on weekends, I had spent an enormous amount of time writing it. It's amazing how many drafts it takes to get a book to sound like you talk. *Hardball* earned solid reviews, my favorite appearing in the *Wall Street Journal*, which called it a "must-read textbook that should be read with a marker." It was written by Chicago's Democratic political boss, "Fast Eddie" Vrydolyak. George Will called me "Half Huck Finn and half Machiavelli," in what he described as a "great guide to the great game of politics."

I sent a copy to a number of journalists and politicians, including Vice President Bush, who responded with a handwritten note: "Thanks for the warm inscription in *Hardball*. I immediately flipped to the index and went through pages 36, 77, 95–96, 202, 206. Having emerged unscathed, I'll now happily read the full book." He was admitting to the common DC practice of reading a book from the back, checking first to see if you're mentioned. It was a part of this future president's charm that was very hard not to like.

My book tour ended on the eve of the California primary. The *San Francisco Examiner* sponsored a debate for the remaining Democratic hopefuls: Michael Dukakis and Jesse Jackson. It was a chance for me to grill the candidates. The moderator was John McLaughlin. A former Jesuit professor from New England, he ran his high-powered political TV talk show with the same tyranny that he and his fellow Jesuits enjoyed running their classrooms.

For this, my years at Holy Cross had prepared me well. Appearing on *The McLaughlin Group*, those Saturdays became a highlight of my early years in journalism. "Take Pat's seat," he once welcomed me, referring to the far-right conservative Pat Buchanan. "The Uzi and rosaries are under the seat."

By midsummer, Democratic presidential candidate Michael Dukakis seemed headed for victory in November. The 1988 convention would be the first I'd cover as a reporter. As is so often the case, the person giving the best speech at the Democratic convention wasn't the candidate. Just as Ted Kennedy had wowed the delegates in New York in 1980, and Governor Mario Cuomo had done in 1984, the Reverend Jesse Jackson grabbed the Democratic heart in Atlanta. He talked of the underpaid attendant who tended the sick in a major hospital but ended up unable to afford a bed for herself when her own time came.

The more enjoyable convention to attend that year was the Republican get-together in New Orleans. One factor was the city itself; the other was the surprising performance of the GOP presidential nominee. I had been following George Bush's career for years. What I remember most was the forlorn sight of him standing outside an office in the Longworth House Office Building, one of three Washington office buildings for members of the House. It's how I think of Bush over the years: always waiting. He lost two races for US Senate down in Texas, served as ambassador to the United Nations, chairman of the Republican National Committee, envoy to China, and director of the Central Intelligence Agency, all the time hoping to get his shot at the big prize.

That Thursday night in the Superdome changed all that. In a powerful acceptance speech, George Herbert Walker Bush made it clear that he had finally arrived. What got to me was the part where he admitted that he was not an eloquent man but that his heart was with the country.

"I may sometimes be a little awkward, but there's nothing self-conscious in my love of country," he said. "I am a quiet man, but I hear the quiet people others don't. The ones who raise the family, pay the taxes, meet the mortgage. I hear them, and I am moved."

Up in the stands, I was misty eyed. Though crafted by Peggy Noonan, the speech captured his love of country, his courage as a young man putting off Yale University for the navy, where he protected his country in World War II flying a small fighter plane out over the Pacific.

The GOP convention marked a rapid change of fortune for the Republicans in the 1988 campaign. An NBC–*Wall Street Journal* poll taken in late July showed Michael Dukakis in the lead by 18 points, but on Election Day, George Bush beat him by 8. This meant that 25 percent of the electorate had changed its mind between the conventions and voting day. That same poll had shown Bush's lead peaking at double-digit levels at one point in the closing weeks. The shift was driven by a devastating negative Republican campaign against Dukakis. It hit him on a trio of issues: his refusal to fine Massachusetts teachers for not leading their classes in the

Pledge of Allegiance, his "card-carrying" membership in the American Civil Liberties Union, and, most potently, his support for his state's prison furlough system, which allowed inmates serving life sentences without the possibility of parole to be given temporary releases after serving a certain amount of time imprisoned. In one notorious case, a beneficiary of the system, an African American named William Horton, never returned to prison. Nearly a year later, while still on the lam, he was arrested after having held a young couple hostage, raping the woman, stabbing her boyfriend, and then stealing his car.

To exploit the case and portray Dukakis as soft on crime, Bush's media consultant, Roger Ailes—who, in the early twenty-first century made Fox News a ratings juggernaut through highly partisan programming aimed at a conservative audience—produced a TV ad that showed actors dressed as prisoners passing through a revolving door as if leaving a hotel. Massachusetts's furlough system, highlighting the Willie Horton story, became a blazing element in the Bush campaign. "If I can make Willie Horton a household name," Bush campaign strategist Lee Atwater said, "we will win the election."

While the official Bush campaign ads showed faces of various ethnic backgrounds passing through that revolving door, a pro-Bush group linked to the National Security Political Action Committee ran an ad spotlighting Horton himself and his rape of a white woman following release on a "furlough." The ad was flagrantly about race. It's one thing to criticize the idea of temporary releases for prisoners who'd been sentenced to life without parole. It's another to play so clearly to white fears of the violence Horton had committed.

Each Republican attack on Dukakis targeted him from a different direction. The Pledge of Allegiance issue portrayed him as lacking in gut patriotism. Calling him a card-carrying member of the ACLU appropriated a term associated with charges of Communist Party ties. The Horton ad appealed to base racism.

As a coup de grâce, the Republicans ran a commercial of Dukakis riding around in a tank wearing a giant helmet while the announcer listed the weapons systems he had opposed. The image evoked the cartoon character Rocket J. Squirrel of *The Adventures of Rocky and Bullwinkle*.

The Thursday before Election Day, the *Washington Post* invited me to offer my prediction on the outcome. My method was to study the states, especially those that were harder to call, and figure out who was going to win each one. Although I got several wrong, my mistakes neatly offset one another. Pitted against a dozen other political observers, I made the lone accurate prediction of the electoral vote between Bush and Dukakis and very nearly nailed the popular vote.

Looking back, the election was less Bush versus Dukakis than it was about Ronald Reagan versus change. People felt comfortable with the eight years they'd shared with the former motion picture and television personality. They liked his old-time patriotism, his gift for political Technicolor, the feeling about this country that he was so good at sharing. That was the essence of the 1988 election: the voters' verdict that what they had was better than trying something altogether too different. For the third consecutive presidential contest, the GOP candidate trounced his Democratic rival: 426 to 111 in the Electoral College, and 53.4 percent to 45.6 percent in the popular vote.

Although I supported Michael Dukakis in my column, I was not terribly unhappy with the result. The fact is, I admired George Bush's devotion to this country and his reverence for high public office. Asked once what he found so meaningful about serving as president, he gave what I felt was the right response. Bush said it was the "honor" of it. Wherever a president intends to take the country, an instinctive reverence for the office is a good starting point.

At the end of the election year, I had a syndicated twice-a-week column with the *San Francisco Examiner*, a weekly commentary role on CBS, and was showing up on *The McLaughlin Group*. Meanwhile, Kathleen was an on-air reporter at WJLA and substitute anchor. With two young boys, and a daughter on the way, I was counting my good fortune. But storm clouds loomed.

The Washington journalist establishment was about to strike back. It began with a lecture given by the *Washington Post*'s David Broder. He spoke of journalism's "determination to keep its distance from government, not only to avoid censorship but to avoid co-optation. Subversion by seduction. The insidious inhibition of intimacy. The blurring of the lines between journalism on one side, and politics and government on the other."

A few years earlier, Broder had signaled his concern for cozy relationships between journalists and politicians. Stopping by the *Post* newsroom to pick up my friend James Rowe for lunch, Broder offered a friendly warning about journalists getting too close to the people they are covering. Rowe, who wrote on economic issues, covered the Senate Budget Committee. As Jim would tell you, I spent hours impressing upon him and other national reporters the new panel's historic mission to gain better control over congressional fiscal policy.

Broder reprised his lecture in a column that spoke of a new, dark presence: a "new hybrid creature" who is "one day . . . a public official . . . [and] a journalist or television commentator" the next. He was talking about those who moved from political and government roles into journalism. In other words, he was talking about me.

Broder didn't name this "hybrid" or "androgynous" figure he had in mind, but his *Post* colleague Richard Harwood soon did:

Christopher Matthews served ably on Capitol Hill for a number of years as a press agent and propagandist for retired House Speaker Thomas P. "Tip" O'Neill. He had previously toiled in the stables of Democratic senators and as a speechwriter for President Jimmy Carter. When Mr. Matthews left the hill a couple of years ago, he quickly found employment as a commentator for the Mutual radio network. . . .

He was hired by the *Examiner,* he said, because its editors wanted "my inside perspective on how politicians think." And it was not a hindrance that after 20 years as a Washington politician, he had what we in journalism call "connections" and "access." He was, in short, a legitimate member of what David Broder described last week as "a power-wielding clique of insiders . . . a clique where politicians, publicists, and journalists are easily interchangeable parts.

Harwood went on to cite others who moved from public or political positions into journalism—Diane Sawyer, Pat Buchanan, Henry Kissinger, George Will, John McLaughlin—calling them "switch-hitters." He said that the "incessant bed-hopping" between the two roles was doing damage to the "image of independence we cultivate and cherish."

What these critics overlooked was my objective analysis of the 1988 presidential campaign. I called it as I saw it, even if my former Democratic associates in the Dukakis campaign resented it. I won the *Post's* Crystal Ball Award, in fact, with my exact and independent predictions of the results that November.

The Harwood column ran on Sunday. The next day, I charged into the *Washington Post* newsroom and headed to the glassed-in office of executive editor Ben Bradlee. Why, I demanded to know, was the *Post* bashing me? Bradlee and his wife, Sally Quinn, had been exceedingly warm and welcoming to Kathleen and me, inviting us to their celebrated New Year's Eve parties. He seemed taken aback by my brashness but, then again, not the least bit intimidated.

"What did you come in here for? To lift your leg on me?"

With that classic Ben retort, spoken in the crusty language of the World War II naval officer, it was hard to sustain my outrage. If this great man whose leadership had taken down a president during Watergate saw this as just another battle between newspaperman and upset subject, what was I to say?

Ben then laid on the charm. He said it didn't make any sense to be angry with someone like Dick Harwood, a US Marine who had fought at Iwo Jima. He wasn't one of the elite types around the *Post* but a regular guy like me.

Exactly a month later, the *Washington Post* splashed a huge article on the front page of the Style section: "Trading Places: The 'Insiders' Debate." It began, as Harwood had, with me.

"Christopher Matthews, pink and dogged in the morn, has his back up to the high wood partition in the narrow breakfast booth. His coffee is getting cold."

I was sitting across the table from reporter Charles Trueheart in my favorite Washington pub, Martin's Tavern in Georgetown.

"I will not defend what I'm doing," the reporter quoted me as saying ("never unbuttoning his smile"). "It's not a guild. It's not the Masters of the Cloth Hall. It's a free market. It's a free country."

"Matthews, 42, admits to the charge he's been lucky. 'I never dreamed I could do what I'm doing,' he says. Neither have most journalists; a tinge of envy may lurk within their ire."

"Being a speechwriter is an exact apprenticeship for writing a column," I argued. Who do you want to hear, I challenged the interviewer, "guys who've spent their lives hanging out in hallways" or "guys who've spent their lives in back rooms"?

The article ended with me rather brashly saying that I didn't have to defend wanting to become a full-time journalist. Free speech was my God-given right.

"I feel like doing it," I told the *Washington Post* reporter. "That's my defense. I feel like doing it."

After glorying in the big article, which featured countless well-known journalists who'd also worked in politics to one degree or another, I quickly called up Bradlee and thanked him for the piece, which I took as a makeup for the Broder-Harwood double-teaming. Even on the phone, I could see Ben's poker face. He was neither admitting a connection nor denying a role. Like everyone else, I just wanted the great man's approval, even if tossed at me backhanded. I felt that, at least in his eyes, I had become the florid-faced columnist who could duke it out with a Richard Harwood. Of course, I loved it.

In its February 1989 issue, *Washingtonian* magazine keyed a big story entitled "Washington's Top Fifty Journalists." It was Kirk O'Donnell who warned me, "You're in trouble now." Close pals with a tight-knit set of political reporters, he'd gotten word how upset they were about yours truly being on the exclusive list.

Bannered "Today's Journalism Establishment," the full-page article featured some of the most celebrated figures in newspapers and television— Benjamin Bradlee, David Brinkley, David Broder, Sam Donaldson, Howard Fineman, Jack Germond, Al Hunt, Ted Koppel, Andrea Mitchell, Robert Novak, William Safire, Lesley Stahl, Judy Woodruff, Bob Woodward— and in the middle of them all, "Chris Matthews, *S. F. Examiner*," and my smiling face. The article began, again, with me:

> Election Day wasn't a typical day for politico-turned-pundit Christopher Matthews. But it wasn't atypical, either.
>
> That afternoon, before the returns were in, the former speechwriter and aide to Tip O'Neill wrote a next-day column on how Dukakis blew it. Then he dashed over to Mutual radio's studios in Crystal City, where he and Larry King provided commentary for nine hours. Matthews, who is Washington bureau chief for the *San Francisco Examiner*, also conferred by phone with his editor on the West Coast throughout the evening.
>
> At 2 a.m., he jumped into a waiting limousine, which got him to New York in time to take a shower and read some wire copy before appearing on the *CBS Morning News*. Then it was back to Washington, where he pounded out another column on the election.
>
> Matthews, 43, is a new face in big-time Washington journalism— and a prime example of today's reporter-as-empire-builder.

I had wanted to write about the country's fight for political leadership and its position in the world. In spite of some headwinds, I was doing it.

CHAPTER TWENTY-NINE

WHITE HOUSE DINNER

One figure in the Washington establishment who might have thought I had done a fair job covering the 1988 campaign despite my Democratic background was the man in the White House. In the spring of 1989, President and Mrs. Bush invited Kathleen and me to the White House for dinner and a movie. Initially, it looked like we would have to miss it. Dad called to say that he and Mom were driving back from their winter trip to Florida, and they'd be arriving the same night we were to be at the White House. About to convey our regrets, Kathleen got ahold of our friend Lois Romano, a reporter at the *Washington Post*. Hearing the situation, Lois called up the White House social director, described our predicament, including the fact that Mom was experiencing the early onset of Alzheimer's. We were told the appeal went to the president himself, who gave the green light.

I have thought at times of this president taking the time to make that call in our family's favor. There was a kindness in it, a gentleness, totally in character with the human qualities he had championed in his acceptance speech. True to his word, this was George Bush, the *man* as well as the president, honoring that very decency.

When we arrived at the White House and walked up those historic stairs to the family residence, the president and First Lady were standing there alone to greet us. They quickly divided us up. The president took my parents under his wing, while Barbara Bush included us in a group of other guests who'd arrived already. The next I saw of Dad and Mom that evening was when the First Lady took us out on the Truman Balcony to see the view overlooking the South Lawn. Through the French doors, I glimpsed one of the glorious sights of my life: the president, Dad, and Mom chatting away like old family friends.

When we had a chance to compare the tours, Dad was amazed by how much the president had wanted to show Mom and him. Bush took them into his private bathroom, his closets, everything. A gentleman of the old school, Bush was offering his guests a true "open house." Over the buffet dinner in the main hall of the residential quarters, Dad looked at me, smiling and quietly, distinctly forming the words of his verdict: "Greatest night of my life."

I've wondered over the years exactly why President George H. W. Bush gave our family the honor of the invitation that night. My one hint came when the First Lady, showing us into their bedroom, described how a White House staffer threw the morning newspapers onto the bed as they watched the morning news programs. My hunch has been that the president watched *CBS This Morning* and saw my regular commentaries.

This shows how different the times were back then. Here I was, known to be a recent assistant to the most powerful Democrat in the country, offering up an objective assessment of the 1988 presidential race. The same independence that drove the Dukakis people wild may have impressed the Bush side, including the candidate. Again, I called it as I saw it.

The guests around us in the family residence showed the breadth of Bush's world: Bill White, the National League baseball president; Republican John Tower, the former Texas senator who had been Bush's nominee for secretary of defense; and Democrats Tom Foley, the House majority leader, and Congressman Marty Russo of Illinois. Each one of them, as I could figure it, was a personal friend of the president's.

Somewhere over dinner, the president directed his attention to us. Something he said suggested he thought we were a Democratic family, much as the Bushes are down-the-line Republicans.

"Mr. President, actually my family are all Republicans," I said.

"What happened to *you*?" he hit back.

Dinner over, we headed down to the Family Movie Theater in the White House basement. After the Bushes passed out bags of popcorn, we saw *Chances Are*, starring Robert Downey Jr. and Cybil Shepherd, a romantic comedy set in DC. I loved it. How could I not be smitten on an evening like this, one on which I was able to bring the parents who had worked so hard to bring me up?

A couple of months later, I was sitting in the Roosevelt Room in the West Wing, where the Carter staffers used to have our morning meetings. Veteran Hearst journalist Joseph Kingsbury-Smith had arranged a briefing for the bureau's reporters. For the next hour, I couldn't tell if Bush remembered who I was. All that changed afterward when he made a point of rounding the long table and walking up to me with a question that sounded like it had been lingering in his mind. "Has your Dad changed your mind about things yet?"

This ability to remember not just people's names but also something about them is what sets the old-style politician apart from others. Bush's pal Tip O'Neill certainly had it. Whatever you may say, it shows that person cares about real human beings, not just about his "fellow Americans" or "society." It's my belief that it matters.

"Please be nice to him," my Dad said with real feeling that night as we left the White House.

I couldn't, of course. It wasn't my job.

Looking back, that fine man who hosted my parents grows with history. He made hard decisions and, at the time, paid for them in terms of his public popularity. But in important cases, when he raised taxes to reduce the federal deficit and when he chose to limit the war with Iraq's Saddam Hussein, George Bush's judgment was in the country's best interest, not his own.

CHAPTER THIRTY

HUNGARY

Ｂy the late 1980s, the European order left by World War II had been frozen for four decades. The Iron Curtain that had separated the Continent between the democracies and those under Moscow's thumb seemed indestructible. There was freedom on the western side, Communism on the other. In America, regardless of our politics, people thought that the way things were by the late 1940s was the way it would remain.

On Easter 1989 I got my firsthand look at the Soviet Union's control over Eastern Europe. It was just in time to see it begin to die. Having watched the decline of one empire, the British in Africa, I was now about to witness the fall of another. I had grown up regularly crouching under my desk at St. Christopher's, fearing the fall of Russia's atom bombs. Every Sunday we prayed for our despised foe's conversion.

This explains my excitement about traveling to Budapest in the spring of 1989. My friend Jerry Rafshoon had gone from being Jimmy Carter's media consultant to producing movies. He was producing a four-part television drama of William L. Shirer's book *The Nightmare Years,* one of his accounts of Adolf Hitler's rise in the 1930s. Jerry was filming in the Hungarian capital because its old buildings matched those of pre–World War II Berlin. I decided to join him and bring along our oldest son, Michael, who was six.

When I was growing up, Hungary was the heroic country that rebelled against Russian domination in 1956. Our first taste of that national spirit came in our own capital. It showed itself in the welcoming reception Kathleen, Michael, and I received at the Hungarian ambassador's residence. They made a festive event of our stopping by to collect the visas for Michael and me. It was clear that Hungarians, even those in its government service overseas, had no love for the Communists. One way of showing it was the contempt the officials showed that day for hard-line East Germany.

From our first arrival in Budapest, I could see this was not the dark, Cold War picture of Eastern Europe we'd seen on TV. The city was alive with Western culture, from the sidewalk artists' caricatures of Woody Allen, Marilyn Monroe, Charles Bronson, and other Hollywood stars, to the Beach Boys' tunes playing in the elevator of the InterContinental Hotel overlooking the Danube River.

At the foreign information office, I caught another sign of the government's disdain for Soviet Bloc politics. Proudly displayed at the entrance was a photograph of East German dictator Erich Honecker. He was standing in front of a set of deer antlers mounted on the wall behind. It made the Communist boss look like he had horns. That Hungary's foreign information office, visited by correspondents from around the world, would feature such a prank in plain sight stirred my thoughts about the Hungarian political order.

My first meeting in Budapest was with Géza Jeszenszky, a history professor at the University of Leipzig, then called Karl Marx University. I had gotten word that he was active with a group of political reformers called the Hungarian Democratic Forum. His high-ceilinged apartment reminded me of *The Third Man,* the classic Orson Welles film made against the backdrop of grim post–World War II Vienna.

After welcoming us, Professor Jeszenszky began telling me about all the big changes taking place in his country. Political changes. When I showed skepticism that anything would truly change as long as Hungary was trapped in the political and military bear hug of Moscow, he refused to agree.

"Freedom is contagious," he said. It sounded less an argument than a fact. When I asked the source of this optimism, he gave a one-word answer: "Yeltsin." He was referring to Moscow leader Boris Yeltsin, who had dared challenge the old Kremlin order. He then spoke of the Forum movement in Hungary. "Writers and intellectuals are meeting in the countryside," he said with genuine hope, but it didn't shake my doubt. How could intellectuals and meetings overthrow the all-powerful Warsaw Pact, the phalanx of Russia-forged nations that had crushed the Hungarian rebellion in 1956? If cobblestones couldn't stop Eastern bloc tanks, how would *writers*?

With that meeting, though, I began to see something big was happening in Hungary—and not just to the artists on the sidewalks and the people who program the elevator music. A government economist spoke with delight at the hypocrisy of colleagues he'd known for years as hardened Communists now adjusting to the new political conversation. "The road to Damascus is very crowded these days." He was referring to Saint Paul's conversion from ruthless tax collector to true Christian. With our young Michael snapping pictures, the chief of the Budapest Communist Party confessed bluntly to me that "the socialist model" wasn't working anymore.

More striking was a statement by a reformist member of the Hungarian cabinet that the 1956 revolt constituted a true "popular uprising."

"Thirty-three years ago, a Hungarian premier was hanged for saying much the same thing," I wrote in my *Examiner* column. "Today on the same streets of Budapest that once carried free-firing Soviet tanks, the pro-Western urge is palpable, as is the despair of those hard-liners who have kept this nation captive since 1947."

I had found myself an eyewitness to something truly historic. Eastern Europe was moving westward in its politics. The old Soviet empire was coming apart in ways hard to imagine. The USSR, which seemed on the verge of matching the USA in global prowess, was suffering a mortal wound.

My reporting on the political changes in Hungary was interspersed with the glamor of watching the filming of *The Nightmare Years*. Sam Waterston had the starring role as William L. Shirer, the American correspondent based in Berlin during the thirties. Marthe Keller was playing his wife. One period in European history was being exhumed while another was just coming to life.

Our visit to Budapest was my first trip behind the Iron Curtain. It was also the last month that the Curtain would matter. A month after Michael and I returned home, the government of Hungary began to cut down a portion of the wire fence separating it from Austria. It was the first official breach of the Iron Curtain. By 1990, there was a free, democratic Republic of Hungary. Géza Jeszenszky was the country's foreign minister.

CHAPTER THIRTY-ONE

BERLIN WALL

From the day of its construction in August 1961, the ugly barrier between East and West Berlin had been a graphic symbol of Soviet bloc captivity. It was erected for a single purpose: to stop the flow of East Germans from escaping to the West—which by then was upward of three million people. But the Berlin Wall did not stop people from trying. By 1989, news and documentary films had made us all too familiar with the sight of people risking their lives to climb the wall and race through its notorious "death strip." The photographs of those being shot dead became an iconic statement about Communist captivity.

Through the summer of 1989, Hungary took gradual steps to bring down the Iron Curtain. These steps led to an all-out challenge to Moscow and the purpose of the Warsaw Pact itself in September when the government allowed an estimated twelve thousand East Germans to emigrate freely to the West through Hungary. This meant the Berlin Wall could no longer keep people locked under Communist rule. I wrote in my *San Francisco Examiner* column that the Hungarians "are no longer willing to do Berlin's dirty work."

It was clear, reading that column years later, that my old Cold War feelings had been aroused. To me, the Hungarians were once again the heroes of the day. This time I believed we were in a position to offer help. "It's time for America to support Hungary in this dispute. It's time to put the great power and prestige of the world's most robust democracy at the service of a small Central European country that has once again taken risks and suffered abuse championing those values most basic to our own republic."

There were some Americans with far stronger passions about the events in Hungary. Congressman Tom Lantos of California was born and grew up there. A Jew, he lived to survive the German occupation and with it the Holocaust. At sixty-one, serving his fifth term in the US House of Representatives, he could appreciate the wonder of what was happening with the liberation of Hungary and Poland and the opening of the Berlin Wall. It was the victory for those countries left behind in the West's liberation from the Nazis.

"He can see that the long, grim aftermath of World War II is about to end and with it the barbed wire and inhuman captivity of Josef Stalin's whole miserable empire," I wrote that November. "Now, finally, the grimness of the postwar period is rising. The smiling faces that once lined Paris, as our Yanks came marching through, are matched by the faces atop the Berlin Wall. Finally, the freedom promised by victory against Hitler is at hand."

Without asking permission from my editors at the *Examiner* I headed to Berlin. This was history, my history, and I needed to be there to catch it. Arriving at Tempelhof airport, I headed through the Berlin Wall, still being enforced with tedious precision, to the Grand Hotel in East Berlin. From there I walked up Unter den Linden to the Brandenburg Gate and mixed into the crowd. It was rumored that the East Germans were going to open the historic gateway soon.

As I began asking questions of people, I realized quickly that my limited high school and college German wasn't up to the kind of information I was after. I wanted to know what this moment—what this *history*—felt like to these people. Fortunately, I found an American grad student to interpret for me.

I had a simple plan: to ask each East German waiting there on that drizzling evening what *Freiheit*—freedom—meant to him or her. The first to speak was a nurse who told me that it would mean that her fellow nurses would stop leaving East Berlin for the West. After hearing other practical responses, I came upon a young man wearing a surplus army jacket, the kind I wore in college. He could have been a student activist in the "free speech" movement at the University of California at Berkeley in the 1960s. "*This* is *Freiheit*," he said, "*talking to you*. This standing in a public place arguing openly about such things as democracy, capitalism, and socialism."

The nurse joined in. "Four weeks ago, we couldn't have done this." She said that there were only seventeen nurses left on her hospital floor. "It's bleeding us to death." The only way to stop the flood, she said, was through free, multiparty elections. "If we keep working, doing demonstrations, maybe we'll get them soon. We really do believe in democracy. Let us have a chance!"

I asked the people in the crowd what kind of system they wanted: capitalist or socialist? "We want a united Germany where the people can make the choice," the nurse said. A young man had a different response: "We want a socialist country, even if we don't have reunification."

"We know we cannot have what they have over there," another man agreed, referring to West Germany, "without having such a sharp-elbowed society like it does."

"I want the freedom to earn what I have worked for and not be forced to do something because I am told to," said still another.

"As the arguments raged on," I wrote, "it was clear that what a new East Germany may look like was less important—for now—than the freedom to talk and choose."

The next night, I attended a student protest at nearby Humboldt University. Again, I saw the conflict between capitalism and socialism. Where the East German people agreed was on the need for a true democracy. As far as specific demands, they began with reform of the university itself. The student leaders wanted a public accounting of how its money was being spent. They wanted professors hired and given tenure based on their performance, not political connections. They wanted more instruction in English, less in Russian.

This demand for reform went well beyond the campus. A protest organizer said he wanted a full accounting of how the East German government had let the economy disintegrate. For too long, he said, the country has been ruled by a Communist Party elite. "The citizens of this country were never authorized to do things on their own without permission of the government," he complained.

What became obvious to me was how the calls for freedom of political expression were driven by anger at the East German government. People felt subjugated. Having been in the country only a few days taught me why so many were leaving. They wanted to work and get paid fairly for it.

"It's one thing to treat human beings like rodents on a treadmill," I wrote. "The Socialist Unity Party, known here as the 'SED,' adds humiliation to the spectacle. Each day of his life, the citizen of the German Democratic Republic is reminded of his serfdom. He gets the message from the currency he is required to use.

"The hotel where I am staying is a case in point. The Grand will not even accept what its haughty clerks derisively call 'local.' This was the economic heart of the East German's humiliation. Those who work at tourist hotels, those who drive taxis or wait on tables, are the privileged people. Those who work in factories or otherwise serve the needs of the citizenry are stuck with a form of payment that has become a joke even within the country's own borders."

In interviews with factory managers and school principals, I learned that even the rare chance to travel abroad could be humiliating. Seeking a vacation, an East German had the choice of two destinations: Poland or Hungary. Those were the lone nations where their country's weak, propped-up currency was accepted.

"The result is a two-class East German society. At its top stands an elite class able to get its hands on foreign currency. At the bottom is the great captive 'socialist' workforce that must suffer the added insult of being paid each week in a currency that its own hotel clerks consider too worthless to put in their cash registers."

That Friday, I ventured out to Lake Wannsee on the outskirts of Berlin. On a leafy lane, with the lake visible through the trees, I found the headquarters of the Aspen Institute. It was built on the very spot where Joseph Goebbels and his family lived. I thought about the spectral contrast: between the beauty of the place and the ugly horror that Hitler's chief propagandist tried to hide.

Also visiting Berlin at this historic time was John McLaughlin. On Saturday he and I stood at the Berlin Wall opening at Potsdamer Platz and watched the people of East Germany pass through. The grim figures looked like characters in a black-and-white film walking into a movie in Technicolor. "This is where forty years of Stalinism has gotten them," remarked our proud West German driver, "standing in line for biscuits."

It was a nasty but accurate observation of Communist suppression. The desperation of the East Berliners was vivid. "The contrasts between those arriving and those greeting them could hardly be greater," I reported. "It was as if members of the same family had been separated at birth. One group went to California, the other to Siberia.

"'Look! You can see the difference!' our West German driver insisted as we rubbernecked later at the packed sidewalks of the Kurfürstendamm, West Berlin's dazzling downtown. 'See that woman with the hat,' he said as he pointed to a 30ish pedestrian wearing what looked like an inexpensive watch cap. 'See the ones wearing those jeans, and the badly made shoes!'" He seemed determined to point out the shoddiness of the arriving East Germans.

Unlike him, I was looking at Cold War history coming to an end. "If the East Germans felt underdressed for the occasion, they didn't show it," I wrote. "They were too dazzled by the world of commercial wealth they suddenly found around them. A few hundred yards behind them was the grim world of Marx and Stalin. Around them loomed a world as sleek as Rodeo Drive and as wide open as North Beach.

"It has been 44 years since the two worlds were first divided near the filled-in bunker where Adolf Hitler's dreams finally died. For the last 28 years, they have barely seen each other through the barriers of concrete and barbed wire."

What struck me in those historic days was how powerful had been the influence of the Communist regime on those coming through the wall.

"For all the excitement of recent weeks, a visitor is still struck by the defeated look on so many faces. When the lines get long, no one complains—not even when someone cuts in. This comes in part from living in a society where the worker is paid in a worthless currency, where the only way to get a good car or a trip abroad is to find some 'hustle' that offers access to hard currency."

The people of East Germany had been injured, insulted, and now discarded by their own "People's" government. It's not the theory of Communism that failed ultimately; it was the practice. To the bitter end, they were being denied that most basic human right: the right to escape. I had grown up watching scenes of East Germans being shot climbing the wall or racing to freedom after they had. I now crossed through the Berlin Wall at the Friedrichstrasse checkpoint twice a day as a matter of course. Each time, I had to go from one stale cigarette–smelling shack to the next, from one member of the Volkspolitzei asking questions to another VoPo asking the same questions. Even as it passed into history, the wall was still being held together by red tape. Stupid bureaucracy was now the vestige of the watchtowers and the death strip.

The next day, John and I took a daylong driving tour of East Germany. We began in Potsdam, where Allied leaders Truman, Churchill, and Stalin met in the summer of 1945 to decide the fate of defeated Germany. At the site of the conference, we found a brochure that conveniently set the beginnings of the "anti-Hitler coalition" in 1941, the year Germany attacked the Soviet Union. It neatly canceled out the years 1939 to 1941, when Moscow maintained a nonaggression pact with Hitler. The propaganda had the Nazis surrendering to a Red Army field marshal in 1945. There was no mention of an American general named Eisenhower.

The authors were not satisfied in ignoring the US role in winning World War II. They condemned us as war criminals, arguing that President Truman dropped the atom bombs on Japan not to end the war but for the sole purpose of intimidating the Soviet Union. "In the interest of American plans to rule the world and the policy of pressure on the Soviet Union," the glossy Potsdam handout declared, "two flourishing Japanese cities had to perish, about 300,000 people had to die."

Late that afternoon, at a visit to the Nazi concentration camp at Buchenwald, where tens of thousands of Jews had been killed, an old guard adorned in war medals told of the atrocities committed there against Soviet officers. "Were there any Jews killed here?" McLaughlin asked. No, he assured us, the chief victims in Buchenwald were Communists.

One of our last stops that day was the ancient church in Wittenberg. It was on its high door that in 1517 the monk Martin Luther had nailed his Ninety-Five Theses, an act that began the Protestant Reformation. Once inside, I briefly lost sight of John. I found him standing on Martin Luther's tomb. Through the dust-filled sun rays from the window, he offered up a question: "How did he know?" To John, the wonder of Luther's courage wasn't the doctrinal but the political. It was not what the great Luther envisioned about man's relation to God but what he figured out about power. How did this lone Catholic cleric know that he could stand against the European order and not get himself burnt at the stake like all the other heretics who'd gone down the same path?

Our last stop was at St. Nicholas Church, or Nikolaikirche, in Leipzig. This was the "Peace" church where Monday evenings had been devoted to praying for change in the country. "There was no head of the revolution," a cabaret artist said of the revolutionary events of late 1989. "The head was the Nikolaikirche, and the body was the center of the city. There was only one leadership: Monday, five o'clock, St. Nicholas Church." It was in that sixteenth-century Lutheran place of worship that the hopeful German people sang "We Shall Overcome" in English. In doing so they would help bring down the Communist dictatorship.

That night, John, our drivers, and I had dinner at Auerbachs Keller, the equally vintage Leipzig restaurant. It's where the playwright Goethe had Mephistopheles first talking to Faust. Like the visit to the church in Wittenberg, the restaurant showed what human life is like in the absence of commerce. Left to their basic functions, churches and restaurants retain their pasts.

"No one talks the language of revolution," I wrote upon leaving Berlin, "but everyone does the work of it. No one maps the grand strategy, yet both the government and its critics play out their revolutionary roles. The effect is a chain reaction.

"First, we see the rudiments of a political movement—Solidarity in Poland, the Forum in Hungary, the New Forum in East Germany.

"In each case, the movement makes nonrevolutionary demands. Its only goal is to 'reform' the existing order. It wants to improve, not destroy socialism. . . .

"The chain reaction is what matters," I wrote. "Courageous citizens call for 'reform' but end up denouncing the ruling Communists. They begin as a movement and eventually become a party. . . .

"The rivalry is joined. Elections are held. The public rejects the tainted Communists and chooses the democratic alternative. Only bullets and tanks can stop it, and Mikhail Gorbachev knows that such weapons are suicidal when the targets are the very people who now hold the future of Eastern Europe in their hands."

CHAPTER THIRTY-TWO

A BOOMER AS PRESIDENT

Nineteen eighty-nine changed the way my generation, the early baby boomers, looked at life. From the time we'd opened our eyes to the world, we faced the threat of being destroyed. Even a decade after we'd hid under our desks, President Kennedy spoke of how a "miscalculation" by the United States or the Union of Soviet Socialist Republics would trigger a nuclear war. Films such as *Dr. Strangelove* and *Fail Safe*, both from 1964, warned—one with dark humor, the other in dead seriousness—of how the world could destroy itself. It seemed inevitable that someone, someday, would push a button and blow up life as we'd known it.

What I'd witnessed in Budapest and Berlin in 1989 announced that this specter of Armageddon might be disappearing. The Iron Curtain and the wider global conflict it defined were approaching their end. Falling with the wall was the anxiety over a global Communist victory. If the aggressors in Moscow weren't able to hold Eastern Europe, they were not likely to threaten the rest of the world.

The new decade dawned with other challenges. By August 1990, American security faced a far lesser threat from the Mideast. When Iraqi dictator Saddam Hussein's army invaded and occupied neighboring Kuwait, President Bush declared that the Iraqi aggression would "not stand." He organized a global coalition to push the Iraqi army back across the border.

That winter, I was in Germany reporting on the workings of the country's new, united government. Based on the view from the streets, however, the people of Bonn were more excited by their opposition to the US war on Iraq. *"Kein Blut fur Ol"* signs were all over the capital. "No Blood for Oil."

Our response to Iraq's provocation looked to me like the old Vietnam mistake. We were taking US forces to a part of the world where we weren't prepared to stay. When we left, the situation would revert back to the control of those who remained. Even worse, I worried that sending US forces to the Mideast would be a one-way ticket. Once there, we'd be stuck in the sand.

Initially, Bush's call to war won him public support. That November, the *Washington Post* asked me to predict the results of the 1990 midterm elections. For the second time, I won the Crystal Ball Award, in this case by picking the precise results for the House of Representatives. The Republican loss of nine seats was modest by historic standards for a president's party two years following his election. I also picked the net results in the governors' races but was one seat off in the Senate results.

Politically, the Gulf War won great, if short-term, popularity for President Bush. While the US military performed with excellence, the conflict lacked staying power with voters. After the US-led coalition removed Saddam Hussein's Iraqi army from Kuwait in March 1991, President George H. W. Bush enjoyed a job approval boost to 89 percent. By July 1992, less than a year and a half later, it was down to 29 percent.

Meanwhile, in August 1991 history with far greater consequence was being made in Moscow. Boris Yeltsin stood on a Red Army tank and faced down an attempted coup by die-hard Communists. His heroic stance ended the Soviet Union and with it the Cold War.

One result, it turned out, was that the American presidency was no longer limited to those who'd served in uniform. Dwight Eisenhower, John F. Kennedy, Lyndon Johnson, Richard Nixon, Gerald Ford, Ronald Reagan, and George H. W. Bush were all uniformed officers in World War II, even as they displayed vastly different levels of military achievement.

Jimmy Carter, too young to fight in WWII, was a midshipman at the US Naval Academy in Annapolis, Maryland. He was on summer cruise when the peace treaty with Japan was signed aboard the USS *Missouri*. What mattered to voters is that all these men had met their citizen's duty to serve, especially in wartime.

That standard of military service didn't hold the same power as when we'd been threatened by another superpower.

By the summer of 1992, President Bush's political prospects were dire. Voters were no longer impressed with his wartime record either as a young man in the Pacific or as commander in chief in the Persian Gulf. It was the weakening economy that monopolized their attention.

Fortunately for Bush, most of his likely Democratic challengers had passed on a presidential run. They didn't believe they could match the commander in chief who had beaten Saddam Hussein. Unfortunately for Bush, his most dangerous rival did.

A former colleague at the Carter White House, Tom Belford, had told me to keep a lookout for a Georgetown University classmate of his. He was talking about a Democrat who had been elected governor of Arkansas at age thirty-two.

Tall and physically commanding, Bill Clinton had made all the right moves. He possessed a sunny, outgoing personality. Despite his too-obvious ambition, he had the gifted politician's talent for putting the other person up on a pedestal. He could make that person believe that he or she was all Bill Clinton could think about.

In fact, Bill Clinton never allowed himself to be distracted from his main purpose in life: what he would call his "political viability." After graduating from Yale Law School, he didn't join the flock heading to Wall Street or Washington, DC. He went straight home to Arkansas. Why? Because that maxim of Tip O'Neill's, "All politics is local," is an excellent guide for starting up a political career.

Back home, Clinton lost his first race for Congress against a Republican incumbent. He bounced back quickly and got elected Arkansas's attorney general. Winning statewide office put him in an even better political position than if he'd won that seat in the US House of Representatives.

Elected governor in 1978, however, Clinton soon lost his way. It was a matter of style and culture. He and his wife, Yale Law classmate Hillary Rodham, struck Arkansans as too cool for school, and, like many Democrats in 1980, he was swept out of office. After his two-year term was over, so seemed the Clintons.

The young ex-governor studied his loss and saw the mistakes. So did Hillary. They were about to show Arkansas and the country that he was the "Comeback Kid." Clinton picked himself up, exhibited some humility, and beat the guy who'd beaten him two years before. It was a Clinton sequence of conduct the country would come to recognize: hubris, followed by defeat, followed by stunning personal and political recovery. He went on to be reelected Arkansas governor in 1984, 1986, 1988, and 1990.

By the spring of 1991, just three months after the US victory over Iraq, Clinton was readying his run for president, positioning himself as a centrist, even conservative, alternative to the man most Democrats expected to be the 1992 front-runner: the liberal governor of New York, Mario Cuomo.

In May I went out to Cleveland to cover the annual conference of the Democratic Leadership Council, the group of moderate governors, members of Congress, and lobbyists. The DLC was created as a reaction to the Democrats' defeats of 1980, 1984, and 1988. The group believed the party had swung too far left over those years, their reputation killed by Jimmy Carter's weakness on national defense, candidate Walter Mondale's call for tax increases, and the image of Mike Dukakis letting prisoners out for the weekend.

The headline of my column from Cleveland read: "Democratic Conservatives Find a Voice." That voice was Bill Clinton's, at least before a gathering of right-leaning Democrats. "We should demand that everyone who can go to work *do* it," he asserted. "Forty percent of our welfare dollars would not have to come out of taxpayers' hides if the men who owe child support and can pay it, did it!"

Finally came the kicker: "I'll let you into a little secret: governments don't raise children, people do. And it's time they were asked to assume their responsibilities and forced to do it if they refuse."

"Never before," I wrote in my *San Francisco Examiner* column, "has such a prominent, mainstream national Democrat won such resounding applause on such a conservative message."

As I began covering the 1992 presidential campaign, I started looking for a TV platform from which to cover it. My CBS gig had run its course with the departure of executive producer David Corvo. I now went up to New York to meet with Jack Riley, the executive producer of ABC's *Good Morning America*. I convinced Jack to make me a regular commentator for the upcoming campaign. From his office on the Upper West Side, I walked to a public telephone and called John McLaughlin. I told John about *GMA* signing me up and asked to get back on his show, from which I'd been absent for months. His producer called later that week with an invitation for the Friday taping. I was back in the saddle.

With the Iraq War and the Cold War behind us, voters' minds were now firmly on the economy. While the 1990–91 recession had technically ended, jobs were coming back slowly. The country was experiencing something new and depressing: a "jobless recovery." Families worried if another round of layoffs might cost them their jobs as well as their health insurance. These concerns animated the political landscape.

To introduce themselves to New York's influential Democrats, Bill and Hillary Clinton were invited as guests at my friend Bob Schiffer's breakfast group at the Regency Hotel on New York's Park Avenue. What I remember most from that morning was the speaking order. Hillary went first and gave a robust performance; she then introduced her husband.

I had a powerful sense watching their teamwork that the two Clintons were onto something new politically. They were offering themselves not so much as candidate and spouse but as an electoral ticket. It was Hillary, notably, who spotted the campaign consultant who would carry them to victory: James Carville.

James and I had dinner in December 1991 to talk about the coming race. His focus that evening was the frustration that working people felt toward their own government.

"This country told me when I was born into this world that there was a set of rules that I was supposed to go by. I was supposed to go to school. Basically, I had to pass every grade. I could go to trade school or business school or college. And if I did those things that society expected of me, then in return for that, I would get a job.

"There were some minimal things that society, government, was supposed to deliver for me: the opportunity to buy a house, a street I could walk down, a park my kids could play in, to have a better life for my kids down the road and so on.

"And people say now, 'I did all that, and the other end of the bargain hasn't been held up.'"

Carville, the master political consultant, was saying pretty much what my Peace Corps buddy from Pittsburgh, John Catanese, had said years before. "People don't mind being used; they mind being discarded." Voters are neither greedy nor vengeful, they simply resent being shortchanged on the basics of the American dream. They're not out to soak the rich, only to get what they need themselves and have worked a lifetime to expect. They don't like seeing their president so distracted by world events that he can't connect to what matters most to them.

"The truth of the matter is that the most successful Democratic campaigns are about big ideas," Carville argued to me over dinner. This was his: it was time to bring the American presidency back from George Bush's design for "a New World Order" to the basic needs of the people.

"It's the economy, stupid!" became the winning slogan of the 1992 presidential campaign.

The Clinton campaign began unsteadily. In late January came the Gennifer Flowers story. The Arkansas singer held a press conference in

New York to say she'd had a longtime affair with the governor. Then came the "draft" story. A letter emerged that Clinton had written the commandant of the University of Arkansas ROTC thanking him for "saving" him from the Vietnam-era draft.

On the night of the New Hampshire primary, Team Clinton held a big rally at 9:05 p.m., well ahead of the 11:00 news programs—and well ahead of the other candidates. Its purpose was to declare victory, to give Bill Clinton the headline no matter what the arithmetic determined. "New Hampshire tonight has made Bill Clinton the Comeback Kid!" declared the kid himself. After holding a giant lead in a *Boston Globe* poll a month earlier, he had just lost this first primary of the presidential race by roughly 8 percentage points to former Massachusetts senator Paul Tsongas.

How did Clinton pull it off? How could he declare victory? The next morning, I got a clue. I was sitting in the greenroom of WMUR, ABC-TV's Manchester, New Hampshire, affiliate, waiting to do my *GMA* hit. In walked a candidate acting every inch the winner. Surrounded by a throng of aides, he headed straight for a platter of glazed donuts and dug in. Clinton had the confidence of a candidate on a sure course toward victory.

A few minutes later, another candidate, toting a schoolbag, arrived. He had a single aide with him and seemed not all that sure of himself. He asked me if it would be all right if he took a donut. It was the winner of the New Hampshire primary, Paul Tsongas.

How much is political success based on self-confidence? The answer was right there on display in that *Good Morning America* greenroom.

There was another big story the morning after the New Hampshire primary. On the Republican side, archconservative Patrick Buchanan, known primarily as a debater on CNN's *Crossfire,* had just finished a strong second to President George H. W. Bush with 37 percent of the vote. His success at the ballot box was prophetic for his party and the country. For the first time since isolationists used it just prior to World War II, we heard the slogan "America First!" Buchanan was appealing to the nationalist sentiments of a region rocked by job losses. He blamed it on foreign trade and on the financial and academic elites who saw only the benefits of economic globalism. Pat Buchanan ran that campaign as anti-trade, pro-life, and pro-gun. He was an avatar of the right-wing leader who champions the cause of the working guy. Listen to him in that campaign: "These people are our people. They don't read Adam Smith or Edmund Burke, but they come from the same schoolyards and the same playgrounds and towns as we came from. They share our beliefs and our convictions, our hopes and our dreams. These are conservatives of the heart."

A quarter century later, another presidential candidate would raise up the Buchanan banner and appeal to the same people, the same resentments. Already in 1992 a maverick Texan, Ross Perot, appealed to the same base of antiestablishment voters. Seeming to have it in for Bush personally, he announced his intention to run as an independent two days after Bush had managed to beat Buchanan in New Hampshire. Perot then dropped out of the race in July only to return to it just five weeks before the November election. Promoting himself as an unassuming Washington outsider and successful businessman, he would end up with 19 percent of the vote. His final entry was clearly seen as hurting Bush more than Clinton even if it didn't alter the ultimate verdict.

I had several close-up encounters with Bill Clinton in that '92 campaign. One was an extended on-air interview with him before the California primary in late May. To his credit, he answered every question I threw at him. My second encounter was alone with him in Texas just after he'd accepted the nomination. He and his running mate, Senator Al Gore of Tennessee, were on their postconvention bus tour. As we sat in the back of the bus, Clinton said he was worried about something. He sensed the Republicans were about to dump something on him; some bit of embarrassing dirt meant to destroy him.

That afternoon in Georgetown, Texas, I caught a reporter's glimpse of how 1992 was going to end. I walked to a modest motel to use the restroom. On the way out, I asked the clerk at the front desk who he thought was going to win the election.

"I kinda think those two boys," he said in a local accent. *Those two boys.* It was a salute to Clinton's decision to double down on his southernness. In those few words, this local guy was saying that the "boy" from Arkansas had been darn smart to pick that "boy" from Tennessee as his political partner.

At a stop later that day, just around sundown, I watched Clinton work the country crowd, fielding questions in full southern accent.

"You, over there in the flat!" he called to one questioner in the outdoor crowd. *"You, over there in the flat!"* The Georgetown student sufficiently urbane to land a Rhodes scholarship was now the guy calling the Friday-night high school game. Or the auctioneer at the church fair. It was the local boy talking local. Could you imagine him talking like this up in New York?

Clinton's entire campaign was like this: talking to people where they're at. He was for "people who work hard and play by the rules." That was pure James Carville, and Clinton knew its truth. People who played by the rules were those people James was telling me about at that Italian restaurant the previous December. They were the people who worked to get through school, paid their taxes, and now all they wanted was a job to help them keep their family together.

Clinton was talking to people like me, too. He was promising to make abortion "safe, legal, and *rare.*" That was a direct pitch to those who accepted the moral teachings of their church but accepted the Supreme Court's ruling on what's implied in the Constitution. Clinton had a good sense of the undecided voter and the cultural factors that moved him or her. And that's how a Democrat beat a Republican president who just months before enjoyed a near 90 percent job approval rating.

I was in Little Rock on election night, writing my column. "In the early morning hours after victory here, Bill Clinton arrived torturously late to a rally of campaign workers. With confetti clinging to his coat, the president elect came to seal a covenant. He would not become, he swore, another prisoner of the White House. Rather than command we read his lips, the new leader committed himself to read ours.

"But who will make sure that he does? Who will whisper to him beneath the lilting strains of 'Hail to the Chief' that the music and the big-picture summitry and the White House itself are incidental to the job of rescuing the American dream?"

I was warning this young, newly elected president to avoid the hubris that brought down the man he'd just beaten. George H. W. Bush had won the presidency with the help of Peggy Noonan, the eloquent speechwriter from middle-class roots in New Jersey, and Lee Atwater, who had made his name running South Carolina campaigns against people named Turnipseed. But he turned to others when he took office.

If Bill Clinton is smart, I wrote, "the Arkansas governor will stay within complaining distance of those campaign folks who helped put him in a position to make that presidential promise."

What I didn't report that night was that William Jefferson Clinton had taught me a vital lesson for anyone in a public career: never let political adversaries or armchair critics, whether they're right or wrong, take you down.

CHAPTER THIRTY-THREE

A FAREWELL IN
NORTH CAMBRIDGE

I awoke in early January 1994 with a phone call from a producer at *Good Morning America*. Tip O'Neill had died overnight and they wanted me to talk about him. Once on-air, I became so emotional that my friend Charlie Gibson had to turn the camera from me.

Not long after, I received word that the O'Neill family wanted me to be an honorary pallbearer. With the funeral set for that Friday, Vice President Al Gore offered Kathleen and me a ride up to Boston on Air Force Two. It would be held at St. John the Evangelist Church, where the Speaker had been christened and where he'd married Millie. An honor guard of horses stood outside the church in the frigid cold. His son Tom's eulogy was warm, witty, perfect. The morning was altogether Irish, Catholic, and North Cambridge, a neighbor's funeral made national by the man's legacy. President Carter was there. So were the Republicans Bob Dole and longtime Illinois congressman Bob Michel, the men with whom he'd once shared the country's leadership.

I wrote about my boss in that day's *Boston Globe*:

O'Neill took pride in serving as Speaker of the House for the longest, unbroken stretch on record. . . . [But he] spoke not just to the House but to the American people. . . .

. . . Every cabdriver knew where he stood: for the little guy.

In a decade that applauded greed, Tip O'Neill made the unfashion-able argument for its victims. When [President] Reagan cut programs for the sick and the old and the poor, he beat the drum to save them. When the cuts stuck, he felt for the injured. . . .

Thomas P. O'Neill Jr. would have settled for a more traditional speakership.

More than any politician of his era, he loved the backroom jostle, the back-and-forth between close colleagues, the peacemaking, the deal making, all the indoor sports of politics best played without a camera in the room.

Going on television is something he did not for his ego but of necessity. His beliefs, his party, even the institution of the Congress, were under attack. He had no choice but to defend them.

Because he had the courage to stand alone, because he had beliefs, because he was a man of honor and color and good humor and great heart, he will go down as the Speaker of the century.

I have always been warmed by the experience of having stayed close to Speaker O'Neill in the years after he left office. He would invite me to lunch at the Palm, across from the law office he shared with his son Kip. Walking into that "power" restaurant with him was an honor. You could feel the noontime crowd watching the great man.

I have kept in touch with the O'Neills. They have so much right to be proud of the father they shared with the country.

That young guy who brought me into politics, Wayne Owens, once gave me a great bit of advice. He said that I should associate with good people. I am proud when people think of me as Tip O'Neill's guy. It says something about me—a truth about what I have done in life.

CHAPTER THIRTY-FOUR

BRINGING DOWN APARTHEID

I n 1948 the white voters of South Africa elected the National Party to power. With it came the enforced racial segregation known as apartheid. It instituted the principle and practice of white supremacy. Four decades later, the worldwide hostility to the South African government had made it a pariah. Many countries banned the nation from trade, entertainment, and, most important to many South Africans, sports.

In 1985 I accepted an invitation from Congressman Bill Gray and other African American members of Congress for a fact-finding trip to South Africa. Its purpose was to build the case for sanctions. I sat alongside the American delegation as it went face-to-face with President P. W. Botha, an apartheid hard-liner. The topic was the future of his country.

In 1989 a pragmatist, F. W. De Klerk, replaced Botha. Like Mikhail Gorbachev in the last months of the Soviet Union, his selection would prove historic, especially his decision the following year to release Nelson Mandela after twenty-seven and a half years in prison. What convinced me personally of De Klerk's sincerity was his removing the ban on both the African National Congress and the South African Communist Party. After the lifting of the Iron Curtain, De Klerk said that South Africa no longer needed to fear Soviet ambitions in the region. Legalizing the

ANC meant that the great black majority of South Africa would soon be in power. The new face of South Africa was about to emerge.

Nelson Mandela, sentenced in 1964 to life in prison for his antigovernment activities, stood as the most celebrated figure in his country, if not the world. He'd spent most of those years in an eight-by-seven-foot cell on Robben Island. He had refused to be set free until the ban on the ANC had ended. He wanted true national elections open to all races.

When De Klerk came to Washington in 1990 and met with reporters, I was not one of the skeptics. I knew there was no way Pretoria would legalize the ANC and the Communist Party if it intended to backslide. The whites of South Africa, led by De Klerk, had recognized the unstoppable power of history. Once the ANC offered candidates, the game would be over for De Klerk's Nationalists. The country was going to be ruled now by its black majority. By sheer numbers, the black vote would decide any election. The "winds of change" that British prime minister Harold Macmillan had foreseen in his 1960 address in Cape Town were finally sweeping across the land of the last holdouts.

The first all-races balloting was set for April 1994. ABC's *Good Morning America* sent me to cover it. It was another extraordinary chance to witness history. Soon after our arrival, the country was hit by violence. Right-wing terrorists were planting bombs to disrupt the arrival of black rule and, with it, the inevitable choice of Nelson Mandela as the country's president.

Our *Good Morning America* team began Election Day at the chapel of Archbishop Desmond Tutu in a leafy Cape Town neighborhood. There were just nine of us when he said a six o'clock morning Mass. His words were of reconciliation: "Thank you for bringing us to this day when all the people shall be able to vote for their elected government. We pray that you turn the hearts of those who want to use evil methods."

To sanctify that call for peaceful unity, Tutu spoke the words of the consecration in his native Xhosa and then in Afrikaans, the language of his oppressors. The Mass concluded, Tutu's car raced from the driveway to Gugulethu, one of the most desperate townships in the province. It's where a young American volunteer had been murdered by a mob, demonized during her killing as a "settler."

"He prays three times a day," an American divinity student told me as our car tried to keep up with the archbishop's. He was explaining that Tutu was sustained all those years by the power of his pulpit to pierce the silence that Pretoria had enforced on South Africa's opposition parties with guns, tanks, and prisons.

At sixty-two, he was now rushing to cast the first vote of his life. To cover that personal milestone, an ABC producer had put a microphone on Tutu to record his reaction on entering the voting station. "Yippee!" he cried out for dramatic effect as he relished the moment that had finally arrived.

"It is real," he said, slipping his marked ballot in the large metal box. "Friends, here we are. This is what we were all working for. Today we are all two or three inches taller."

I spent much of that morning with the archbishop as he journeyed from one voting area to another. Before us were lines stretching from one horizon to the other. Mixed in among the many blacks were a few white voters, including a young woman. "This is the day I've waited for *my* whole life," she said with the voice of a true believer.

Back at his residence, Tutu wanted to talk about the evil of apartheid. "It is very difficult to tell you how I felt," he said of being a black South African through all those years under white rule. He told me about returning home after his theological studies in London and how his young daughter, who had been born in England, spotted some children playing on a swing. She asked if she could, too. "And you had to say, 'No, darling, you can't.' And she didn't understand."

He spoke of the feeling he got at that moment "of being emasculated, dehumanized, because you couldn't look into the eyes of your child to tell her, 'No, darling, those swings are for the white children.'"

Tutu recalled witnessing a young white girl calling his headmaster father "boy." "And there was nothing much my father could do about it.

And you could see him grow small in your very presence, because he was embarrassed this was happening in front of his child.

"That was what apartheid has done, but it's done the same also to white people because it has made them undermine their own humanity."

That day of true national voting in South Africa had come at the demand of one man: Nelson Mandela. He had insisted on the right of his party to compete in the democratic process. He wouldn't leave prison without it.

That was this great man's legacy: a democratic South Africa. Many of us feared that change would come to South Africa only through horrific bloodshed in an all-out racial war. Mandela had insisted on a peaceful democratic transition of power.

Awaiting the results, I had a chance to interview Mandela in Johannesburg. With votes still to be counted, he was not ready to lay out his first steps in leading the country. "Well, I am reluctant to count my chickens before they've hatched." That said, he was quite ready to declare his and the ANC's principles.

Mandela envisioned "a South Africa that belongs to all its people . . . a country without racial discrimination. . . .

"We have used diversity to build a strong nation, unlike the National Party, which used those diversities to keep us divided and to foment racial hostility among South Africans. My vision of South Africa has been one which has a Bill of Rights which guarantees the right of every South African, regardless of race."

Mandela then offered a remarkable tribute to the United States: "The very first head of state to welcome me when I came out of prison and invited me to his country was President George Bush. . . .

"President Clinton has continued with that policy. He is one of those who listens very carefully to our requests, and he responds positively."

The American people, he continued, "have been among the most implacable, uncompromising enemies of racial discrimination generally, and in particular apartheid." I assumed he was referring to the tough economic sanctions in the Comprehensive Anti-Apartheid Act that members of the Congress such as Bill Gray and Mickey Leland had passed over Ronald Reagan's veto.

Mandela would invite three of his prison guards to his inauguration. "Even in the grimmest times in prison," he told me, "when my comrades and I were pushed to our limits, I would see a glimmer of humanity in one of my guards, perhaps just for a second, but it was enough to reassure me and keep me going. Never again shall it be that this beautiful land will again experience the oppression of one by another."

With our assignment completed in South Africa, my producers, crew, and I had a great wine-drenched lunch at the Mount Nelson Hotel, where my hero Winston Churchill had stayed after his escape from the Boers. We then headed over the border to Swaziland to do a story on the country where I'd spent those two life-changing years a quarter century before.

CHAPTER THIRTY-FIVE

TELEVISION

So much of my life has been driven by events and the people I've met. That was a rule in my first book: *It's not who you know; it's who you get to know.*

In the nineties, good fortune struck again. I went to dinner one evening at the Grill on the Alley in Beverly Hills with my college hero Joe McGinniss. He was researching a book on Senator Ted Kennedy. With dinner finished, he invited me to join him afterward at the Four Seasons, where he was meeting someone for drinks.

When Joe said it was Roger Ailes, I resisted. "He's the enemy," I said. He was the guy who'd cooked up the whole Republican assault on Mike Dukakis; the media consultant who helped craft the production of that "revolving door" ad about Willie Horton and the Massachusetts prison furlough system. Before that, Ailes had worked for Richard Nixon and Ronald Reagan.

Agreeing to join the two, I ended up telling Ailes about an idea I had for a half-hour weekly show. It would cover anything big that happened the previous seven days. It could be politics, popular culture, sports, whatever. It just had to be an event that would have merited placement in a time capsule or, at least, an old-time movie newsreel.

Roger picked up on the concept, taking the project seriously. When I visited him several months later at his communications firm in New York, he had worked it into a formal written proposal.

From there, events took hold. In 1993 Roger was named head of the four-year-old business news cable channel CNBC. Soon he took charge of a second cable channel that was christened America's Talking. It offered a full range of talk shows, many of them quirky, such as *Am I Nuts?*, featuring both a resident psychologist and a behavioral therapist; *Pork*, a show on government waste; and *Bugged!*, which highlighted all the things that aggravate people. Watching this carnival come to town, I called up Roger and prodded, "What about that show?"

Again he was quick to act. Ailes gave me the six-to-eight-o'clock evening time slot, the traditional news hours. He christened the program with a stately title: *A-T In-Depth*. He paired me as coanchor with Terry Anzur, a TV journalist who had gone to Stanford with Kathleen.

I was as disturbed and shocked as anyone to learn years later that Roger Ailes was a dark figure. A wealth of direct testimony describes an executive who again and again abused his power. The victims' accounts show a powerful man criminally robbing those under his authority of not only their human dignity but also their very *personhood*.

While short lived, America's Talking provided an opportunity for new people, me included, to get their start on TV. After calling Will Hearst, publisher of the *San Francisco Examiner* and getting his approval to do TV, I began a new daily ritual. I'd work at the Hearst bureau all day, and race from Pennsylvania Avenue over to the K Street studios for my second shift, arriving precariously close to *In-Depth*'s showtime. It was a familiar splitting of my day, something I'd done since being a Senate staffer in the morning and Capitol policeman in the evening. I was Clark Kent by day, a high-flying cable guy by night.

What made the daily preparation easy in those early months was the recurring story we were covering night after night: O. J. Simpson. The former pro football star was being tried for the murder of his former wife, Nicole Brown Simpson, and her friend Ron Goldman. Monday through Friday, we presented updates and arguments on the "Trial of the Century," which certainly lived up to its name. Every cabdriver had his or her radio tuned to the O.J. trial.

Covering the case, I noticed with each evening's edition the fickleness of our lawyer guests. In the greenroom, they spoke of the case being open and shut: O.J. did it. Once on camera, however, they would execute a predictable one-eighty. I have to assume they were hanging out their shingle. Potential clients are not looking for someone to dispense clear-eyed justice as much as they want someone to get them off.

The O.J. trial reached its climax in October 1995, when the jury, after about three hours of deliberation, stunned the country with a verdict of acquittal. The different reactions to that verdict would foretell the coming debate over the fairness of our criminal justice system. It showed how race, class, and money can weigh heavier on the scales than the facts of actual guilt.

Our day-to-day coverage of the trial exhibited something new in American journalism. Unlike other news programs, shows like *A-T In-Depth* were able to take a story like the O.J. trial and run with it. This allowed the most passionate viewers to follow the trial continuously, getting to know the case inside out. It showed what cable television could deliver: a daily look at the defendant, a sense of the other personalities, the twists and turns of the testimony. Cable TV was a new way to tell such stories.

Ernest Hemingway wrote of how much he enjoyed sitting in a Paris café catching up on the latest crime story in the newspapers. Every edition would deliver the latest developments in the case. In this way, there was always something to look forward to when you sat down in a café. This is precisely what it was like for the regular viewers of an evening cable show like we were doing for America's Talking.

I should add something about the impact of cable. People who like what you say—your *take* on the news—become your audience. It's the awesome human connection of television. Knowing the audience is out there becomes your company, just as you have become theirs. That bond of trust, even of affection, is in very human ways the best part of the job.

CHAPTER THIRTY-SIX

MOM

Mom died in September 1996. It had been a long time coming. She had suffered fifteen years from Alzheimer's. The symptoms had come quietly but undeniably. In the earlier days at their home in Ocean City, I found a bit of paper with a sentence she had tried, again and again, to complete but couldn't. It trailed off—brutal evidence of what was happening to someone who had done so much for us. Dad performed valiantly and patiently, caring for her to the height of his soul's endurance.

"How's Mom?" we'd ask.

"Classic," he'd answer. Thank God he'd read enough on the disease to recognize the pattern, to connect the clinical with what he was seeing. It saved him from self-doubt. Yet it's hard to think of all those times he got Mom in the car and drove around the block because Mom was so desperate to get "home." Or to imagine him alone with his thoughts as he bathed her and kept her clean. He hid so much of it from us. It was all a testament to the tough self-reliance of his Northern Irish mother. Dad was true to his deepest belief: you do your duty.

Dying the way Mom did was a long goodbye for Dad and my brothers. The memories fade as the distance grows, but not all. A good part of her remains with me. It's the Irish rebel that never quits, who struggles because it's what history requires.

Paying tribute to this gutsy Irish American we were lucky to have for our mother, I wrote in my column:

I have a picture of my mom, who died last week, from that grand trip we took to Washington in 1954. She's standing with her three oldest boys at this country's one, true national shrine, the Lincoln Memorial.

The picture tells quite a story, not just of four sunny days in Washington, but of my mother's aspirations for her five sons.

It is, I can see now a very American story. . . .

My mother had ambitions, most of all for her sons. When Dad got out of the navy at the end of World War II, she encouraged him to get his bachelor's degree under the GI Bill.

She and he made the even bigger jump of moving from the old church-dominated neighborhood to an area of converted farmland near Bucks County my grandparents would forever view as "God's country."

The move was symbolic of wider aspirations that would reveal themselves in the years to follow. . . .

. . . It was not the size of my dad's paycheck but the way both my parents . . . somehow managed to raise their children as upper-middle income.

My mother had known a far different childhood. College had been out of the question. The minute she graduated from high school, she was made to work and pay "board," turning over each pay envelope to her Depression-weary mother. . . .

The greatest restriction was on what she could do with her life. Ambition, like college, was not discussed. She was not expected to have any. She was expected to live just as she was raised herself.

Mom had other ideas. Just as she hoped, her greatest gift to us, her most loving legacy, was that most American of all notions: that the way things are is not necessarily the way they are going to be.

People, given the will, can choose to live very much differently than their parents did.

For Mom, and so many women of her generation, the obstacles to building her capabilities and realizing her dreams were insurmountable. Many of the doors that opened to me in my career did not open for women or for people of color, and still don't. The career privileges I enjoyed were not equally distributed, by any means.

CHAPTER THIRTY-SEVEN

CLINTON REDUX

In November 1994 the voters of America delivered Bill Clinton a come-uppance. It was much like what happened to him in Arkansas in 1980, when the voters there evicted him from the governor's mansion. Here again, he'd overplayed his hand. Two years earlier, Americans had chosen him as their president, a young newcomer who connected with them. He had campaigned as a champion of the working family. His slogans about sticking up for "people who work hard and play by the rules" struck a chord with moderate Democrats and independents.

In office, Clinton took a more progressive stance. Some of his actions would afford him his place in history. One of these was naming women's rights pioneer Ruth Bader Ginsburg to the Supreme Court. Her heroic record on behalf of gender equality has more than passed the test of time. It glows in the wide ambitions of young women who benefited from the horizons she widened.

Our family has witnessed the country's progress in this arena. When Kathleen played on the Stanford University tennis team, women were relegated to inferior courts, and members had to personally pay for travel to away matches. The enforcement of Title IX in 1972 would end such discrimination. Justice Ginsburg carried the fight forward. For our daughter, Caroline, who has earned degrees from the University of Pennsylvania, the John F. Kennedy School at Harvard University, and Stanford Business

School, Ginsburg is a larger-than-life figure, and young women like her face a better future.

Clinton's other first-term actions, while worthy as public policy, wrought electoral damage. He was criticized for raising taxes, and Hillary was excoriated for her ambitious but failed effort to create a national health care system.

The bottom line is that Bill Clinton's party took a beating in the '94 midterms, losing eight seats in the Senate and *fifty-four* in the House of Representatives. The Republicans won total control of the Congress for the first time since Dwight Eisenhower's first election in 1952. Democrats lost a dominance on Capitol Hill they had enjoyed back to the New Deal.

Clinton now acted to correct his course. Having lost confidence in his team, he brought in Dick Morris, a right-leaning media consultant, to tell him what to do. He signed a Republican-designed welfare reform bill, submitted to Speaker Newt Gingrich's push to lower federal deficits, and signed the Defense of Marriage Act, which defined marriage as between a man and a woman and allowed states to refuse to acknowledge same-sex marriages that occurred in other states. All this was to reposition himself politically for 1996.

What struck me, as the election approached, is how politically expedient the Clintons became. My feeling about some of the Clintons' behavior grew worse as I watched them invite wealthy campaign contributors to spend nights at the White House. They were using the historic residence as a Motel 6 for those rich enough to pay the fee. I didn't like the sleaze of it.

To secure a second term, the president was doing it all over again, including moving to the political center, where the decisive voters resided. To Clinton's credit, he refused to surrender on affirmative action; he stuck with his commitment to the cause of racial equality.

Clinton's opponent in 1996 was Bob Dole, a cloth-coat Republican like Dad, whose politics were not driven by tax bracket. There was nothing elitist about the man. His Republicanism was all *heartland*, all balanced budgets and prairie self-reliance. I liked him except when he was taking partisan shots at my boss Tip.

As usual, I was in New Hampshire for the 1996 primary. Our son Thomas was with me, getting his picture taken with many of the figures of American political lore. They included Senator Eugene McCarthy, the hero of the 1968 primary, who was working with a documentary team. Thomas was up on my shoulders when Senator Dole passed by after giving a speech. He asked me to call the primary. I didn't have the heart to tell him what I sensed coming. I gave him a verbal thumbs-up even though my reading of the polls told me Pat Buchanan was going to beat him. Which he did.

I believe Bob Dole, the man, never realized the affection so many people like me had for him. Like other World War II veterans, he was reserved in his emotions. Perhaps one reason he never blossomed as a presidential candidate is the lack of inner joy Americans like to feel from their leaders.

That November I voted for Bill Clinton. I did so despite his casual readiness to do whatever it took to get and stay ahead. Perhaps that's what it takes to reach the top.

By 1996, I was doing my own show on America's Talking. With that channel about to shut down, Ailes shifted *Politics with Chris Matthews* to CNBC. He himself began the process of starting Fox News. With the 1996 election behind us, Bill Clinton having easily won a second term, my new CNBC boss decided that politics alone couldn't carry a nightly show. He said I needed to change the direction of my program and, with it, the title.

So what would it be? Without hesitation, I suggested the name of my first book. On the spot, he agreed. For the next twenty-plus years, it was going to be *Hardball,* which was more centered on politics than ever.

What I didn't realize yet was how that name would mark the show's insistent character. *Hardball* was meant, by its nature, to push beyond what the politicians and their flacks were saying. It didn't mean combat, not necessarily, but it demanded toughness.

There was a well-learned reason for this approach. It arose from a vital insight picked up from my years working for politicians, one that was now driving me in my new role.

I knew that the words politicians speak are the best case they think they have. If a story is *better* than what you're reading in the newspapers or hearing on the TV news, you can count on the politician and his surrogates having told it. If the reality is *worse*, which it often is, they'll keep what they know to themselves.

That's the awful truth, and the reason I pressed hard all those years even at the expense of looking and sounding like a dentist leaning in with his drill. For that kind of persistence, I've learned there is a lone but great reward. It's when someone stops you in an airport or on the street to say, "I like the way you don't let them get away with anything!"

In early 1998 I was down in Saint Augustine, Florida, giving a lecture for an old friend at Flagler College, when the Bill Clinton–Monica Lewinsky story broke. It was just as I was about to mount the stage that I learned that the president had been caught in a scandalous relationship with a recent White House intern.

In his usual, well-practiced way, the second-term president found a timely escape route. Standing in the Roosevelt Room of the West Wing, he offered a blunt declaration of innocence: "I'm going to say this again: I did not have sexual relations with that woman . . . Miss Lewinsky."

That got him through the peak of the heat. Had he admitted guilt at that point, Clinton could well have faced a phalanx of Democratic leaders demanding his immediate resignation. By denying the relationship with Lewinsky outright, he forced his fellow Democrats to choose: they could either withdraw their attacks or call their president a liar.

By the time the evidence forced Clinton to confess, the pressure for him to resign had fizzled. He had outlasted the country's attention span, survived its moral opprobrium. His House impeachment in December 1998 didn't lead to conviction, only to a largely partisan vote in the Senate.

Looking back, I don't think many serious people thought Clinton should have been impeached. When the November 1998 midterm elections arrived, the Lewinsky story still dominated the news. Normally the party holding the White House loses seats in these elections, especially in second presidential terms.

But 1998 was the first time since 1822 this was not the case. The Democrats didn't lose a single seat in the Senate and netted five seats in the House. People thought the Republicans in Congress had overplayed their hand. This wasn't Watergate or anything like it.

You might call it a case of nationwide jury nullification. Whatever the evidence, Bill Clinton's misconduct was not seen as dangerous to the country. Besides, the forty-second president was popular, the economy was good, and, for the first time in decades, the federal government was operating at a surplus. This country's verdict on Bill Clinton was to keep him on the job.

CHAPTER THIRTY-EIGHT

GOOD FRIDAY

The dream of most Irish Americans, like me, has been to see their old country free, united, and at peace. As the end of the twentieth century approached, Ireland was divided and at war. In Northern Ireland, the nationalists, mostly Catholics who wanted the province to be reunited with the rest of the island, were treated as undesired, second-class citizens. The Protestant majority, called the unionists, was determined to remain within the United Kingdom.

The thirty-year war between the two sides was both bloody and cruel. By the late 1990s, nearly 3,500 people in Northern Ireland had been killed in an armed struggle that was called in ghastly understatement the Troubles.

It was hard for me to see this conflict apart from my own family's history. Dad was born to an Episcopalian father from England and a Presbyterian mother from Northern Ireland. Mom's parents were Irish Catholic, with American roots going back to the nineteenth-century potato famine. Mom and Dad married in defiance of all this. Whatever their positions on the marriage, both our sets of grandparents took my brothers and me into their hearts and kept us. We were theirs, and that was it.

I wanted the same peace back in Ireland. When news came in the spring of 1998 of the Good Friday Agreement, I was anxious to get over there. Ireland was at the precipice of a solid, positive step to peace between both sides—a real chance to end the Troubles and take Northern Ireland in the direction of true power sharing. Fortunately, I got the go-ahead from my editor at the *Examiner* to cover it.

Before heading off to Belfast, I picked up on the politics of the agreement from two of the top combatants in the thirty-year struggle. Martin McGuinness was once chief of staff to the Provisional Irish Republican Army, while David Ervine had once been affiliated with the Ulster Volunteer Force, which had planted bombs for his side. Despite their roles in the bloodshed, both supported a "yes" vote in the coming election. Both wanted an end to the violence. The killing had gone on too long and was getting nowhere. It was time to end it.

McGuinness made clear that his ultimate goal hadn't changed. He wanted a united Ireland but accepted that it would have to be done by the consent of Northern Ireland voters. In my column, Ervine expressed his support for the Good Friday Agreement somewhat differently. "We have to find a way to manage our enmity," he said. No one was going to forget the violence of the other side; they simply were going to now fight it out politically.

In Ireland, I interviewed people unwilling to forget, much less forgive. A Protestant in the unionist seaside town of Killeen told me what happened to his teenaged sons on a recent night in Belfast. They were surrounded by a group of young men who demanded to hear their religion. When they claimed, out of sheer fear, to be "Catholic," they were given a test: recite the rosary! Knowing they couldn't, they ran for their lives.

A leader of a women's peace group sized up the struggle with bitter succinctness: "We killed each other randomly because we didn't like the look on your face or your religion or your neighborhood."

The Good Friday Agreement, named for the day of Christ's crucifixion, was meant to end the Troubles. It resulted from strong pressure from the United States. Four leading Irish American politicians—Senators Ted Kennedy and Daniel Patrick Moynihan, Speaker Tip O'Neill, and New

York governor Hugh Carey—had joined together to oppose the violence. They'd taken a hard stance against the gunrunners, those Irish Americans who sent money to the Irish Republican cause irrespective of how it was to be used. They demanded that the conflicts in Northern Ireland be settled by politics and, for that, the flow of money from American sympathizers needed to stop. There could be no more arming the IRA. For their brave stand, they won the nickname "the Four Horsemen," an homage less to those figures of the Apocalypse than to the famous Notre Dame football team's backfield of the 1920s.

The Northern Ireland leader who recruited these men to the nonviolent cause was John Hume, who headed the Social Democratic and Labour Party. When I arrived in Northern Ireland in the days before the Good Friday referendum, I caught up with John as he was out canvassing. He was arguing the case for peace, if only on economic grounds, telling a small crowd that ending the Troubles would open the door to greater tourism. To do it, the people of Northern Ireland needed to accept that there are people who identify as British and those who identify as Irish. The way forward was for both sides to accept this fact.

My few days in Northern Ireland, rushing from one political event to the next, showed that Hume was hardly alone in wanting peace. I stood in Belfast's Ulster Hall as Protestant workingmen cheered the call for a peaceful end to sectarian fighting. The emotion in that room was strong, passionate, and from what I could tell, genuine.

However, the strains of resistance were also on vivid display. Its weapon was the same I'd witnessed in South Africa four years earlier: the bomb. The violence by dead-enders who were unwilling to compromise showed the resentment the peace agreement was likely to face, even if approved by the voters.

Religion was at the heart of it. The Protestant guy driving me around gave me a taste of it. He asked me why the Catholics in his country insisted on having their sons and daughters wear such colorful school uniforms. "Why can't they wear the same black-and-white uniforms as the Protestant kids? And why do Catholics insist on genuflecting every time they walk past a church?"

Well, the good guys won. In late May 1998 the people of Northern Ireland voted for the peace agreement. It created true power sharing between nationalist and unionist, declaring that any unification with the Republic of Ireland was decided by people in the voting booths. The Irish bloodshed was being replaced by a method of combat at which the Irish excel: *politics*.

CHAPTER THIRTY-NINE

MILLENNIAL

In January 2001 Bill Clinton left the country in sound economic shape, giving the Democrats good bragging points. The federal government recorded surpluses in fiscal years 1998, 1999, 2000, and 2001. After years of being denigrated as "deficit spenders," the Democrats had a president deserving of a victory lap for fiscal rectitude. Clinton's admitted misconduct with a young staffer, on the other hand, would leave the next Democratic nominee vulnerable, especially if it was his vice president.

The year opened with healthy fights in both parties. On the Democratic side, veep Al Gore was challenged by New Jersey senator Bill Bradley, the former basketball star at Princeton University and for the New York Knicks. Texas governor George W. Bush, the oldest son of George H. W. and Barbara Bush, faced Arizona senator John McCain.

It would be my fourth presidential election for the *San Francisco Examiner*. My first stop was to watch Governor Bush formally open his campaign in New Castle, New Hampshire. On spotting my arrival, Governor Bush let rip that the "big shots" were starting to show up. It was Bush the frat boy snapping his towel at me in the locker room.

One word had impressed me with Bush in that early going. It was his call for *humility* regarding the country's foreign policy. To me, that was a positive signal. After Ronald Reagan's adventures in Lebanon and Grenada, Bush's father's decision to fight the Gulf War, and Bill Clinton's leadership of the NATO air campaign in Kosovo in the late 1990s, I believed that America's penchant for resorting to war was becoming far too routine.

That winter, I followed our family ritual. This time it was Caroline's turn to travel along as we caught as many speeches as we could. Our youngest, just ten years old, proved quite the political analyst. "Do you know, Dad, what the difference is between Bill Bradley and George Bush? It's that Bradley has something to say, and George doesn't."

Caroline's assessment was shared by the Granite State's Republicans if not its Democrats. Bush lost, but so did Bradley.

John McCain now became the man to beat in the next primary, South Carolina, forcing the McCain-Bush battle into the center ring of the national media. For us, the premier event in South Carolina was the *Hardball* College Tour at Clemson University. Of all my nights of live television, these campus visits tended to be the most exciting. This turned out to be the most exciting of all. Sitting there onstage, with the Clemson band blaring and John McCain making his way up the aisle, I belted out the show opening: "From Clemson University, it's the *Hardball* College Tour!"

The next sixty minutes were the stuff of great live television: the bright lights, the music, the gung-ho candidate delivering answers to the hot questions of the moment.

This bringing the top candidates with us to college campuses was the best thing we did on *Hardball*. I thought it had a wonderful premise: a good way to bring young adults into the political conversation is to bring politics to them.

To make it a true meeting of minds, we let the students ask most of the questions. When the candidate refused to give a straight answer, I was ready to jump in and pursue a better answer.

As I said, Clemson was a great night for *Hardball*. When Senator McCain entered that auditorium, the hall exploded. He was greeted like a rock star!

The Vietnam War navy pilot, who'd been shot down over the enemy capital of Hanoi and then spent six years as a POW in the infamous Hanoi Hilton, was a great "get" for the evening. He was also a feisty guest. He gave the college crowd what it came for.

"We're going to take the influence of big money and special interests out of Washington," he promised. "We're going to break the iron triangle of money, lobbyists, and legislation and give the government back to these young people. They're the ones that deserve it, and they're the ones to get it when I'm president of the United States."

McCain was making the same appeal that I had a quarter century earlier as a young candidate taking on Philadelphia's downtown political machine. And it had the same appeal to the young in 2000 as it did in 1974. If the voters would take away power from the entrenched campaign donors, they could take back their democracy. The people would be calling the shots. The regular people, who get out there and work for the candidates, would be the fat cats. Sadly, McCain's full-throated case failed to achieve the goal. Campaign contributions continue to open doors on Capitol Hill. Lobbyists continue to work the iron triangle of fund-raising, grateful lawmakers, and special interest legislation.

Later that night, after our big show at Clemson, Congressman Lindsey Graham took my executive producer, Phil Griffin, and me to a rural restaurant for spaghetti and meatballs. It was along a railroad track and couldn't have been more hardscrabble America. I thought that night Lindsey's friend and candidate was going to really shake things up in the country. After watching the delight and excitement of the Clemson crowd, I wondered how anyone could beat John McCain, this maverick who'd just beaten a president's son in New Hampshire.

I was on the verge of discovering that there were larger, darker forces operating in South Carolina. "A more menacing storm of anger belts through South Carolina these days before the February 19 primary," I wrote in my column. "It's the wild and angry forces of the GOP establishment. It's the Republicans that McCain's insurgent campaign has threatened and aroused. It's the corporate power boys who don't mind paying the toll in DC as long as they get value for it."

To ensure that the McCain campaign died in South Carolina and stayed dead, Bush's allies were waging a race-baiting campaign from the bad old days. The story was pushed out that the McCains' adopted daughter, Bridget, born in Bangladesh, was, in fact, his natural daughter by an African American. As an added touch, a story was sent around that McCain's wife, Cindy, was a drug addict.

South Carolina Republicans ended up voting for whom they had been told. The smears worked. It's a fact of politics I don't like but have come to recognize. Once dirt is thrown on a candidate, it's hard to get it off. Once a suspicion is raised, through whispers or push polling (the tactic of spreading a story by presenting it in a question) or social media, it stays raised. What was done to Michael Dukakis in 1988 had been done to John McCain. Once again it was race. The specter of Willie Horton had been replaced by the age-old fear of miscegenation.

That fall of 2000, with the presidential election just over the horizon, attention shifted to the three scheduled debates between Vice President Gore and Governor Bush. The matchup that mattered most, I decided, was the last one. I've watched a particular moment of it again and again on YouTube. It's when Gore left his stool and walked across the stage to Bush, then stood there in his face.

"What about the Dingell-Norwood bill?" he demanded. Gore did so as if the huge national TV audience, or his opponent, had some notion of what he was talking about. In fact, he was referring to long-pending legislation that would regulate the practices of managed health care plans. In political terms, he may as well have been asking, "What about the Easter Bunny?"

Bush's reaction was to offer a light, sarcastic bow of recognition and continue talking. The audience broke into laughter. That audience reaction matched my own. The vice president of the United States had attempted a power play that had just fallen flat.

The numbers prove it. In the month before the debates, Gore led Bush 47 to 44 percent in the Gallup poll. In the fifteen days afterward, Bush led Gore 47 percent to 44 percent. Some awkward fumbles would cause Gore to throw away that lead by the election.

Anchoring the year 2000 election results would mean a long night for me. At 7:50 that evening, November 7, NBC called Florida for Gore. Other networks followed. CNN then retracted its call, saying it was too close to call. The Associated Press did the same.

At 2:16 the next morning, the networks, but not the AP, began calling Florida and the election for Bush. Gore, operating on the same information as them, called his opponent to concede.

But by 4:00 a.m., however, NBC and ABC had retracted their call for Bush, agreeing now with the AP that it was too close to call. Gore, again responding to the changing situation, called Bush back and retracted his concession in a testy exchange between the two men.

Bush, striking a superior pose, acted now as if Gore had broken a gentleman's code. Surrounded by his parents, his attitude struck me as dynastic. How dare this Gore fellow think he has a right to take back a victory he had already conceded? Bush was acting as if Gore's words on the phone counted more than the actual vote.

I remember seeing the sun come up outside 30 Rockefeller Center. And with it, I recall with the same delight, came a box of glazed donuts. It had been a hectic, hungry night.

For the next five weeks I stayed in New York. I increasingly admired the job MSNBC was doing covering the recount in Florida. Thanks to people on the ground like our friend Alan Fein, a politically active Miami attorney with whom I had worked at the White House, we were getting an excellent, up-to-date picture of the Florida drama.

This was best exhibited when a Democratic vote counter held up a disputed ballot to a light and pronounced it for Gore. He was followed by a Republican holding up the same ballot to the same light and declaring with equal seriousness it was a vote for Bush.

It wasn't just individual certifiers who were counting the ballots differently. The Florida counties were. This was the justification for the US Supreme Court's getting into it. On December 12, it ruled by a vote of 7 to 2 that Florida's recount, which was based on counties using different standards in certifying ballots, violated the Equal Protection Clause of the Fourteenth Amendment, which requires states to treat an individual in the same manner as others in similar conditions and circumstances.

The high court ruled that it wasn't fair to have one county declare a voter's intention valid and another county saying a similar ballot was not.

But then, by a 5-to-4 decision, it declared that, given the Electoral College deadline, there was no alternative but to accept the election result certified earlier by the Florida secretary of state, the one showing George Bush the narrow winner. Despite his having lost the national popular vote by 547,398, Florida's 25 electoral votes propelled Bush just over the 270 threshold needed to win. The last time a candidate ascended to the White House under these circumstances, losing the popular vote but winning in the Electoral College, was in 1888, when Benjamin Harrison lost by 90,000 votes but defeated President Grover Cleveland.

Before 2000 I found it hard to imagine a candidate who finished second in the popular vote could strut comfortably into the presidency. George W. Bush crushed that notion. He took his victory with an air of easy entitlement. Al Gore conceded his loss in the Electoral College with patriotic grace. He did so in words and cadence that paid homage to that greatest appeal for healing, Abraham Lincoln's second inaugural address, in which he spoke of how neither side wanted the great struggle between North and South, but then "the war came." Gore said that neither he nor Bush anticipated the long and difficult recount, "yet it came."

The 2000 election saw the triumph of another figure from the recent presidency. Hillary Rodham Clinton could have rested on her laurels as a former First Lady. Instead, she stuck her neck out and ran for the US Senate from New York, a feat equal to what Robert Kennedy did on leaving the attorney generalship in 1964.

There is little doubt, however, that Bill Clinton's misconduct in office damaged his vice president's chances. From the outset of the campaign, Bush promised that if elected, he would uphold the "honor and dignity" of the office. Everyone saw it as a direct shot at both Clinton and Al Gore, who had boldly defended him the day of his impeachment by the House of Representatives.

Gore, apparently relying on the same research as Bush, had decided to keep his distance from Clinton. One candidate was pushing the "Monica" story in voters' minds, the other trying to push it aside by banishing Clinton himself to the sidelines. I think Al Gore would have been a stronger candidate had he broken with Clinton on the Monica affair at the time of the impeachment and teamed up in defending the president's *policies*. That would have been masterful. Sadly for Gore, he did the opposite, cheerleading for Clinton the day of his impeachment, but then separating from him throughout the 2000 campaign.

The approaching new millennium—January 1, 2001—would bring an epiphany that, for a good while, would unite us. It was a healing force that rebounded from an attack on the country itself.

CHAPTER FORTY

ATTACK ON A SEPTEMBER MORNING

In just one morning, nineteen foreign terrorists used four American passenger planes to murder nearly three thousand people. At little financial cost to the perpetrators, they destroyed those towering symbols of this country's economic power, the World Trade Center. They struck the command center of the US military, the Pentagon. Were it not for the courage of passengers in the Pennsylvania sky, they might have demolished the Capitol as well.

Like everyone else, I remember where I was when the World Trade Center news hit. For me, Tuesday, September 11, 2001, began normally. I was on the phone with executive producer Phil Griffin. We both had the *Today* show on our televisions when a plane crashed into the North Tower. At first, it was assumed to be the result of a flying accident involving a private plane. That notion died a sudden death when the second jet slammed into the South Tower. Americans knew they were under attack.

Kathleen and I were headed that morning to a funeral service for our friend Joan Gardner at Saint John's Episcopal Church, located on the north side of Lafayette Square, across from the White House. When we sang "America the Beautiful," it was with special meaning, particularly the lines "Thine alabaster cities gleam / Undimmed by human tears!" I don't imagine any of us could get out of his or her mind what was happening up in New York. All we knew was the news we'd seen before our arrival at the church—that and the noise of sirens and general commotion through the walls.

Once out on Sixteenth Street, we could see people all caught in the same moment of uncertainty. The news about the Pentagon, right across the Potomac River from us, getting hit was now all around. Somehow I made it to the NBC studios out on Nebraska Avenue and went to work.

We spent the day watching the towers crumble. We shuddered at the horror of those who'd been stranded on the upper floors. We began, each of us, gauging the malice of those who would coldly design and execute such a plan.

In the hours and days ahead, we would also contemplate the courage shown by the firefighters who climbed the stairs of the towers as others raced down.

The Friday after the attack, President Bush flew to New York to visit Ground Zero. He had come to thank those working in the recovery effort, still searching through the rubble for human bodies.

"Thank you all," he said through a bullhorn. "I want you all to know that America today is on bended knee in prayer for the people whose lives were lost here, for the workers who work here, for the families who mourn."

Then came a moment that elevated the American spirit.

"I can't hear you!" a recovery worker yelled from well in back.

Now came Bush's roar.

"I can hear *you*! The rest of the world hears you! And the people who knocked these buildings down will hear from all of us soon!"

From all around, we could now hear the cheering. "USA! USA! USA! USA! USA! USA! USA! USA!"

Here was a stunned nation coming out of its shock. Here was a leader's guarantee that action would be taken, that we were not at the will of our enemies, that we, the people of the United States, were going to now take charge. President Bush was voicing the country's resilience. As I wrote:

"For the first time in our collective national memory, mainland American civilians know what it's like to be on the punishing end of battle. We have been hit, hurt, and, say what you will, humbled. . . .

"The question now is how to carry out justice toward those who attacked us without stirring further spin-offs of hatred, terrorism, and death."

Bush soon sent forces to Afghanistan, the country that had harbored the terrorists of 9/11. Here at home, if ever so briefly, we became a different country. You could feel it on the streets and subways of New York.

I was now writing for the *San Francisco Chronicle,* which the Hearst Corporation had bought to replace the *Examiner.* A late-September column dealt with how the emotional reaction differed from the days after the assassination of President Kennedy. "September 11, 2001, brought life to our sense of nationhood," I observed.

"This feeling is the silver lining to this cloud of gloom."

A Gallup poll showed that Americans accorded the highest moral prestige to two professions: firefighters and nurses. I wrote of the changes in New York itself. "There's better eye contact out in the streets than there used to be. People are talking to the people they meet in the elevator, the bar, the coffee line. 'Hello' has replaced the averted glance."

There was something else: an urban serenity. I heard it in the wail of the saxophone a guy was playing on a New York subway train. Was it the sense of being in this thing together, like Londoners during the blitz? Like the horror in Dallas four decades before, the country had been wounded in its certainties.

But what next? Before the month of September was out, I began worrying about where the American reaction to 9/11 would take us. I feared our actions could only lead to something worse. As a run-up to the Gulf War, we had put our troops in the sacred land of Saudi Arabia. Then, in its wake, we had placed economic sanctions on Iraq. In the Middle East, both actions were being used to recruit terrorist fighters against us, like those who hit us on September 11. Wouldn't a larger US response lead to more recruitment?

By early October, the US and its allies had combat forces arrayed in Afghanistan. Their mission was to overthrow the Taliban government that had been harboring the terrorist organization Al Qaeda, cofounded by the mastermind of the 9/11 ambushes, Osama bin Laden. By mid-December, our mission was accomplished. The Taliban was out of power.

I worried Bush was being encouraged to go further. I had gotten a tip that Deputy Defense Secretary Paul Wolfowitz was openly pushing war with Iraq, a country with no known involvement in the September attacks. He had raised the issue, only to be quieted, at the president's first post-9/11 meeting at Camp David. I hoped this talk of "Iraq" had been stopped. My big fear was that we would repeat the Vietnam experience, digging ourselves into a wider war in the Islamic world.

By November, I was voicing my fears on *Hardball* about a US attack on Iraq. "We should not go to war with Iraq unless we have solid evidence they were connected with the September 11 attack," I asserted.

That December, I kept it up. "Like victors before him, President Bush is being tempted with greater glories in the days ahead," I wrote. "He is considering following his triumph in Afghanistan with a more magnificent destruction of Saddam Hussein.

"It's a bad idea. If it was in my power to stop him, I would. . . .

"I have given up trying to understand the thinking of those who agitate for such a wrong and tragic course against Saddam Hussein. They try—and fail—to blame him for September 11" . . . "Yet their inability to nail him only adds to their resolve."

The year was not over yet, and we were already on the death track.

CHAPTER FORTY-ONE

A WAR OF OUR CHOOSING

I was afraid of where the war hawks were taking us and that the passions of this country were being exploited. We had gone into Afghanistan to punish those who had given haven to the 9/11 terrorists. Now we were being pushed to another agenda that preceded the 2001 attack.

In 1998 the advocates for war with Iraq had pushed the Iraq Liberation Act through Congress. It called for the United States to support efforts to remove the regime in Baghdad. As we now entered 2002, the drumbeat for war with Saddam Hussein had grown louder, more persistent. All my life, we had seen the aggressor as the bad guy. It's why we had fought the Nazis and Japan in World War II; why we opposed the Soviet Union. Yet the White House was talking about going to war with a country that hadn't attacked us. What had happened to George W. Bush's call for "humility" in foreign policy?

"I worry that the United States is going to invade Iraq," I commented on *Hardball* in February. By August I had begun to write about the coming loss of lives on both sides if the conflict led to war. "I worry about huge casualties by us, greater casualties by the Iraqis."

The op-ed pages were packed with voices calling for war. Why were the American people being pushed so blindly into this fight? Was there evidence that Iraq had something to do with 9/11? Did we have proof that Saddam Hussein had nuclear weapons and might arm a terrorist group?

"If we still have to figure out why we're going to war with Iraq," I argued, "don't we have a problem right there?"

Vice President Dick Cheney kept offering arguments for military action against Saddam's regime:

"We know he's got chemical and biological."

"We know he's working on nuclear."

Again and again, the Bush war hawks exploited the acronym WMD—weapons of mass destruction—to suggest without proof that Saddam Hussein possessed nuclear weapons.

On September 8, 2002, the *New York Times* ran a headline, "US Says Hussein Intensifies Quest for A-Bomb Parts." It quoted "American officials" as saying that Iraq was trying to buy specially designed aluminum tubes needed to help produce nuclear material.

That Sunday, Dick Cheney showed up on *Meet the Press* to push the bogus "aluminum tubes" story. "We don't want the smoking gun to be a mushroom cloud," National Security Adviser Condoleezza Rice warned those wanting harder evidence of an Iraqi nuclear weapons program.

That claim about the aluminum tubes was leaked to the *Times* by people who knew better. There was no hard evidence of an Iraqi nuclear weapons program because there *wasn't* any such program. What did exist was a president, a vice president, and a band of like-minded hawks who wanted war with Iraq far more than they wanted the truth.

Once the Congress passed the resolution authorizing the use of force against Iraq in October 2002, the die was cast. The only question about the invasion of Iraq was the date. "What's to stop the president now?" I challenged the Democratic senators such as Hillary Clinton, Joe Biden, and John Kerry, who'd all voted for the resolution. "You gave him a blank check."

The United States invaded Iraq in March 2003. The president took the congressional Iraq War resolution as constitutional justification. More than four thousand Americans were killed in the Iraq War. A minimum of a hundred thousand Iraqi soldiers and civilians would die in the conflict.

Near the end of his life, Senator Ted Kennedy would call his "nay" vote on the war resolution the most important vote of his Senate career.

What I found calamitous was that a president of this country was able to change the standard by which we, the American people, go to war. We had chosen to attack another country, overthrow its leaders, and kill anyone who got in our way.

Why did so many Democratic senators go along with this? Why did the media cheerlead with such docility? Why did this country allow a clique of ideologues to sell the argument that this war would advance the cause of "freedom"? Why did a phrase like "regime change" become an American goal? Why did we allow WMD to mean nuclear weapons? How did the suspicion that a country had WMD justify a war? And why did we ignore the prime lesson of Vietnam: that the people who determine a land's future are those who remain when the outsiders have left? Where were the hawks when America was taught this lesson on the streets of Saigon?

During the run-up to the Iraq War, I found myself making a difficult transition professionally. NBC had awarded me a new weekend broadcast in addition to *Hardball* on MSNBC Monday through Friday. The combination of anchoring weekday evenings and taping the new show each Friday for Sunday broadcast made it impossible to turn out quality work for the *San Francisco Chronicle*.

New York Times columnist Frank Rich, who went on to produce the hit TV series *Veep* and *Succession*, once compared writing a column to living under a windmill. Yet it was those twice-a-week deadlines that charged me—not just keeping up with the news but also thinking *through* it. And yet I couldn't do it all.

I made a point to use my last *Chronicle* column to speak out strongly against the attack I saw Bush launching on Iraq:

So, I'll say it. I hate this war that's coming in Iraq. I don't think we'll be proud of it. We Americans are reluctant warriors. We fight when attacked. We didn't invade Cuba when we learned the Russians had missiles there. We didn't want to do to them what the Japanese had done to us.

I'm afraid this crowd about President Bush would have. They also would have gone to an all-out war a generation later when those Iranian students grabbed our diplomats.

I oppose this war because it will create a millennium of hatred and the suicidal terrorism that comes from it. . . .

Maybe it's the Peace Corps still in me, but I don't think we win friends or—and this is more important—avoid making dangerous enemies in the third world by making war against it.

CHAPTER FORTY-TWO

BARACK OBAMA

By 2004, this country had witnessed 9/11, a US attack on Afghanistan in 2001, and another on Iraq in 2003. We were looking for a leader to soften our division, remind us of our moral strength, our *specialness*. We needed a spiritual pick-me-up.

For me and millions of others, it appeared before us at the 2004 Democratic convention in Boston. Through the influence of Louis Susman, a major Democratic backer from Chicago, presidential nominee John Kerry had chosen an Illinois state lawmaker running for the US Senate to deliver the keynote address.

That evening, young Barack Obama showed the power of gifted oratory.

"Let's face it," he said to break the ice, "my presence on this stage is pretty unlikely." He was drawing the audience to what it knew already: his remarkable background as the son of a Kenyan father and a midwestern American mother. Just as important, he was telling them that he, the guy up there on that podium, knew *precisely* how he was being seen.

With that self-aware opening, Obama was honoring the Bobby Kennedy rule to *always hang a lantern on your problem*. Don't leave an audience to whisper about what sets you apart; spell it right out for them. He spoke of how his father, "born and raised in a small village in Kenya," had won a scholarship to study "in a magical place, America, which stood as a beacon of freedom and opportunity to so many who had come before." It was the immigrant's story: the story of aspiration. He was including himself not as part of an ethnic minority but as "part of the larger American story."

Obama then gave the greatest tribute to what, in my opinion, is the heart of our country's prized exceptionalism: "In no other country on earth is my story even possible." He was introducing himself not only as witness to this exceptionalism but also as its living, glittering incarnation.

> Tonight we gather to affirm the greatness of our nation, not because of the height of our skyscrapers, or the power of our military, or the size of our economy. Our pride is based on a simple premise, summed up in a declaration made over two hundred years ago, "We hold these truths to be self-evident, that all men are created equal. That they are endowed by their Creator with certain inalienable rights. That among these are life, liberty and the pursuit of happiness."
>
> This is the true genius of America, a faith in the simple dreams of its people, the insistence on small miracles. . . . That we can say what we think, write what we think, without hearing a sudden knock on the door. That we can have an idea and start our own business without paying a bribe or hiring somebody's son.

Anchoring that night for MSNBC, I had come across a rarity: a genuine political hero. Here was this guy a generation younger than me radiating what I wanted most to hear: the hope of a united country, one that was ready to include a Barack Obama at the very top.

"I have seen the first black president there," I declared from my anchor chair in Quincy Market, "and the reason I say that is because, I think, the immigrant experience, combined with the African background, combined with the incredible education, combined with this beautiful speech. . . . That speech was a piece of work."

I made that assessment after years of seeing the great speeches at Democratic conventions, the best inevitably delivered by someone other than the nominee. They included Eugene McCarthy (1960), John Pastore

(1964), Barbara Jordan (1976), Ted Kennedy (1980), Mario Cuomo (1984), and Jesse Jackson (1988).

Obama's speech, which joins that list, wasn't broadcast live by the major networks, ABC, CBS, or NBC. Fortunately, we at MSNBC did put it on the air. I doubt we will see another speech like it for some time.

When Obama stood at the podium in Boston that night, he had not yet been elected to the US Senate. It was soon after the 2004 election that he decided not to stop there.

CHAPTER FORTY-THREE

DUEL

In 2004 I was the lone MSNBC anchor covering the Republican convention at New York's Madison Square Garden. Our base of operations was an outdoor studio on Herald Square, several blocks away. We had Broadway traffic on both sides and a revved-up crowd watching from the curb.

Even with the anchor desk and security to protect us, we were exposed. On one night, a protester dressed in a peaked hood and dark gown, to resemble the abused prisoners at Abu Ghraib prison in Iraq, jumped across the guard fence and directly onto me. Chris Pietrich, the security professional who was serving as my bodyguard, threw him to the ground so fast it caused my colleague Howard Fineman to execute a perfect Hollywood double-take.

But the moment most *Hardball* viewers remember is what came the third night of the GOP convention. The person chosen to deliver the convention's keynote was a Democrat, Senator Zell Miller, who would be retiring from politics come January. The former Georgia governor had announced earlier that year his intention to support President Bush. A stem-winder of the old school, Miller got right to his point.

"My family is more important than my party," he began. With that bugle call echoing through the Garden, he listed one national defense system after another that Democratic presidential candidate John Kerry had voted against. He told how each of those weapons, starting with the B-1 bomber, had been crucial to US military action in the Gulf War, Afghanistan, and the 2003 assault on Iraq. He asked how Kerry intended to defend the country. "With spitballs?"

It was the classic keynoter, aimed at firing up the party loyalists, stirring the delegates and those watching from home. Where I felt Miller crossed the line was not his bellicosity against Kerry, Ted Kennedy, and the Democrats generally. It was his shot against the media.

"It's the soldier, not the reporter, who has given us the freedom of the press."

It struck me that Senator Miller's comments bordered on militarism—that we owed our rights to those in the government who'd been issued guns. Didn't the Declaration of Independence say we were endowed liberty "by our creator"?

Just as bad, Miller suggested the media was guilty of undercutting those at the war front; that those of us who wrote or spoke out against the Iraq War had American blood on our hands.

Minutes later, the man who made these charges appeared on the giant TV screen before me as my guest on *Hardball*. He was clearly ready to fight. Based on what followed, Miller wasn't the only one.

"I want to ask you about the most powerful line in your speech, and it had so many. Do you believe that John Kerry and Ted Kennedy really only believe in defending America with spitballs?"

"Well, I certainly don't believe they want to defend America by putting the kind of armor and the kind of equipment that we've got to have out there," he replied.

"I'm just asking you, Senator, do you mean to say—I know there's rhetoric in campaigns—that you really believe that John Kerry and Ted Kennedy did not believe in defending the country?"

"Wait a minute, I didn't . . . I didn't question their patriotism," he responded.

"Do you believe they don't believe in defending the country?" I pressed.

"I question their judgment."

Things were about to escalate.

"I want to try to be as nice as I possibly can to you," he said. "I wish I was over there where I could get a little closer up into your face."

On hearing these fighting words, the crowd leaning in from the sidewalk started to go wild. I now attempted to reach common agreement. I asked Senator Miller to agree that Democrats often call Republicans "heartless" for voting against massive spending bills. Weren't he and the Republicans now doing the same thing on defense spending, calling the Democrats pacifists because they don't go along with big Pentagon bills?

I don't think he was picking up on my point. Maybe he couldn't hear it through the din.

"You're saying a bunch of baloney. . . . You've got to quit taking those Democratic talking points," he said.

"No, I'm using your talking points and asking you if you really believe them."

"I think we ought to cancel this interview."

"Well, that would be my loss, Senator," I said. "That would be my loss." And I meant it.

By now, the crowd was roaring. My executive producer, Tammy Haddad, was, as usual, connected to me by my earpiece. Now I heard the voice of Rick Kaplan, the MSNBC president.

"Savor it," Rick encouraged me, hoping I would not let the fish off the hook. *Stretch it out.* He was counting on that odd symbiosis that gives those watching another channel time to realize there's something happening elsewhere and go looking for it.

I now asked my guest why he had said in his speech that it's "not the reporter" who fights for freedom of the press but the "soldier." Was that just "an applause line" against the media at a conservative convention? A cheap shot?

"You're hopeless," came Miller's answer. "I wish I was over there. I wish we lived in the day . . ."

"I've got to warn you," I interrupted. "We are in a tough part of town over here. But I do recommend you come over because I like you."

That teasing of mine now elicited the line of the night, the week, perhaps the year, certainly on *Hardball:*

"Get out of my face! If you're going to ask me a question, step back and let me answer. *I wish we lived in the day where you could challenge a person to a duel. Now, that would be pretty good.*"

Hearing him throw down the gauntlet, I upgraded my invitation for him to join me over at Herald Square. "Can you come over? I need you, Senator. Please come over."

"You get in my face," he now threatened, "I'm going to get back in your face."

"You'll help our ratings tremendously if you come over tomorrow night because everybody thinks you are going to beat me up."

I was working now, as I usually was, for the NBC team.

TV Guide would call that over-the-top exchange among the most "unexpected moments in television history." For weeks thereafter, *Saturday Night Live* did sketches poking fun at that night's spectacle, especially at Senator Miller.

In all honesty, I worried that it was for real; that Miller was so overwrought that he might mean that stuff about a duel. I imagined myself, like the fated Alexander Hamilton, standing on a bluff over the Hudson River with someone asking me to choose in this latter-day contest between a pair of old Confederate pistols.

The next day, I got the verdict on my bout with Senator Miller. It came from an unlikely umpire. California's Republican governor, Arnold Schwarzenegger, who had addressed the convention earlier, was on the phone. "He gave you a million dollars in publicity!" he said. "He should be having lunch with you right now, making friends."

Years later I wrote to Senator Miller. I told him how I admired and respected his service as a marine and later in public office, and didn't think our encounter in New York was worthy of it; that I didn't feel right about how it came off.

In return, I received a powerful letter from the retired senator. He said that night had been bothering him all the years since and that he appreciated my sharing my feelings with him. He was admitting that, like me, he knew what it was like to have had a bad night, to say things that, upon minimal reflection, you would have avoided. Miller's letter was warm, generous—an elevation for both of us. He died not long after.

CHAPTER FORTY-FOUR

A FUNERAL IN ROME

In April 2005 I was given the historic opportunity to go to Vatican City for the largest gathering of world leaders outside the United Nations since the death of British prime minister Winston Churchill. Ten kings, six queens, and at least seventy presidents and prime ministers came together for the funeral of Pope John Paul II. As a journalist, it was my chance to cover one of the great world occasions. As a Roman Catholic, being in Vatican City for those days was powerfully spiritual.

Politically, John Paul II had been a figure of history. Everyone from Mikhail Gorbachev to President George H. W. Bush, both of whom attended the funeral, credited the late pope as a vital catalyst to the fall of the Iron Curtain. His election by the College of Cardinals in 1978 and his dramatic return to his native Poland the following year gave a powerful thrust to those wanting Eastern Europe liberated.

I spent the week of the funeral anchoring from Gianicolo, the hill overlooking St. Peter's Square, which gave me a direct line of sight on the long procession of people waiting to view the open casket of the late pope. What impressed me was their sacrificial patience. They were packed so tightly together they could barely move.

I wondered at the Romans' devotion to this Polish pope. That week I learned a partial reason for it. All politics is *local*. John Paul II, I was told, had taken his role as bishop of Rome to heart. Each week, he would try to visit one of the Eternal City's parishes. He would have dinner with the priests on Saturday night, say Mass on Sunday morning, then meet with the children in the parish hall. By the time he died, John Paul had paid weekend visits to most of the city's three-hundred-plus parishes. The Romans remembered this.

Next in line were the Poles, men and women who held a deep devotion to their compatriot and had traveled by bus and car to be there. They, too, waited for hours to see their liberator a last time.

Joseph Ratzinger, dean of the College of Cardinals, delivered the funeral oration. Listening to his address, I felt pulled back into my role as political pundit. I had the powerful sense he was setting himself up for succession. It reminded me of Mark Antony's funeral oration for Julius Caesar. Indeed, two weeks later, he was elected to replace the beloved John Paul II, as Pope Benedict XVI.

What I remember most of those nights on Gianicolo was the music that played in a loop through the week. We would go live at eleven at night Rome time to hit our five o'clock *Hardball* showtime on the East Coast. I had the same feeling on those nights that I would reliably get whenever I'm in Rome or Jerusalem: a sense of being in the right place for me—in this case, at an important time. As a Catholic, it was one of my life's great honors.

A year later came another funeral, one closer to home. Kathleen and I were in Rhode Island for the wedding of our nephew Brian, son of my brother Jim and his wife, Karen. Dad was so excited about the occasion bringing the whole extended family together. He said it was the "happiest night" of his life. At midnight, when we returned to the hotel, Dad didn't want it to end. Though Kathleen and I had decided to call it quits, my nephew Jimmy told me Dad stayed out until two in the morning.

Two hours later, I got a call from his wife, Trude, whom he'd married soon after Mom's death. Dad had suffered a heart attack. He died in the ambulance, with my brother Jim holding tightly to his hand.

All my adult life, my father had been a model for me. Like so many of his World War II generation, he made no excuses, made no complaints, and did his duty to country and to our family. Mom and Dad maximized what they could do for their five sons, minimized the luxuries they accepted for themselves. If love can be measured in service, the two of them gave all they could. I think of Dad, in particular, whenever I reread *The Giving Tree* by Shel Silverstein. He gave all he could for my brothers and me. He took care of Mom to the end, never complaining of this unexpected burden. He found happiness in what was left to him. He loved his sons, his friends, his life. He found happiness in what was his. I wish I could have brought myself to tell him all this when I could. That goes for Mom, too.

CHAPTER FORTY-FIVE

THRILL

On a February day in 2007 in Springfield, Illinois, Senator Obama announced his candidacy for president. It was below twenty degrees that morning. I had heat pads in my shoes and an electric heater at my legs. I couldn't help but think of my cameraman, who had none of this protection against the brutal elements.

There before us was the radiant Obama family—Barack, Michelle, Malia, and Sasha—all in gorgeous overcoats as they mounted the platform arrayed before the old State Capitol. Across the street from Abraham Lincoln's law office, the Illinois senator was beginning his successful march to the American presidency. From that frigid morning, it looked to be a long one.

Three months later, I moderated the first Republican debate for the coming 2008 election. I owe the assignment to host the event, held at the Ronald Reagan Presidential Library in Simi Valley, California, to former First Lady Nancy Reagan.

Mrs. Reagan and I had become good friends over the years. It began with a discussion about our families' histories with Alzheimer's disease. She once told me that losing her husband to the disease was "worse than the shooting." I knew what she meant. It's one thing to have a close call with death; it's far worse to lose someone's good company forever.

Nancy and I had a number of dinners together at restaurants she and her "Ronnie" liked. I remember her giving the old waiter at Chasen's a hard time when she saw that her husband's picture wasn't on the menu with other old Hollywood stars. Watching her make her case, I could see how she kept the Ronald Reagan legacy so bright.

The 2008 primaries now involved a heavyweight battle between Obama and early favorite Senator Hillary Clinton. Covering the Iowa caucuses, however, I saw the challenger's magic. Actually, I *felt* it while watching him in action from the back of high school auditoriums. There was an electricity in those rooms that I've never experienced in a political meeting. When he won Iowa, he spoke to history:

"They said this day would never come. They said our sights were set too high. But on this January night, at this defining moment in history, you have done what the cynics said we could never do."

For a few days, it looked like Obama would sweep through the primaries. Then, a week later in New Hampshire, Hillary Clinton upset him by winning the popular vote. She did it through sheer persistence. I watched her stand in a giant hall the Saturday before primary day, answering every question thrown at her. She refused to quit.

Clinton would win the popular vote again in Nevada. Now it appeared that she, not Obama, was on the way to the nomination. What turned the victory to Obama was his strategy. Instead of working the big primary states, he concentrated his campaign on picking up delegates in the smaller caucus states. His team simply had a sharper eye for the prize.

I had become a strong supporter of Obama. One big reason was Iraq. His words of triumph the night after winning the Maryland, DC, and Virginia primaries, were especially stirring.

"A war that should've never been authorized and never been waged. That's what happens when we use 9/11 to scare up votes, and that's why we need to do more than end a war—we need to end the mind-set that got us into this war."

I was physically thrilled by what I was hearing. It was *real* patriotism, not the jingoism we'd gotten day after day from the Bush hawks. Finally, we had a leader ready to spell out the awful truth: that the United States had been led in a terribly wrong direction, one that betrayed our principles. He talked of restoring this country to its proper role as an enemy of aggression, not a perpetrator of it. It gave me hope that the America I loved was still with us. Something pure had come back. Hope.

Just before Election Day 2008, Obama barnstormed his way through my home city of Philadelphia. The first stop was in an economically depressed area of North Philadelphia. The crowd was African American, and the neighborhood had not gotten past its days as an arrival point for people of the great inner-migration of the 1950s and 1960s. Obama spoke at the exact location—Progress Plaza—where I had gone just before leaving for the Peace Corps to pick up ways to promote small business. Sadly, there had been little economic progress in the forty years since.

Yet the words from Barack Obama that most grabbed people that morning weren't about economics. It was his promise of unity and inclusion that caused the crowd to erupt. After nearly 250 years of slavery, 100 years of Jim Crow, and a half century of uneven, frustrating progress, all people really wanted was to be included—fully included—in American society.

Obama's opponent that November was John McCain, the Republican many of us in the media had rooted for in his fight for the nomination eight years earlier. He reminded me of that history at that October's annual Al Smith Dinner, an occasion that brings together candidates of both parties in a spirit of fun and good fellowship. I was attending as a guest of former governor Hugh Carey. "[Chris Matthews] used to like me," he told the audience, "but he found somebody new. . . . Maverick I can do, but messiah is above my pay grade."

I worried that 2008 would be a replay of what had happened twice in California elections for governor. Tom Bradley, the mayor of Los Angeles, was favored in the polls both times he was the Democratic nominee. In both cases, the results fell short of his preelection numbers. Some people had told pollsters they were going to support him, an African American, but didn't vote that way in the booth.

In November 2008 the voters displayed a reverse of the "Bradley effect." A higher percentage of people voted for Obama than told pollsters they intended to. Anchoring on election night, we saw the powerful scene in Chicago's Grant Park, where thousands gathered to cheer the Obama–Biden ticket's commanding victory. I thought of the pictures of that same park during the 1968 Democratic convention, when students and police battled each other through the tear gas. This time there were only tears of joy.

Perhaps it was the inspiration of this moment that got me thinking about running for office again, this time for a US Senate seat from Pennsylvania. In late 2008 the *Philadelphia Inquirer* led with the headline "*Hardball* Host Edges Closer to Senate Run."

"In recent weeks, Matthews has ramped up his exploration for a 2010 campaign as a Democrat against Sen. Arlen Specter (R-PA). He has discussed the dynamics of a possible run with prominent Democratic fund-raisers, strategists, and leaders across his native Pennsylvania, according to several people who have spoken to Matthews during the last several weeks."

My problem lay right there in that article. I couldn't have a conversation with anyone without it appearing in the media. As a journalist, that put me in an untenable position. How could I cover politics while at the same time preparing to jump into it myself?

In early January I pulled the plug, which again made the *Inquirer*'s front page. It was a difficult decision. Old dreams die hard.

During the early months of 2009, I watched President Obama tame the Great Recession left to him by the Bush administration. He had inherited a giant, burst housing bubble, a huge number of foreclosures, and rising unemployment. He met this dangerous combination by stimulating the economy, the very opposite tactic of the fiscal austerity being tried in Europe. He was just as successful in passing the landmark Affordable Care Act in 2010. One of the people he owed for that was Nancy Pelosi, the first woman Speaker of the House in US history. Having worked for

Tip O'Neill all those years, I can appreciate her strength in keeping the Democrats together. I believe she incorporates the twin tests of a great leader: she is feared but not hated. That requires a master's political touch, and Pelosi has proven it again and again.

A plan for national health care had been a careerlong goal of Senator Ted Kennedy, who died of brain cancer seven months before Obamacare's enactment. What people don't know about this great man was his *personal* interest in people's health. In 2005, when I received a diagnosis of diabetes, Ted telephoned to wish me well. I have no idea how he learned of my condition, but he came across as fully informed. He stayed on the phone, telling me about all the friends and family who were in my situation. He could not have been warmer or more considerate.

Strangely enough, I got that phone call from the senator just as I was going through my first episode of hypoglycemia. For several frightening moments, I wondered if I would black out. As Kennedy went on about those other people he knew who had diabetes, I couldn't get him off the phone. Again, it was a case of one human being trying to buck up another.

By 2012, I was out in Iowa covering President Obama's reelection effort and his potential opposition, including Mitt Romney, his ultimate rival. Romney was the moderate Republican governor of Massachusetts who'd inaugurated the health care plan on which Obama had modeled his. He had served his Mormon mission in France and carried the air of the well born. After all, his father had headed up American Motors, been governor of Michigan, and was thought well enough of to be a popular, if brief, candidate for president. When I approached him as he was autographing posters, I asked if he could say "Let them eat cake" in French. Seeing the setup, Romney answered discreetly, "I can, but I won't!"

He showed the same wary goodwill when we met up at the Al Smith Dinner late in the campaign. This was after he had dominated Obama in the first of two debates but had taken tough treatment from the media. He was equally generous in remarks about the president, speaking of his rival's "fine and gracious moments" as chief executive, adding that he had many gifts and a beautiful family any man would be proud of. "In our country," he said, "you can oppose someone in politics and make a confident argument against his policies without any ill will."

When it came to Obama's turn, the president alluded to his weak performance in the first debate and the hammering he took for it, including from me. "Four years ago, I gave him a thrill up his leg. This time I gave him a stroke."

CHAPTER FORTY-SIX

KATHLEEN MATTHEWS FOR CONGRESS

Just as my wife had encouraged me in my career leaps, I tried to do the same for her. Two years after we married, I encouraged Kathleen to go on-air. I thought she had everything it took to be a great news broadcaster. She started by taking freelance assignments, while remaining a producer.

In 1982, pregnant with our first child, Michael, Kathleen was hired by her station as a full-time reporter specializing in education. Over the next decade, she rose to top anchor. I could see from the reaction on the sidewalk the regard and affection people held for my wife. After a quarter century of reporting and anchoring the news, she took a sabbatical to become a fellow at the Institute of Politics at Harvard's John F. Kennedy School. Soon after, in 2006, she was recruited by the legendary hotelier J. Willard "Bill" Marriott Jr. to be his corporation's executive vice president for global communications. She would hold that position for nearly a decade.

Our children were also moving ahead. Michael graduated from Brown University, then, after working for the Clinton Foundation in Rwanda, earned his master's degree in film at New York University's Tisch School of the Arts. Thomas graduated from NYU in acting and was in the cast of HBO's acclaimed drama *The Newsroom* as the young producer Martin

Stallworth. Caroline was at the University of Pennsylvania. From there she went to work for Google, then earned a double master's degree at Harvard's Kennedy School of Public Policy and the Graduate School of Business at Stanford University.

With Michael married to Brown classmate Sarah Staveley-O'Carroll and living in Los Angeles, Thomas acting in LA and New York, and Caroline off getting her final degrees, Kathleen decided to make another leap. In June 2015 she declared her candidacy for Congress for an open seat in Maryland. Having broken barriers in journalism and business, she wanted to do it in politics.

She ran a strong, impressive campaign but came up short on primary night. Not that it would have been a game changer, but I was prevented by MSNBC from doing anything significant to help. I would have loved simply going door-to-door telling everyone what a committed, progressive, brilliant candidate she was.

Kathleen later served as state Democratic Party chair and as an elector for Joe Biden and Kamala Harris from Maryland in the 2020 state-by-state presidential tally.

CHAPTER FORTY-SEVEN

TRUMP

No one could have truly foreseen how badly the presidency of Donald Trump would end. All of us witnessed how it began.

In the 2016 primaries, he bullied one Republican after another off the debate stage. In the general election against Democrat Hillary Clinton, he did it again, because it's all he can do. He destroyed his opponents with ridicule, a talent that is worthless in the job he was seeking, that of American president.

What Trump showed me in my earliest encounters was his casual resorting to deceit. I began having him on *Hardball* during the Clinton presidency. Even in those years, he was what show bookers call a good "get." The New York real estate developer and casino operator knew how to make news. Name a subject, he had an opinion. He struck me as a figure from the comic books—perhaps a "downtown Gotham businessman" in the *Batman* strip.

Much of what Trump had to say in those early *Hardball* appearances was a preview of the awful business to come. In 1998 he offered some telling advice to President Clinton on how to deal with the Monica Lewinsky scandal. Trump said Clinton should have taken the Fifth Amendment protection against self-incrimination and justify not testifying by hurling charges against independent counsel Kenneth Starr. Trump imagined how he would have played it: "I don't get along with this man, Starr. He's after me. He's a Republican. He's this. He's that."

Of course, this was precisely the Trump game plan during his four years as president. He condemned anyone who crossed him, whether it be a GOP rival for the nomination, a judge who didn't rule his way, or a member of the press who printed or broadcasted the truth.

As I saw it, Trump made no effort back then to cloak his ruthlessness. When I asked him about the 2004 Swift Boat Veterans for Truth attacks on John Kerry's admirable war record as a navy lieutenant serving in Vietnam, he called the slimy charges "brilliant." Trump seemed less taken by the lying and smearing of a man who had faced enemy fire for his country than their effectiveness with voters.

"They've taken all of that war hero thing away from Kerry. And they've almost given it to Bush. And Bush, frankly, was not serving."

Frankly?

In 2005 I invited Trump to join us on our *Hardball* College Tour. We hosted it at his alma mater, the University of Pennsylvania's Wharton School of Business. I had good working relations with him back then. He would respond to my calls and, on many occasions, come on the show.

For years, Trump's loyal assistant Rhona Graff would assure me on the phone that her boss was truly getting ready to run for president. Then he wasn't. By the run-up to the 2016 election, I had begun to feel like Charlie Brown in *Peanuts,* with Lucy forever frustrating his chance to kick the football. I began to buy into the quadrennial argument that Trump's talk of a presidential candidacy was simply ballyhoo for his real estate and television enterprises. Then he fooled us all and actually ran.

On the eve of the 2016 Wisconsin presidential primary, he agreed to appear on *Hardball.* I would now have a chance to interview him as a candidate for high office. A *politician.*

The big news that night in Green Bay came when an audience member asked where he stood on "a woman's right to choose" regarding her own reproductive health. He answered by saying he was "pro-life." I decided to call his bluff. I had a hunch that Trump didn't know what he was talking about.

"What should the law be on abortion? Should it be a crime for the woman who has one? If so, how severe a penalty?" Here's how it went from there:

"Well, people in certain parts of the Republican Party and conservative Republicans would say, yes, they should be punished."

"How about you? You say you want to ban it. What does that mean? Do you believe in punishment for abortion, yes or no, as a principle?"

Trump replied, "The answer is there has to be some form of punishment."

I pressed, "For the woman?"

"Yeah, it has to be some form."

He was clearly in over his head. He had signed on to the pro-life stand without checking with its advocates to find out what that means. I decided to drill further.

"What about the guy that gets her pregnant? Is he responsible under the law for these abortions? Or is he not responsible for an abortion decision?"

"Different people, different feelings. I would say no."

I assumed these answers would explode under Donald Trump's feet, destroying his presidential candidacy. In the minutes after the program, everyone I talked to thought that his calling for a woman to be "punished" for having an abortion amounted to political suicide.

Everyone was wrong. Trump's appeal wouldn't stand or fall on his ability to give the right answer to a TV anchor. Nor would it be shaken when, just weeks before the November 2016 election, an eleven-year-old behind-the-scenes videotape from *Access Hollywood* was made public. Trump could be heard bragging about his ability to assault women sexually and get away with it. Or when he said he could "stand in the middle of Fifth Avenue and shoot somebody" and still keep his followers. His supporters accepted all this because Donald Trump, for all his crassness and lack of qualifications, was mocking the elite figures they most resented.

To win in 2016, Trump had done what no candidate of the Right had done quite so successfully before. He had made himself a tribune for those Americans sharing a whole cluster of resentments, from economic to cultural.

With this strategy, Trump borrowed from the nativism of the nineteenth-century Know-Nothing Party, the assaults on the liberal elite championed by Senator Joseph McCarthy in the mid-twentieth century, and Patrick Buchanan's protectionist anger of the 1990s. What Trump added was the pizzazz of a talented TV performer and a mastery of social media.

From the day of his inauguration in January 2017, beginning with his claims of larger crowds, Trump played solely to his aggrieved audience and to his own wounded psyche. In choosing this course, he abdicated a US president's most honored role: leader of the American people. Instead of trying to unite the land, he resorted to four years of scorched earth.

His dishonesty was most lethal when it came to the deadly pandemic that hit the United States in January 2020. Informed early about the dangers posed by the coronavirus, Trump decided on a policy of appeasement. He would let the pandemic spread as long as it didn't threaten him politically. He hid the health dangers to the country to avoid the political peril to himself. In the end, it was his undoing.

After losing the 2020 election, Trump tried every legal and PR trick he could to overturn the results. Well past the ratification of the vote in the Electoral College on December 14, he continued to insist to his 74.2 million voters that he had won in a landslide, when, in reality, Democratic candidate Joe Biden had defeated him soundly, 306 to 232, in the Electoral College, and in the popular vote by a margin of more than 7 million.

In those last months of 2020, I thought that was the worst thing he could do as president. What I watched in January 2021 told me I had been wrong. I'm talking about the American carnage on the sixth of that month, as Congress was ratifying the electoral vote, when Trump's supporters stormed the Capitol with the wicked calls of an American president urging them on.

The only thing worse would have been if he'd gotten himself reelected. Four more years of this guy might have been a national horror impossible to fully obliterate. Fortunately for our ancestors who loved this country so deeply, for we the living, and our progeny, demagoguery has not been a good career choice.

CHAPTER FORTY-EIGHT

HARDBALL

This book has been about learning from history as it takes place around you. *Hardball*, my show on MSNBC, covered a good stretch of that history.

I had a special ambition with the program. It was to give viewers a clearer look at what they were witnessing. It was drilling down to find the truth, especially from the news makers who were determined to keep it from us.

It wasn't that hard a job. Lots of those watching programs like mine know the right questions to ask. They've got it in their heads, even on the tips of their tongues. What they hate is when the person running the show won't ask it. Why? Because it's maddening to watch a politician hiding something, and the person whose job it is to get it out of him or her doesn't even try. So, I've seen my job as working for the viewer. Through all my years on TV, my favorite accolade comes from people who stop me in public and put it on the line:

"I love it that you don't let them get away with anything."

But grilling politicians can be a dangerous profession. Their supporters *hate* it. They want their candidates to be permitted to make their assertions unquestioned, then depart the show with their mission accomplished. No one wants to watch his or her hero being cross-examined.

But I believe no one seeking the voter's approval should get a pass. No politician should be assumed to be telling "the truth, the whole truth, and nothing but the truth." Why? Because most of the time, they are there to make their case. The second reason is that a serious effort to get the truth out of a professional pol is the job I signed up for.

You either like watching a tough interview or you don't. Most people do, as long as it's not their hero getting the third degree. It's why so many of us love courtroom dramas. There's something bracing about getting to the truth after a little suspense. It avoids having a program become predictable.

As John McLaughlin once observed years ago, I'm a tummler. That's the Yiddish word for the performer at the old summer resorts in New York's Catskill Mountains who kept people entertained and engaged even on rainy days. Whether it's at a dinner party, or a production meeting, or on the air, I try to enliven the moment.

These signature factors have definitely produced memorable moments: the near duel with Senator Zell Miller; my on-the-spot prophecy declaring that Barack Obama would be the "first African American president"; my interrogation of candidate Donald Trump that yielded his maladroit call for "punishment" of women who have abortions.

Over the years, people have asked how long it took to prepare for that hour on-air. The short answer is a daily ritual on show days that included reading the newspapers and daily online briefings; getting the latest scuttlebutt and intelligence from my great producers; one production meeting around noon and then another an hour before showtime; writing on deadline a closing commentary and editing the script. Finally, a few minutes of respite getting my makeup put on. That's the calm before the storm; a chance to settle down before going on-air.

Then there's the long-term answer to how I prepare to dissect the day's news. That's what I've spent this book revealing. That's the life I've led, the witness I've been to history, the passion I've had for politics. I know what it means to be one of the very first boomers. I watched Dad get his degree from Drexel on the GI Bill. I was in one of the families heading to the suburbs and the middle class after World War II. I cheered when the Hungarians stood up to Soviet tanks. I cheered for Fidel Castro when he overthrew a rotten Cuban dictator, and then was betrayed by his genuflection to Moscow. I lived the Cold War through it all: Hungary, *Sputnik*, Cuba, the Missile Crisis, Vietnam, and, finally, the fall of the Berlin Wall and the breakup of the USSR. It was my country's history, and mine personally.

What I brought uniquely to the show was my many years inside the country's political life, both as part of it and covering it for the news. Even those two years in Swaziland taught me valuable truths: how people even in small countries treasure their national independence.

As a journalist, I learned perhaps the most glaring lesson of politics. It's that governments fail when they fail the needs of their truest believers. I saw that in East Germany when the wall was coming down. I saw it in our own 2016 elections when the old, reliable Democratic voters of Pennsylvania, Wisconsin, and Michigan proved the old rule I learned from my Peace Corps buddy John Catanese: people don't mind being used; they mind very much being discarded.

I was at every Republican convention from New Orleans in 1988 to Cleveland in 2016, every Democratic convention since George McGovern's catastrophic nomination in 1972 to Hillary Clinton's in Philadelphia. I have followed every single presidential election since 1952. And I have enjoyed covering them all, including the long recount of 2000.

In the fall of 2019, we celebrated the twentieth anniversary of *Hardball* on MSNBC. Executive producer Tina Urbanski and the other producers assembled the highlight moments going back to 1999. It was a great time to remember all that we managed to achieve in a run that covered four presidencies. The guest list was a parade of Americana: Jimmy and Rosalynn Carter, Jeb Bush, James Baker, Ben Stiller, Woody Harrelson, Barbra Streisand, Michael Moore, Harry Belafonte, Rob Reiner, and Kamala Harris, the future vice president.

But I began 2020 with a foreboding. Senator Bernie Sanders was leading in the early contests. His self-description as a democratic socialist promised electoral catastrophe. While he would point to Denmark and other Scandinavian countries as his model, Sanders was known for making positive remarks about Cuba's Fidel Castro and Nicaragua's Daniel Ortega and the Soviet Union itself. Based on history, a Sanders candidacy would repeat the Democratic disaster of 1972. Like George McGovern, he lacked the Cold War sensibility of every American president since Harry Truman.

With the arrival of 2020, Senator Sanders seemed headed for the Democratic nomination. He won the popular vote in Iowa, New Hampshire, and, by a wide spread, in Nevada. With each victory, I became increasingly frustrated, especially with the liberal media. No one seemed disturbed by the Democrats offering up such a vulnerable challenger to President Donald Trump. Worse yet was the separation I felt from a party that I had supported since my first presidential vote in 1968, the year I headed for Africa and the Peace Corps. It was as if people with whom I had voted alongside for decades were heading unthinkingly toward an electoral cliff. My one regret, a familiar one, is that I made my antipathy of Senator Sanders's views far too personal. I painted him in a way he doesn't deserve. The fact is, we've had fine democratic socialist leaders in this country for more than a century. One was Michael Harrington, a Holy Cross guy who in 1962 authored the book *The Other America: Poverty in the United States,* which inspired President Lyndon Johnson's War on Poverty. My friend Rick Hertzberg was also a confirmed socialist. I should have treated the Vermont senator with more decency even if I feared where he was taking this country in early 2020.

What I couldn't see coming in those winter months was the abrupt turn about to take place among Democratic primary voters—and also in my career that would keep me from covering it.

South Carolina was long anticipated as the 2020 contest of Joe Biden's last resort. If he didn't win there, he'd be finished. As it turned out, the former vice president won big in that primary. His victory solidified his position as the one moderate Democrat who could win the presidential nomination and go on to defeat Donald Trump in November. That was made clear by the decisions of Minnesota senator Amy Klobuchar and South Bend, Indiana, mayor Pete Buttigieg to leave the race. The party's more centrist wing was now united around Biden. Even some on the progressive left now saw him as the one Democrat who could carry the banner successfully through the fall.

Down in Charleston the afternoon before the primary, I confronted a turn of events closer to home.

I've spent my life observing history. That means recognizing its inflection points, including those moments, often long overdue, when wrongs need to be righted. One area is gender equality in the workplace, and the need to recognize women on the basis of their talent and performance. I believe in that principle and have sought to champion women who are my professional colleagues in their careers. I believe that is evident in the people I've had as my top producers and the guests we have sought for the program.

On Monday, March 2, 2020, two days after the South Carolina primary, I said that I had not always honored that standard in words, that there had been instances over the years when I have made reference to a person's appearance. What led to that on-air testimony was a Friday report that, four years earlier, I had remarked on a *Hardball* guest's appearance as she was being prepared in the makeup chair. It never occurred to me to deny that it had happened or condone what I'd said. After a conversation with the network, I decided, at age seventy-four, to move up my retirement.

That Monday, the day before Super Tuesday, I began the show by announcing it would be the last *Hardball*. That farewell commentary, brief as it was, addressed two vital matters, each related to the other. One was a tribute to the young people I've been able to bring along professionally:

> The younger generations out there are ready to take the reins. We see them in politics, in the media, in fighting for their causes. They are improving the workplace. We're talking here about better standards than we grew up with, fair standards.

My second topic referred to the circumstances of my ending *Hardball*:

> A lot of it has to do with how we talk to each other, compliments on a woman's appearance that some men, including me, might have once incorrectly thought were okay were never okay, not then, and certainly not today. And for making such comments in the past, I'm sorry.

I stand by that. I've spent my career talking. I know more than others the influence of words. I must and will hold myself to a higher standard. It took me too long to realize this is a matter of human fairness.

I'm happy to be part of a country that wants to get better with each generation. *Hardball* has been proud over the years to introduce and showcase serious young talent. That starts with Joy Reid, who now holds my old time slot on MSNBC. Norah O'Donnell appeared back when we were still on CNBC. She is now chief anchor for CBS News. The *Washington Post*'s Robert Costa rose to host *Washington Week* on PBS. Yamiche Alcindor, formerly of the *New York Times*, is also with PBS. Heidi Przybyla is with NBC. The *Washington Post*'s Jonathan Capehart has a show on MSNBC and debates David Brooks on *PBS NewsHour*.

The *Hardball* College Tour was another hit. Over the years, we took the show to Stanford, George Mason, Chapman, Fordham, Iowa State, Georgetown, West Chester (PA), and Harvard University. We got young people into politics by bringing politics to them.

The other point I made on that last *Hardball* was directed to the people of my generation. I spoke about the young people who'd stop me at airports and talk about their parents or grandparents who watched me faithfully. Or the spouses who said, "My husband watched you to the end."

On that last *Hardball,* the evening of March 2, 2020, I said to all our faithful watchers that it wasn't goodbye "but 'til we meet again." I wish that here again to all those millions of people who stuck with me all these exciting years, all those who share my love of this country and its democratic spirit.

CHAPTER FORTY-NINE

THIS COUNTRY

What people want is very simple. They want an America as good as its promise.

—US Congresswoman Barbara Jordan (D-TX), 1977

The title of this book, *This Country,* comes from a phrase I associate with President Harry Truman. He believed there was a shared national *feeling* and was confident in his ability to hear the American people. This might explain his conviction that he, a distant underdog, was going to win that first post–World War II election in 1948.

Truman may have been inspired by the way his country responded to the Japanese attack on Pearl Harbor. Once the security of the country was at stake, the long debate over US entry into the European war was over. We were of a single mind and heart, united in purpose, spirited by a great leader.

Joe Alsop, the legendary Washington columnist, was in Hong Kong when President Roosevelt spoke to the country the day after the surprise attack on Pearl Harbor. He was lying on the floor of his apartment as Japanese planes dropped bombs, but wrote later that he knew, listening to FDR's voice as he spoke of that "date which will live in infamy," that we would win the great world war on which we were embarking.

I think of the presidents in my day who have spoken with the same confidence. John F. Kennedy did so when he told us to "ask what you can do for your country," and spoke for this country's freedom-loving soul when he told the people of West Berlin that he, the American president, was one with them. I think, too, of President Ronald Reagan and what he said that tragic afternoon in 1986 when the *Challenger* space shuttle exploded in the sky shortly after lifting off from Kennedy Space Center: how its young crew carried this country's pioneering spirit. Or the second President Bush when he spoke from the ruins of the World Trade Center.

One could argue that it takes a romantic to believe this country has a mind and heart to which a president can give voice. Fair enough. But the office brings with it that power. As Theodore Roosevelt said, our elected national leader has a bully pulpit for speaking to the country. Not every president has had the character to use it, because it demands speaking not for himself—or herself—but for the American people as a whole.

I think of the closing scene in the 1993 political comedy *Dave*, starring Kevin Kline and Sigourney Weaver, when good-natured Dave Kovic, an exact look-alike standing in for corrupt President Bill Mitchell, admits to scandal and resigns: "I think there are certain things you should expect from your president. I ought to care more about you than I do about myself. I ought to care more about what is right than I do about what is popular. I ought to be willing to give up this whole thing for something I believe in."

This is not a fantastic notion. George Washington, the first to hold the office, impressed even King George III in this regard. Having defeated the greatest army in the world, he gave up command and went back to his home in Virginia. He did the same after serving his two constitutional terms as president. A man who could easily have become a dictator for life cared more about the republic that he had fought to create. Abraham Lincoln, just weeks before the end of the Civil War as well as his death, called us to "bind up the nation's wounds." In this, his second inaugural, he looked to a future of healing and a national unity. "With malice toward none, with charity toward all."

There are, of course, issues that perpetually separate us. They are the conflicts that drive and energize any free people. They stand at the border between the rights of the individual and the goals of society. I have been arguing on this terrain since I wrote an article at La Salle College High School on the two contending events of 1789, the French Revolution and the adoption of the American Constitution. I was still studying this perennial tension when I spent the summer of 1966 in Worcester digging into anthropology for some natural order: Is it free markets or socialism? It was the same question I put to the desperate yet hopeful East Germans in 1989.

It remains a lively one today. How much freedom can the individual retain as we advance the economic cause of society as a whole? How much should government grow? I confess to a bias toward the rights of the individual. I have been in autocratic countries, East Germany and Cuba, and, in the faces of human defeat, I didn't like what I saw and felt. We Americans love our freedom, a fact never more palpable than when it is being denied.

Adlai Stevenson II, twice a gallant Democratic candidate for president, in 1952 and 1956, put it best. "When an American says he loves his country he means . . . that he loves an inner air, an inner light in which freedom lives and in which a man can draw the breath of self-respect."

The hard facts of life make social progress imperative and change, therefore, unavoidable. We need to address the great disparity between rich and poor. We need to find a way to universal health care. We have to build a society that provides for the sick and old and those among us who simply never get a break.

As I write this, America has begun a national reckoning on race. I have often called it the San Andreas Fault of our politics. It's the set of tectonic plates that shift and collide at unpredictable times. People of my generation grew up in a country that was strictly segregated. The same doors I got through were tightly closed to women and people of color.

The passage of time has not come close to ending the injustice. After almost 250 years of legal slavery, 100 years of Jim Crow, followed by a half-century struggle for civil rights, is there anyone who can honestly deny our need to address this divide that holds back so many of our fellow Americans? As long as fear and anger still work their way through this country's life, optimism for a postracial America alone will not do the job.

The Black Lives Matter movement has offered hope. Even as it has reflected unrest, it has raised the right questions. Would those police officers allegedly involved in wrongful deaths of black men have performed differently in dealing with a white person? And, if so, what does that say about this country? After reading so many front-page stories about police shootings, all these years later, how could anyone see this as acceptable? Somehow we have to end the economic and social entrapment that makes racial difference the basis of a caste system. To be a good American in the twenty-first century requires more than not doing bad.

One area of cultural progress concerns sexual identity and orientation. Beginning in the 1980s, I spoke or served as moderator at numerous events for the Human Rights Campaign. I was, like a majority of Americans, thrilled by the Supreme Court's recognition of marriage equality in 2015. At the same time, I respect the country's ongoing debate over abortion rights. I've publicly backed the pro-choice position since I ran for Congress the year after *Roe v. Wade*. That said, I think it is healthy to have voices raised about the moral issue of abortion itself, especially late term.

That balance is the fulcrum of my political interest generally. I have a tendency to quietly root for the side that's losing. It's my natural pugnacity.

I don't like being in the pack. I want balance, the eternal struggle over government versus the individual, between beliefs about personal morality and the individual freedom to make decisions. I want to right the boat, not swamp it in one direction or the other. It's what my favorite teacher, Gerald Tremblay, told us once. He said he tended to root for the side that's losing the argument. If that keeps up the noise level, that's what I'm talking about. I like conflict and relish differences of opinion. It's the sound of our democracy working. As I've said, it's the system I believe in. I love the human competition for office, the continual debate in the Congress over what kind of country we want to live in.

My life in American politics has shown me the weaknesses in our democracy. Start with the money that pays for TV campaign ads, money that comes too often from those who want to pick and then manipulate the eventual winner. It's what I crusaded against for Ralph Nader and later as a congressional candidate a half century ago. I believe it has distorted not just our policies at home but also abroad.

And yet, through all the imperfection, I can hear the American voice in our elections. Every two years, a vast electorate speaks and, yes, it is heard in Washington. I remain committed to this country, its national politics, and its capital city.

When I drive home from downtown Washington at night, I look out across the Potomac River. I look for that small flickering light at Arlington National Cemetery, that eternal flame that an American president's widow asked to be placed there. Each time I pass, I look to it perhaps for assurance, and when I catch that little glitter on the hill across the river, I am calmed to see it still there. It's a symbol of our democratic republic, and I want to see it aglow.

Peter Mooney, who graduated from Holy Cross one year ahead of me, recently sent a letter to the school about a youthful memory:

"Back in those days, if you came into the college cafeteria after class, there would often be a raucous group at one of the tables. Something was being debated, all right, but instead of anger or rage, there was rollicking laughter. In the midst of this mirth, one tall, thin guy, clearly enjoying himself, his face reddened with laughter, would be holding forth about something or other—politics or sports (perhaps his hapless Philadelphia Phillies) or society in general. That would be Chris."

Reading that description of me from a half century ago, I see the unaltered focus of my life, one that is unlikely to change. My fascination with politics is part of me. You might say it's a gift. I remember watching Dick Cavett interview the great film director John Huston, the director of *The Maltese Falcon, The Treasure of Sierra Madre, The African Queen*, and *The Man Who Would Be King*. Huston was now hooked up to an oxygen tank. Dick asked what kept him going. "Interest!" the great man blasted back. "Interest!" What he most sought in life, even at this precarious stage, was something that excites him: an idea, a notion, whatever.

For me, that interest has been in the political life and its heroes, many of them described in this book. Winston Churchill has loomed large in my imagination ever since I returned from two years in Africa and saw all those shelves of books about him in the stacks of the Library of Congress. I say that as one who knows most of his faults but also of his great virtue. He sounded the early alarm in the 1930s about Adolf Hitler when others were blinding themselves to the truth or refusing to speak it. Had Great Britain taken his warnings to heart, the Second World War might not have come. One person who believed that, ironically, was Nazi propaganda chief Joseph Goebbels. On May 9, 1941, he wrote in his diary about Churchill: "This man is a strange mixture of heroism and cunning. If he had come to power in 1932, we would not be where we are today."

If Churchill is my guide in politics, Ernest Hemingway is mine in life's adventure. He once said that all great literature began with Huckleberry Finn. For me, that's ironic. Hemingway was my Tom Sawyer. Just as Tom got his friends to see the fun in whitewashing a fence, Hemingway got me hooked on an entire geography: Paris in the 1920s, Spain in the 1930s, Africa anytime. He created charm for me in Key West, Cuba, and even Ketchum, Idaho. Wherever he chose to spend time has become for me a place of romance. His spirit has greeted me in such places as I ventured abroad. I felt his presence at the Portuguese bullfight in Lourenço Marques. There was the Mbabane tearoom where the owner asked if I "knew the Hemingways" after seeing me with one of his books. There was the Safari Hotel in Arusha, Tanzania, where Steve Hank and I found the guy with his tales of having boxed the great writer in that very bar.

I think often of getting back to Africa; back where so much began for me out there on a dirt road in the *lowveld* of Swaziland, looking to the great escarpment to the east.

I have another trip in mind, one I'll never take but forever hope for. I imagine coming back to this country a few hundred years from now and finding it still what our founders bequeathed to us. It will hold elections every two years for Congress, every four for president. There will be more equality, a greater comity. People will be happier with one another. Race and ethnicity will no longer stand as barriers to shared freedom and equality.

I want all history to matter. Much like the British who keep the bodies of their monarchs, good and vile, in Westminster Abbey—from King Henry VIII to Queen "Bloody" Mary I—I want to know it all. There is a special good in knowing the history of this country. We should know ours, including the current era, because it makes us better. That includes, perhaps especially, all the crises and the pain.

But as we acknowledge the old, we must be ready to admit the new. Hostility to immigrants isn't unique to this country. Nativism—and its demagogues—is common on every continent. What makes us different is that we are not a land forged on ethnicity or tribe. What makes arrival to the United States exceptional is a person's ability to become truly American.

Many hold differing notions of American exceptionalism. This is mine: what's unique, what is truly *America,* is that ability of a newcomer to be accepted. This country is one place where you can arrive and become a true citizen, an American, like my Grandmom-in-Chestnut Hill.

I'm so glad that it was Joe Biden, the forty-sixth president of the United States, who has saluted this openness to newcomers as the reason for this country's well-recognized ability to rejuvenate itself.

The battle between left and right, with luck, will not fade. We need it, because even as we strive for a better life for the worst off of us, we must battle for the maximum liberty of the individual American. It's my faith that, countless years from now, we will be in a fairer country, a truly free country, still, after all the years, trying to get it right.

ACKNOWLEDGMENTS

Writing a memoir demands a worthy search into the past. Just as the archaeologist digs to the lowest soil to find the lost times, so does the writer to the most distant recesses of memory.

One great gift of the effort was the list of those who helped me on my life's journey. It begins with my parents and four brothers, then continues through my grandparents and aunts to my teachers.

For my wealth of early career adventures, I must thank President John F. Kennedy for founding the Peace Corps, Congressman Wayne Owens, Senator Frank E. Moss, President Jimmy Carter, Richard Pettigrew, Hendrik Hertzberg, Congressman Tony Coelho, Marty Franks, and the Honorable Thomas P. "Tip" O'Neill Jr.

For getting me started as a writer, I thank Gerald Tremblay and Hendrik Hertzberg. Also, editor James Silberman and reporter Bob Woodward for getting me to write *Hardball* back in 1988. For starting me as a journalist, I thank *San Francisco Examiner* executive editor Larry Kramer for offering me a full-time newspaper job, and Jimmy Breslin and George F. Will for encouraging me to take it.

For getting me on broadcast television, I thank Sir Howard Stringer, David Corvo, and the late John McLaughlin. Most important, I thank Nancy Nathan, who created and executive produced *The Chris Matthews Show* all those weekends for twelve years.

I want to thank the top executives who've led me over the years: Comcast president and CEO Brian Roberts, NBC president Bob Wright, NBS news presidents Andy Lack and Noah Oppenheim, and MSNBC president Phil Griffin.

For all those faithful viewers of *Hardball*, I hold a lifetime of affection. Topping that list of those who helped me bring the show to life each night is executive producer Tina Urbanski. Her brains, loyalty, and unmatchable competence made it all possible.

Also high on my list is the redoubtable Ann Klenk, who preceded Tina as executive producer. Former producers include Rob Yarin, Phil Griffin, and Tammy Haddad.

Robert Zeliger served not just as *Hardball* senior producer but as great company. I always knew that the professional working in the next office was there to help and cheer me on.

Julia Clancy, who joined me later, excelled both as a frontline *Hardball* producer but also at helping me gather research for this book. What a pro!

And now the team of segment producers who made the show work all those years: Will Rabbe, Tiffany Mullon, Valerie McCabe, Jonathan Helman, Nkechi Nneji, Bridget Mulcahy, Michael LaRosa, Geet Jeswani, and Rachel Wiktin.

The *Hardball* crew was a team of solid professionals. They were my partners in getting the show on-air. They were led by my floor director and close and honorable friend Derbin Cabel. Joining us were Tim Cote, Gary Lynn, Burt Thomas, George Toman, Julie Pearl, Chester Reis, Terry Kelley, Rose Procopio, and Alicia Majeed. They were my friends as well as committed workmates.

Up at 30 Rockefeller Plaza in New York, the *Hardball* team was led by director Ray Herbert, senior producer Lorena Ruiz, Pete Fall, Robert Lyon, Adam Garnett, and Lauren Raposa. For getting me ready for airtime I must thank Alisa Gunari and Tanya Miloscia.

I want to thank Katherine Cunningham, my teaching assistant at Vietnam's Fulbright University, for her professional help in this project as well.

ACKNOWLEDGMENTS

At Simon & Schuster I want to thank President and CEO Jonathan Karp, Publisher Dana Canedy, Deputy Publisher Richard Rhorer, Director of Marketing Stephen Bedford, and Associate Editor Emily Simonson for each of their commitments to the project. I must give a special tribute to Senior Editor Stuart Roberts for sharpening an overlong manuscript. He possesses the editor's gift for getting the story told fully in the author's own words.

I want to thank my TV representation over the years: first that of Richard Leibner, later with Ari Emanuel, Michelle Bohan, and especially Henry Reisch. For my literary representation I owe the excellent Jennifer Walsh and Eric Simonoff.

Finally, I want to thank Kathleen, herein cited as The Queen, for her wise reading of the manuscript and for decades of wisdom, support and, most of all, love.

INDEX

ABOUT THE AUTHOR

Chris Matthews is the author of the *New York Times* bestsellers *Bobby Kennedy: A Raging Spirit; Jack Kennedy: Elusive Hero; Tip & the Gipper: When Politics Worked; Kennedy & Nixon: The Rivalry That Shaped Postwar America;* and *Hardball: How Politics Is Played—Told by One Who Knows the Game.* He is the former host of MSNBC's *Hardball with Chris Matthews.*